Never Stop

Never Stop

a memoir

Simba Sana

BOLDEN

AN **AGATE** IMPRINT

CHICAGO

Printed in the United States

Never Stop
ISBN 13: 978-1-57284-192-5
ISBN 10: 1-57284-192-3
eISBN13: 978-1-57284-809-2
eISBN10: 1-57284-809-X

First printing: September 2017

10 9 8 7 6 5 4 3 2 1   17 18 19 20 21

Bolden Books is an imprint of Agate Publishing. Agate books are available
in bulk at discount prices. For more information, visit agatepublishing.com.

Contents

Life contains a fundamental goodness that informs our lives. My mother, based on how she cared for me, was keenly aware of this. I've been fortunate to have a wife who possesses this same knowledge, and it's a reassuring thing to see that our children know this as well.

This book is dedicated to them!

Foundation

MY MOTHER NEVER TOLD ME ANYTHING ABOUT HER past—not one thing! This may be hard to believe, but she talked to herself more than she ever actually spoke to me. I grew accustomed to this at home, but as I got older, I became keenly aware that her habit of engaging in intense conversations with herself was not ordinary behavior.

My aunt and uncles, who only saw us from time to time, knew something was wrong, too, but they never spoke about it, at least not to me, and their attempts to reach out to my mom were often rebuffed. My mom, being very stubborn, was generally unwilling to allow people into our lives. Including family.

It wasn't until after my mom's death that her past began filtering its way to me, primarily from four sources. Her King James Bible, I discovered, had a list of family names and birthdates. She also kept documents and photos in an old, sky-blue Hawthorne suitcase. Despite the reluctance of many in my family, my constant questioning over the years gradually netted me some details about my mother's life. And finally, Lucille Hester, a friend of my mother's, shared whatever details she could recall whenever we saw each other in later years.

Lula Arzie Mae Artis, I learned, was born in Wayne County, North Carolina on January 25, 1932. Her dislike of the name Lula was so strong that she scribbled over it on her high school and college diplomas. She was the second youngest of ten children, and the youngest of three girls born to John Henry and Hattie Thompson Artis.

The Artis family faced two tragedies around the time of Arzie Mae's birth. Her sister, Inez, was burned to death in an accidental fire before Arzie Mae was born. It was said that Inez was so bright that she'd begun teaching one of her older brothers how to read. Then, when Arzie Mae was four, her mother died from complications during the birth of her eleventh child, who also died. John Henry, who was a farmer, later remarried a woman named Lucretia, and she treated his children as her own.

Arzie Mae was petite and brown-skinned, with thick, long, dark hair and a face that, as a college student, garnered her a prominent seat in the school's convertible during the homecoming parade. As a little girl, she and two of her cousins would sometimes venture over to the neighborhood market to perform outside. She did the singing while her cousins invited passersby to watch for a small fee. Arzie Mae had a beautiful voice, and her favorite song was the Lord's Prayer.

Whether it was due to the pain from her mother's death, or some other reason, Arzie Mae was not a happy person. Much of her anger was directed at her oldest sister, Irene. She also had problems getting along with other girls, and, in her adult years, she developed a reputation, especially among the women in the family, for being mean.

Arzie Mae excelled in school, however. She graduated from Friendship High School in 1951 with honors and delivered a speech at the commencement ceremony. At North Carolina A&T in Greensboro, she continued to excel in her studies while joining the Alpha Kappa Alpha sorority. She graduated with a bachelor's degree in home economics in 1955.

She earned a high school teacher's certificate in the nearby city of Raleigh in 1959. She also began a relationship with tall, dark-skinned Herman Sutton, who had also graduated from A&T. Sometime after they started dating, Herman was visiting the Artis family home when he blacked out and collapsed to the floor. John Henry came rushing into the room, but no one could figure out what had caused Herman to lose consciousness. A few years later, he had a short stay at the Cherry Hill Psychiatric Hospital in Goldsboro, North Carolina.

Some family members expressed concerns about Arzie Mae dating Herman. Despite this, she continued seeing him, and they married sometime in the early '60s. John Henry died shortly after, in 1963, and a few years later the marriage began to falter. When Herman was offered a position in Michigan, Arzie Mae refused to give up her teaching job to move with him, so they divorced.

Michigan may have been too far for Arzie Mae, but Washington, DC wasn't, apparently. She moved there in 1966 and got a job at Coolidge Senior High School as a home economics teacher, with an annual salary of $5,350. Her older brother Leroy and his wife, Mary, had moved to Riggs Park in the Northeast part of DC in the late '50s. Her cousin Wilbert was also married and living in the city, as was his brother Curtis.

Being the second-youngest sibling and the so-called baby girl of her family, Arzie Mae was always doted on by her brothers, Uncle Leroy perhaps most of all. He was a tough, sturdy-framed man, a veteran of WWII, and one of the best mechanics you could find. He took on a lot of family responsibilities, especially since John Henry was somewhat sickly. It was Leroy's hard-earned money that paid for Arzie Mae's tuition at A&T.

When Arzie Mae came to DC, she stayed with Uncle Leroy,

Aunt Mary, and their two children. Belva, the oldest child, was forced to surrender her room to accommodate her aunt. Her only request was that Arzie Mae not smoke in her room, so that the smell wouldn't damage her beloved wardrobe. Though Arzie Mae agreed to these terms, she would simply close the door to Belva's room and smoke anyway. Aunt Mary and Belva's complaints were ignored by Uncle Leroy.

Before long, Arzie Mae moved into a two-bedroom bottom-floor unit in the Hawaiian Garden apartment complex in Fort Totten. She befriended a fellow teacher in the DC public school system, named Lucille Hester, who lived just a floor above her.

At the age of 35, Arzie Mae mysteriously turned up pregnant, and she attempted to keep it a secret. Even Ms. Hester, who became her close friend, didn't know about the pregnancy. Sticking to her plan of secrecy, Arzie Mae started inviting a guy from North Carolina, who had previously been unsuccessful in courting her, to come visit her in DC. The suitor was surprised but excited by the offer, and he began visiting Arzie Mae. During one of his trips, he became a bit suspicious and stopped by to see Aunt Mary, who somehow knew about the pregnancy. Once the suitor found out what Arzie Mae was keeping from him, he stopped seeing her.

Arzie Mae's fortunes took a bad turn. Sometime in '67 or '68, she stopped working. For years, a rumor circulated within the family that she was fired for misappropriating school funds, but that was never confirmed. Being pregnant and unmarried, with no man visibly present, must have been a difficult burden for her to bear. But despite her predicament, Arzie Mae adopted an inexplicably harsh attitude toward her family. Her brothers had always been a reliable source of aid. Even though they were now saddled with the responsibilities of caring for their own families, they offered whatever support they could give. Arzie Mae, however, rejected their overtures. Desperate and fearful of not being able to feed herself and pay bills, Arzie Mae went to Ms. Hester for help, though she still kept her pregnancy a secret. Ms. Hester, who was pregnant herself, offered to feed her anytime the need arose.

It was under these circumstances that I, Bernard Douglas Sutton, was born in Washington, DC on Tuesday, May 28, 1968, at approximately 9:00 p.m. at Washington Hospital Center. It was almost two months after many inner cities like DC's exploded in violence over the assassination of Dr. Martin Luther King.

Despite Arzie Mae's continued refusal to accept help from family members, one of them must have managed to get the key to her apartment. When she arrived home with me from the hospital on June 1, a crib and several new pieces of furniture were there. She was still unwilling to reveal my father's identity to anyone. In my baby book, my father was listed as the very first person who called the hospital after I was born, but she simply wrote his name down as "father." Every time I looked at my baby book as an adult, that word, *father*, came at me like a closed iron door to which I would never obtain the key.

Shortly after returning home, Arzie Mae told several family members, "I'm not going back to work. And someone's going to take care of me." Untenable as this was, she held to it. She sought aid from the city's Department of Social Services and started receiving food stamps and a monthly welfare check.

It was seemingly happenstance that Ms. Hester found out about me. A baby's cry caught her attention one day as she was walking past Arzie Mae's door. Startled, she knocked, and Arzie Mae let her in and showed her to a little brown-skinned baby, after securing her promise to keep my birth a secret.

The Hawaiian Garden Apartments consisted of four four-story, light-red brick buildings. Of course, I would see much larger apartment buildings years later, but as a little boy, they seemed massive to me. The fact that they were larger than most of the other buildings for at least several blocks around only enhanced this perception. Each building had its own parking lot and they shared a small blacktop playground. My mom and I lived at 4520 Fort Totten Drive, directly across the street from Fort Totten Park. As a little boy out on my own one day, I accidentally started a fire in the park that grew large enough to need fire trucks to quell the blaze. No one, including my mom, ever suspected that I was the one who almost burned down the neighborhood park.

One of my earliest memories as a toddler was lying in bed between my mom and a man who to this day I suspect was my father. The white sheets covering me from head to feet shielded me from the imaginary monsters looming in the darkness. The comfort and security in those moments while lying between these two loving and protective giants overwhelmed me. But, apparently, my giddiness was disturbing their sleep, because they sat up in bed and scolded me until I quieted down. This was the only time I recall experiencing this feeling as a child.

My first recollection of venturing outside by myself occurred when I was four or five years old. It had just ceased raining, and my goal was to make it through all the dampness to the playground. While en route, I encountered a dog standing nearby and watching me approach. I tried to befriend the dog by inching up close enough to pet such a cute and innocent-looking animal. Suddenly, the dog lunged at me with a quick bark that sent me plopping right down into a puddle of water as it darted off. The abruptness of the dog's actions along with the wetness that was now all over the back of my pants brought me to tears, and I wailed for mommy while running back home. From that incident, I developed a fear of dogs that stayed with me for years.

A few years later, when I was still a small, skinny little boy, my mom drove us in her old white Chevrolet to visit a priest at a nearby monastery. As we were standing outside, this massive, furry beast appeared out of nowhere. I took off running frantically across a grassy field, leaving my mom and the priest to fend for themselves. Before I could reach the closest building, this monster tackled me to the ground, blocking all the daylight with its body until my mom and the priest came running up. I was an adult before I realized that this creature was a St. Bernard, my namesake and the world's greatest rescue dog. My running away probably sent it a signal that I wanted to play. As a little boy, however, the incident greatly heightened my fear of dogs.

I was pretty shy and quiet, and dogs weren't the only things that made me fearful. The older boys playing outside often picked on me. One time, two older girls even had me running home screaming for mommy. I was certainly at the bottom of the food chain in the apartment complex. However, an opportunity to raise my stock within the group presented itself when a boy appeared who was visiting his relatives there for a day or two. The boy was close to my size, just not as slim, and all of us were playing in one of the apartment buildings. As was often the case, the older guys started picking on me. This time they forced me into a tiny closet-like compartment underneath the main stairway. Feeling trapped and claustrophobic, I struggled to free myself from the tight, dark, confined space but couldn't overcome the weight and strength of the older guys. I started yelling for the guys to let me out. Peeping through a hole in the drywall, I noticed the contrast of the new boy's light-colored tennis shoes and dark-colored sweat socks as he just sat off to the side watching everything.

After what seemed like forever, the guys let me out. I was surrounded by laughter, and a sense of embarrassment overwhelmed me while I stood there fuming. As the urge to get revenge took over, I quickly assessed my options, thinking to myself: *It'll be better for me to punch the new boy, 'cause that gives me the best chance to vent some frustration and pick up a victory in front of the guys.* So, that's what I did.

My punch had the element of surprise, which gave me the early advantage. But the new boy quickly turned the tide by placing me in a tight headlock. I kept grabbing at his arms to free myself as the guys started urging me on. When I looked over, a few guys were signaling for me to punch him again.

Bap! My punch to the boy's face caused him to loosen his grip. But he responded with several blows to my head, and he tightened his hold on me again. After a minute or so of my squirming in the boy's unyielding headlock, the older guys broke up the fight.

I had vented my frustrations, but suffered another loss for my efforts. The boy slipped away and I was left dejected and adrift over how it all went down. To my surprise, instead of the older guys teasing me, they began giving me some pointers on how I could've done better. I had garnered respect for fighting, and they stopped picking on me. I liked that, but I felt bad about unfairly targeting the other boy—and about the whipping he gave me. It taught me never to pick a fight with an innocent party.

Of all my fears, my fear of death was, by far, the greatest. One day, my second-grade teacher at St. Anthony's grade school, located in the Brooklyn Northeast neighborhood, spoke to the class about the Immaculate Conception, heaven and hell, and everlasting life. None of it made any sense to me, but no one else seemed to share my concerns. So, after the other students left the class, I stayed to speak with the teacher.

"I don't understand," I said, pleading for clarity.

Looking at my troubled face, the teacher tried to console me, saying, "You just have to believe."

What kept tripping me up was the element of time. *How can we live forever?* I couldn't imagine time without a beginning or ending. Just like my own body and mind had a beginning and would one day end, I saw everything else as sharing the same fate. Even worse, the mere thought of leaving my body and everything I'd come to know made me very fearful. The idea of heaven did give me a measure of comfort, but doubt always crept in to open the floodgates of overwhelming fear. At night, I would lie in bed thinking about my spirit leaving my body and living somewhere else, forever. Then questions would race through my mind: *Where was I before coming here? Where will I go after death?* The fact that my mind couldn't answer these questions would sometimes cause me to scream out, "Mama, Mama!" She would come rushing to my bedside. Her presence always calmed me, but I never shared my thoughts about death with her.

Instinctively, I must have known that speaking to her about such things would have been fruitless. I never needed or asked my mother to help with my homework. She never read me any bedtime stories or engaged me in open-ended discussions about what was going on in our daily lives. All of her dialogue with me was about making sure I was fed, clean, and tidy. These experiences at home fit right in with how things were run at St. Anthony's. All students were required to wear uniforms: the boys in blue pants, white collared shirts, blue ties, and casual shoes, and the girls in white collared shirts, plaid skirts or blue pants, and casual shoes. The school was very strict, which on occasion extended to corporal punishment.

My most vivid memory of this form of discipline occurred in Sister Clotilde's fourth-grade class. We had just scuttled back to our desks from recess to discover that our class clown's grandmother was sitting in a chair next to our teacher's desk. Sister Clotilde, the meanest person I'd met at that point in my life, commanded that our funny and beloved clown come to the front, where his grandmother promptly introduced her leather belt to his naked hind parts. Greenish veins strained and protruded along the temples of his light-complexioned skin as the entire class observed in horror what would possibly be our fate if we dared step out of line.

Students were given rosaries and instructed to recite a prayer for every bead on the string before going to bed. Prayer, we were told, was important, so that our souls could reach the eternal bliss of heaven, instead of suffering everlasting damnation in hell.

Parents were encouraged to take their children to the adjoining St. Anthony's parish on Sunday.

My mom took me to church nearly every Sunday. I was much older when I figured out that my mother had converted from being Baptist, like the rest of her family, to Roman Catholic, so that the Archdiocese of Washington would cover my private school costs. Going to Mass didn't interest me in the least. The gloomy-sounding organ and haunting voice of the female choir singer made the hour-long service even more unbearable. For me, the best thing about church was getting to eat the altar bread after the Gospel reading.

Reading fantasy novels became my thing. In third grade, I checked out a copy of *The Lion, the Witch, and the Wardrobe* from the school library. The book was the first in C. S. Lewis's seven-book Chronicles of Narnia series, and it provided me with an important new form of escape. *The Hobbit* was next. After finishing all 316 pages in one weekend, I was hooked on J. R. R. Tolkien. Watching Saturday morning cartoons was my favorite activity, but that weekend it took a back seat to reading *The Hobbit.*

Tolkien's writing totally captured my imagination. Pictures of rolling green hills, dark forests, and tilted mountains entered my mind as I read how this little hobbit creature, with thirteen dwarves and a gray old wizard, embarked on a fantastic adventure. I had no idea that anything from school, much less a book, could make me forgo my Saturday morning animation ritual.

Next I took on Tolkien's *The Lord of the Rings*, which appealed to me like nothing ever had before. Reading those books was, up to that point, the happiest experience of my life. Of course, I wasn't the only person who Tolkien affected this way. The fantasy world he created touched millions of people, especially men and boys, from all around the world, and it spawned a series of games and activities centered on the world of fantasy. Sometimes after school, three or four of us boys would walk to a classmate's house and go on imaginary adventures with the board game Dungeons & Dragons.

Aside from fantasy novels, I delved into Norse, Greek, and Roman mythology. I loved reading about fierce and noble knights, such as Sir Lancelot of King Arthur's Round Table. Some kids were into futuristic stuff, like *Star Wars*, but for me, the older and more ancient the story, the better.

I never shared my escapes into fantasy and mythology with any of the guys back in the neighborhood at Fort Totten. They simply weren't into stuff like that. With them, I played touch and tackle football, trashcan ball (our version of basketball) and hide-and-seek. One of the older guys, Timothy McLean, and I got into electric football and racing. We'd set our little plastic players up in formation, then turn on the vibrating board to get the action going.

Every time I walked into a toy store, my eyes would get as big as dollar pieces whenever I saw an AFX race car set. I owned one of the smaller ones, because that's all my mother could afford, but it was my never-ending dream to one day own one of the big ones.

As it was, I received very few gifts as a child, because money was tight. After my fifth birthday or so, my mom stopped celebrating Christmas. To this day, I have no memory of any birthday cake or present. When her white Chevrolet started going bad, she had to let it go. The rent gobbled up most of our welfare check, and almost everything we ate was paid for with the food-stamp booklets we received monthly.

Sometimes assistance came to us from a generous visitor or two. Mr. Davenport, who lived upstairs, would occasionally drop off a box of Kentucky Fried Chicken and a Rock Creek grape soda for me. The sizzling sound coming out of the glass bottle whenever I screwed off the soft metal top was almost as good as the soda itself, and that chicken must have been as tasty as anything eaten by a mythological god. Mr. Jones (who I remember was the first bald-headed man I ever saw) also came by from time to time to give my mother money, and when he did, he'd generally be leathered down in a trench coat and boots. Uncle Leroy visited us more than anyone—or, at least, he tried to. Most of the time, my mother would speak to him from our front doorstep, opening the door only partially. With the door's chain still attached, he'd mumble his concern for our well-being from the hallway. On the rare occasion when my mother did allow him to enter, he wasn't allowed to stay very long. I could never understand why she treated him so rudely, and despite her actions he never stopped showing his concern for us.

My mom spent much of her time being mad, but Uncle Leroy wasn't the primary culprit. She was angry with the person in her head most of all. Nearly every day she'd start talking angrily to herself in a low conversational tone, barely above a whisper. She never directed her anger toward me, but sometimes I'd get irritated and shout, "Mom!"

Whether it was the sound of my voice or her embarrassment at realizing she was doing this right in front of me, she would suddenly snap out of her trancelike state, at least for the moment. Oftentimes she'd go right back into her rant.

In spite of this, she made sure my life was well ordered. Our apartment was always clean. I always got enough rest for school. My personal appearance was tidy, and she made sure that I was well behaved, never hesitating to tap my behind if necessary.

There was one time, however, when my mom went overboard with the discipline. I was outside with a friend named Wayne, and we stayed away much longer than she told me to. When we got back to my apartment, my mom was upset. I knew I had a good one coming to me once Wayne left. But to my surprise, she took her anger out on Wayne and smacked him across the face. Tears rolled down his cheeks as he quietly left our place. Even at that age, I knew my mom had crossed the line. But she acted like nothing out of the ordinary had taken place.

The next day I was nervous as hell to find Billy, Wayne's oldest brother, fixing his bike under the shade of a tree in the backyard of their house on Allison Street. One of his strong arms was gripping a silver wrench as the other was steadying the wheel of the bike where it was upturned on top of a metal table. Despite this, I felt more embarrassed than fearful. To my relief, Billy didn't seem upset. He told me that he wouldn't make a fuss about it or tell his parents as long as nothing like that ever happened again. I gave him my assurance that it wouldn't. Of course, Wayne and I stopped hanging out after that. This incident represented the first in a series of situations I would periodically face over something my mother did or refused to do.

With very few activities to get into at home, and my mom spending more time talking to herself than to me, I stayed outside as much as I could. One Saturday morning, two buddies turned me onto earning money by hustling grocery bags at the Giant Food, located in nearby Riggs Park Northeast. We stood outside the store and offered to assist shoppers with their grocery bags in order to earn a tip. I got so into plying my trade as a grocery bag hustler that watching my beloved Saturday morning cartoons became a thing of the past. I liked earning money for myself; it empowered me in a way nothing else had before. Having my own money became a real thrill for me. My mother eased up on going to church and Sundays turned into another workday for me. I would try to be the first boy outside at the Giant Food on Saturday and Sunday mornings, generally getting there between 7:00 and 8:00 a.m. I developed a nice little clientele, off-limits to the other boys whenever I was there, which was almost all the time. The older women were generally the best clients, because they often gave me dollar tips.

I began to develop a fondness for music from listening to the radio at home. R&B was what the people around me were listening to, and OK 100 was the most popular station for such music at the time. The Commodores, featuring Lionel Richie, were big, and their "Brick House," was a favorite, as was Chuck Brown's

"Bustin' Loose." Slow jams were my favorite, though. Heatwave had a number of pretty ballads, but "Always and Forever" was their most popular—it was so heartfelt, and I always ended up panting for air after trying, unsuccessfully, to imitate Johnnie Wilder's long, high-pitched note at the end of the song.

My mother would sometimes allow me to visit a neighbor's apartment just down the hall. This guy owned stacks and stacks of albums, and when I'd flip through his music collection, the album covers of Parliament-Funkadelic and Earth, Wind & Fire stood out to me. The vibrant colors and unique imagery grabbed my attention. I was too young to understand the meaning to many of Earth, Wind & Fire's songs, but I thought there was something deep, magical, and unexplainable about their sound, and it touched me more than anything else I'd ever heard.

Jealousy led me to finding my first friend at St. Anthony's. In my second-grade class, I sat next to Alfonso Ronca, one of the few whites attending our predominantly black school. He always got the best grades in class, so the teacher rewarded him with cookies and candy one morning.

Those goodies started speaking to me right from Alfonso's desk, and I instantly became envious. I didn't care about the effort Alfonso may have put into his work or what innate talents he may have been blessed with. I just had to have some of those sweets. During recess, I stole some of his candy and ate it. The teacher discovered my crime later that day, and the pleasure I got from eating Alfonso's candy quickly turned to shame. I apologized to Alfonso with tears flowing from my eyes. Fortunately, he accepted my apology, and we later became friends.

A boy named Rick Gardner transferred to St. Anthony's two years later, and the three of us became real tight. Since Alfonso lived nearby, we often hung at his house after school. His family was Italian and they often spoke their native tongue at home. Rick and I picked up a few Italian curse words that Alfonso taught us.

Since Rick and I took the subway home from school, we often rode the train together despite living in opposite directions from one another. We'd just hang out riding from one end of the Metro's Red Line to the other. His mother often gave him money, and I was earning my own hustling grocery bags, so we'd take turns buying each other snacks. My love affair with popcorn began in those days.

Rick was the first boy I noticed girls openly admiring because of his looks. His light bronze skin and wavy hair attracted a lot of attention. The older girls used to run their fingers through his hair and talk about how *good* it was. Getting girls' attention came easy for Rick. This wasn't the case for me. No one seemed to notice me, because nothing about me stood out. The only way I could meet girls was for me to approach them, but I didn't have the confidence to do that.

Fifth grade was an important year for me. I started finding my rhythm academically. I'd struggled mightily in the third and fourth grades, and, to make things worse, it seemed to me that both of my teachers were mean. But my fifth-grade teacher, Mrs. Fischer, was very nice. At the end of the year, I received the award for the most-improved student in her class.

This was also the year I began voicing concerns at home over the things my classmates and their families had that my mom and I didn't. Most of my classmates' parents had jobs and drove their kids to and from school. When I wanted to learn how to play drums, my mom couldn't afford to buy me an instrument. I went to a few basketball practices with the hope of earning a spot on the school team, but since my mom rarely visited the school, she didn't know any of the other parents with whom I could have carpooled. We lived out a repetitive monthly cycle of poverty. At the beginning of the month, when the welfare check and food stamps arrived, we ran to the store and loaded the refrigerator with groceries. But as the month progressed, a sense of gloom permeated our home as the food began to run out. The money I earned hustling bags didn't bring in enough to solve these issues, and it caused me a lot of frustration. My mom's not working began to bother me. Every time I brought home a form from school that requested my mom's occupation, I'd ask, "Mom. What do I write down as your occupation?"

"Homemaker." That was always her response.

The problem for me was that my mom's being a homemaker wasn't bringing in any money. She seemed fit and physically capable of working, so I began openly voicing my concern about this. Occasionally, my mom would randomly walk onto a basketball court in the neighborhood and ask the guys to pass her the ball. The other guys always enjoyed seeing her shooting baskets, but it started making me upset. One day, after she'd thrown up a few shots as we were on our way to the store, I bluntly asked her, "Why don't you work?"

"It's not for me to work. That's not what God has planned for me." Every time I asked her about work, that's the answer she gave me, and I couldn't come up with a response.

The other thing that greatly troubled me was the mystery of my father's identity. Many of my classmates and friends had dads at home, so I began to inquire. My mom ignored me at first, but I kept peppering her with questions until one day she finally gave me an answer.

"Mom, who's my father?"

"God is your father, and you will live forever. Don't worry, he's gonna move us to a better place." Trusting in what my mom told me, I tried to make sense of it. *Was my birth an Immaculate Conception like Jesus's? Is this why I've never seen my father? Does he not really exist, at least in a physical sense?* My imagination ran wild with questions like these. Even my happy memory of being a toddler sleeping in bed, securely nestled between my mom and the man I assumed was my father, receded to the back of my mind.

For the first time, I gave myself over to believing in God. I went about my days at school with a feeling of contentment, and my bedtime thoughts were peaceful. But this blissful state was disrupted several weeks later, when I came home to an apartment filled with strange men. They were taking our possessions out of the apartment, and they weren't being too nice about it. My mom was just standing there saying nothing. I ran to my room and found my broken-up Oakland Raiders electric football men on the floor. I ran outside to the sidewalk on Fort Totten Drive, where the men had taken our belongings, with tears running down my face. One of my friends, who was a few years older, walked up.

"What happened?"

"I don't know. These men just threw our stuff out here."

"Oh, you got evicted."

I just stood there sniffling. I thought back to the day, not too long before, when I had come home from school and seen an official-looking notice taped to our front door. It was several pages long, and I had wondered why the postal carrier hadn't placed it in our mailbox with everything else. I had snatched the notice off the door and given it to my mom, who had mumbled some angry words after she looked at it. I figured there was a connection between that notice and our getting thrown out, but I was too young to know what it was.

By nightfall, a city official was driving my mom and me to a homeless shelter.

Cornelius Pitts moved to Washington, DC from his hometown of New Orleans in the 1950s. After graduating from Howard University, he earned money as a typist and cab driver, and eventually bought some row houses in the city. His dream was to own a hotel, and, by the end of the 1960s, he had torn down some buildings he owned at 14th and Belmont and opened the Pitts Motor Hotel, right near the U Street Corridor.

Mr. Pitts's years of hard work turned him into an overnight success. The Pitts Hotel was soon recognized as the top hotel for blacks in DC. Its success was due, in large part, to his catering to the city's black elite. Some of the nation's top black entertainers performed at the hotel's Red Carpet Lounge. Dr. Martin Luther King and the Southern Christian Leadership Conference (SCLC) held a meeting at the hotel.

Forces beyond Mr. Pitts's control resulted in the rapid decline of his business. The violence that erupted in 1968 following Dr. King's assassination affected DC as it did many other inner cities. The collective black anger caused many white merchants to move out of the black community. This "white flight" slowed business activity on U Street. Making matters worse, the dismantling of segregation led many blacks to patronize white-owned establishments, taking money out of what had been black segregated areas. The U Street Corridor and other such areas of the city felt that loss.

The economic decline that started in the late '60s picked up during the '70s. The downward spiral led to the U Street community experiencing an influx of crime, drugs, and prostitution. The black elite who once stayed at the Pitts Hotel in its heyday were replaced by guests from the poor and downtrodden classes.

The economic problems that affected the U Street Corridor were felt citywide by the late '70s. Poor people, Vietnam War veterans, and patients newly released from overcrowded mental institutions began filling the streets. Homelessness became a huge problem as the city faced a shortage of low-income housing. City officials desperate for solutions began calling on businesses to help house the city's indigent population. Mr. Pitts, always generous to the less fortunate, began renting some of his rooms to the homeless in an effort to fill this void. Eventually, the once-prestigious Pitts Hotel was converted to a full-time homeless shelter.

The Pitts Hotel was in the latter stages of its transformation when my mom and I stayed there. Our room had a bathroom, a bunk bed, a table, a television, and a large dresser. Cockroaches were often seen on the floor and walls. Rats weren't total strangers either. Despite this, after we arrived, my mother made sure we maintained her standard of cleanliness at all times. Lunch was given to the residents, and usually consisted of a half-beef, half-pork hot dog known in DC as a half-smoke, cupcake, and a soda—my favorite meal of the day.

At that time, the corner of 14th and Belmont was a sight to see. Cheap-looking wine bottles and beer cans were everywhere, and the people who had consumed what was in them were all on the sidewalk surrounding the row houses or sitting on the front steps. Since the Pitts Hotel was located at the top of the street, I had to walk all the way down the block to catch the bus on 14th. People were always hanging outside, even in the morning when I was going to school. By evening, Belmont would be filled with hundreds of people from the top of the hill all the way down to the bottom of the block. The corner of 14th and U Street, just a few blocks from Belmont, was one of the city's hot spots for prostitution. The intersection offered great visibility for the ladies of the night to ply their trade.

Belmont Street, which offered much less visibility, was the drug spot. At that young age, I never noticed any drug transactions. And as I walked along Belmont Street in my school uniform, no one ever approached or bothered me. My mother never said anything about the dangers in the neighborhood, but I was forbidden to venture away from the hotel grounds.

After we had stayed at the Pitts Hotel for several months, Uncle Leroy came to our aid once again by inviting us to stay with his family. Over the years, my mom and I had travelled to North Carolina a few times to see my aunt and uncles, but this was going to be my first time staying with my extended family.

By the late '70s, Riggs Park—known to some as Lamond-Riggs or simply Riggs—was a predominantly black, working-class community. Riggs was built after WWII by Abe Pollin, a real estate mogul and the owner of the NBA's Washington Wizards (formerly the Bullets). The community had been predominantly Jewish, but after the '68 riots, most of the Jews started moving to the Maryland suburbs. Uncle Leroy and Aunt Mary were some of the first blacks to move into Riggs when they purchased their home in 1959. Their place, located at 755 Kennedy Street, was a three-bedroom detached brick house situated among a long, curving row of similarly styled homes in the heart of Riggs. It was late summer in 1978 when my mom and I moved there.

I hadn't known that their son, Leroy Jr., aka Brother, owned a German shepherd. Before I could get to their front steps, the dog started barking at me from behind the fence leading to the backyard. I could've sworn that that dog's eyes were focused only on me. Teeth bared, it could sense my fear, I felt, and it took a lot of convincing from Aunt Mary and Brother to get me to walk up those front steps. This time, Belva was keeping her room. My mom and I slept in the basement. The walls down there were wood paneled. There were also a fold-out sofa, a television, and a half bathroom.

I settled in with Uncle Leroy's family quite easily. Brother helped me overcome my fear of dogs by having me stand outside with him in the backyard while his dog came over and sniffed me up. The dog seemed excited at first, which made me nervous, but Brother standing right there beside me helped me to remain still. Once the dog calmed down, I got more comfortable, and just like that my phobia of dogs was gone.

The house was Aunt Mary's domain, since Uncle Leroy spent a lot of time driving his cab. Aunt Mary, who was also from the South, had a personality as large as they came, and her sense of humor and kind heart made her a joy to be around. One day she bought me some white Nikes, with the swoosh logo in black. They cost $32. That was a day I would never forget.

Belva, who was in her early 20s, had moved back home after graduating from Hampton University in Virginia. She was very intelligent and well-spoken, and seemed wise beyond her years. Her beautiful dark skin and unique attractiveness brought notice from guys, but she had a no-nonsense attitude that kept any undesirables away. Most of her time outside of work was spent helping Aunt Mary take care of the house. She taught me how to play spades, and we spent hours competing against each other at the dining room table.

Brother, who was nearly two years younger than Belva, opted to start working instead of finishing his studies at the University of the District of Columbia (UDC) and was rarely at home. He and his friends would hang out with their buddies or girlfriends. Most of the time it seemed like he was either just coming in or on his way out, much like his father. Where Belva was quiet and serene, Brother loved to talk. He had a cool way of talking that he picked up hanging out in the streets and at Finley's Boxing Gym in DC. I admired and looked up to him like a big brother.

Seeing Brother prepare to go out was quite an event. The attention he put into every detail of his wardrobe was intense. He wore designer jeans, like Jordache or Calvin Klein, and every pair was heavily starched, pressed, and creased. Some of the creases in his older jeans were white from being ironed so much. After ironing his jeans near the dining room, he'd fold them delicately over his forearm and glide back upstairs. He'd come back down with a pair of Hush Puppies on his feet and make his final preparations. He took up his usual position in front of the dining-room mirror, combed and brushed his hair, and talked stuff to me the entire time.

"Shame you too young to step out wit' me."

We developed a very playful relationship. Since I knew he'd spent some time boxing, I'd sometimes throw punches near his face when he stood in the mirror admiring himself. He'd just smile and calmly say, "Don't play or you will lay." One of his buddies would roll up in his car, blow the horn, and Brother would strut out the door. Brother never hit me, but he did find a slick way of getting me back. Since he knew I had given up sweets for the 40 days of Lent, he came into the kitchen one morning and pulled down a box of glazed donuts from atop the refrigerator.

"Mmmmm, this thing is good! You want one?"

Then, he caught himself: "Oh, that's right. You can't eat sweets. Boy, too bad you can't get with one of these here!"

I just hung my head in sadness.

I befriended a neighborhood boy named Lester "Chico" Martin, who was a few years older than me, and who shared my interest in comic books. Being into comics was, for me, a natural extension of my infatuation with cartoons and finding enjoyment in reading about ancient heroes. I really took a liking to reading the Avengers, Thor, and the Silver Surfer comics. Both my and Chico's comic-book collections were somewhat limited, and we didn't have a lot of money. So, Chico introduced me to the art of stealing from stores.

This wasn't something totally new to me. On several occasions when I was just four or five, I had stolen toys out of the grocery store and the old People Drug store. I'd find the toy aisle, grab what I liked, and use my body to hide what was in my hand from the unsuspecting eyes of cashiers. By the time my mom realized I'd pulled a caper, we'd be down the road a ways in her white Chevrolet. She'd get upset and fuss at me but never made me return any of the items.

In my mind, those early acts of thievery had been successes, so what Chico was suggesting seemed like a good opportunity to me. Chico lived a few blocks away on Jefferson Street, so we'd walk over to the nearby Fort Totten Metro. From there, we'd take the Red Line to a comic-book store in Chinatown Northwest.

After we pulled off several thefts with ease, Chico located another store in downtown Silver Spring, Maryland. It was a short ride on the Red Line in the opposite direction from Chinatown.

On our first trip there, it was a rainy day, so Chico unveiled a little trick he'd perfected. As we walked around the store, he hid a few comics in his compact umbrella.

Things were going so well for us that I decided to venture out on my own. I chose the store in Silver Spring as my target, because it was bigger and the main retail space was around the corner from where the cashier generally sat. The store was located on the second floor of a building just a few blocks from the Silver Spring Metro. As usual, there was just one clerk working, and he happened to be engrossed in a comic book. I spoke to him, walked around the corner, and got down to business. After grabbing a few things, I quietly left the store noticing that the clerk's head was still in his comic.

I headed straightaway to the Metro, but before I got off the block, the clerk was calling out to me. He was white and very tall. As soon as I saw him, I took off running, but those long legs of his chased me down within seconds. In my eyes, that white man could have given Carl Lewis a run for his money. After checking my bag and finding the stolen items, he dragged me back to the store. Then he called the police. When a Montgomery County police officer showed up, I admitted to the crime. I also cried, out of a sense of shame and a desire for mercy. As the officer was taking me away, I couldn't resist asking the clerk how he'd known I'd stolen those comics. "Because you didn't say anything to me before you left," he replied.

The officer put me in the back seat of his squad car and took me to a nearby police station. I didn't know what to expect. Once we got inside, he showed me several jail cells, which frightened me more. Then, he sat me down on the other side of his desk and explained that I could end up in one of those cells if my behavior didn't change.

After a few minutes, he drove me to a different Metro station. He pulled out a Metro fare card, handed it to me, and warned me to never steal again. I promised that I wouldn't, grabbed the fare card, and scampered out of the car as happy as could be! Of course, I never mentioned any of this to my mom.

I was so embarrassed by what had happened that I stopped hanging around Chico. My short-lived career as a thief was over. I no longer had any interest in travelling to comic-book stores, especially the two I'd stolen from, and those were the only ones I knew. Since my friendship with Chico was based primarily on stealing comics, we drifted apart.

Many years later, I became friends with Brian Gilmore, an attorney and poet who grew up in Riggs Park. He and Chico had grown up together, and, according to him, Chico got heavily involved with selling drugs. In 1993, Chico's silver Mitsubishi Montero truck was found near the Fort Totten Metro, his body inside, wrapped up in a carpet. Word on the street was that since Chico didn't run with a particular crew of guys, he had become a target for people who may have been jealous of the money he was making.

Riggs Park was closer to the Giant Food than Fort Totten, so I went back to hustling grocery bags and re-established a clientele. I also developed a friendly relationship with the store manager. On one particular Saturday, things just clicked for me. Besides me, none of the regular bag hustlers showed up to work, and the tips were better than they'd ever been. My take by early afternoon was $25. I couldn't believe it! I zoomed home, pockets bulging with quarters, and gave my mom some of the spoils.

My days hustling bags weren't always so great, though. There was a guy named Kevin Fortune who, I'd been told, used to box, and he would give me a hard time whenever he came to the store. He'd ball up his fists and threaten to hit me, so I just kept my distance from him. But one day Kevin caught me walking through the Giant and I couldn't avoid him.

"Gimme a dolla!"

"I don't have one."

"I said, gimme a dolla!"

This time he grabbed the hood of my jacket as I tried to walk by him.

"He said he ain't got no dolla!"

It was my hustling buddy, Li'l Ant, who just happened to be walking by. He also grabbed my hood to make sure Kevin got his message. Kevin was shocked.

"So, it's like that, huh?"

"Yeah! It's like that."

Kevin let go of my hood and stepped off.

Li'l Ant had stood up to Kevin, and his physical stature was even less impressive than mine. He was shorter and skinnier. One of his hands had four fingers, and the other one only had three. Yet, he was much more courageous than me. No one had ever taken up for me like that. At the very least, the incident opened me up to the possibility of having more courage when I was threatened.

Li'l Ant couldn't save me from my mom though. She still ran a tight ship when it came to discipline and obedience. One night she took her belt to me, and all I could do was jump, scream, and holler all over the basement. The next morning, Aunt Mary saw me in the living room. "What was all that singing I heard downstairs last night? Boy, I didn't know you could sing like that."

My relationship with Aunt Mary had a playfulness that never existed between my mom and me, and this made my mom get a bit uneasy. There were times when she made me stay downstairs with her in the basement, even though I wanted to be with Aunt Mary or Belva. I'd see one of them sitting in the living room or at the dining room table and would begin talking to them, only to hear my mom call to me, "Come on down these stairs!" I'd hesitate for a second or two before heading downstairs.

At the time, I wasn't aware of what was going on between my

mom and Aunt Mary. However, I did observe on many occasions my mom coming into the house and not speaking to Aunt Mary. I guess this happened one too many times, because Aunt Mary came to the basement one evening and said to my mom, "You're going to speak to me in my own house." She didn't yell, scream, or utter a single curse word, but she let my mom have it. Then, she looked at me and said, "You're a bright little boy."

After Aunt Mary left, my mom sat on the fold-out sofa and sobbed. I'd never seen her cry before. A heavy jolt of compassion consumed me, but I didn't know how to express it. Anger and frustration were the emotions I was accustomed to seeing my mom display, which had caused our relationship to be physically distant. The urge to comfort her with a hug didn't enter my mind, so I just helplessly looked on as my mom let this unknown side of herself out.

Aunt Mary's words must have finally forced her to accept all the mean things she'd done to her and others. I had felt the force in Aunt Mary's words, things I agreed with but could never have said to my mom at such a young age.

My mom and I didn't last another week on Kennedy Street. As we were packing our bags, Belva and Brother were standing in the dining room with long faces. Before we left, Aunt Mary repeated what she had told me in the basement. Though I was sad about being thrown out, I understood why we had to go, and it certainly wasn't Aunt Mary's fault. Uncle Leroy put us in his cab and took us back to the Pitts Hotel.

This was the second time my mom had caused us to be displaced. Her promise about what God was going to do had not been fulfilled, and the trust I had in her was broken. I still openly respected her and remained obedient, but there was something else beginning to simmer in my heart. I began to doubt the things she told me. She spoke with so much confidence about God. But now I was looking for proof.

I came up with a silly way to test my mom. One morning, I took a hammer that my mother kept around for protection, and hid it under a pillow. Later that day, she inquired about the hammer, but I acted as if I didn't know where it was. I waited for a few hours before removing the pillow to reveal what was underneath. "There's the hammer right there, Mom!"

I pointed at the hammer, acting excited as my mom stood nearby.

She said, "I knew the hammer was there." She was confident as she said this.

"How did you know?"

"Because I put it there."

She put it there? My mom is a damn liar. I'd had enough of this.

I met a streetwise boy named Sean who was also staying at the Pitts Hotel. He and I started slipping off to different parts of the city. The way Sean walked, talked, and carried himself was real cool, and I began to feel inadequate around him. My comics collection was the one thing I had over him. The next time we ventured downtown, I brought some of my most valuable comics and suggested that we go to the comic-book store. This time, I led the way as Sean watched me conducting business with the sales clerk. When the clerk handed me a wad of cash, Sean's eyes lit up. He had no idea that certain comics were valuable, and he was impressed by what I did. I gave him a few bills before we made our way back to 14th and Belmont.

This time, I didn't share any of the money with my mom. My confidence in her had been shaken, and I was beginning to contemplate other ways to make money, and to become more independent. With no other relatives coming to the rescue, this time we stayed at the Pitts Hotel longer than before. But two noteworthy things happened during this time. One afternoon, I was with my mom at an office building somewhere downtown, when she suddenly became all excited. She'd just been approved to receive Social Security. I didn't know what that was, or what it meant, but Mom explained that we were no longer going to be receiving a welfare check and food stamps. My mom was elated.

Sometime later, we were at the Pitts Hotel when someone from the Department of Human Services (DHS) informed my mom that they had found an apartment for us somewhere in Northeast. After months of living in the Pitts, we were finally going to be moving into a permanent home.

Streets

THE X2 AND X4 METRO BUSES WERE LONG, WITH GRAY accordion-looking centers that allowed them to navigate, snake-like, through traffic and tight streets. The bus route ran along H Street, starting uptown in the business district, then moved through some of the rough areas of the Northeast side of the city. Besides H Street, Benning Road and Minnesota and Nannie Helen Burroughs avenues were the main roads along this bus route, which teemed with excitement and more than its share of colorful people.

All of these areas of the city looked war-torn and neglected. Abandoned buildings, litter, and poorly maintained lawns were the standard. Whereas H Street and Minnesota Avenue were busy with people traversing and hanging on the sidewalks like they were on the Vegas strip, the other areas along the bus route were more deso-late. Our apartment was just a block up from Benning Road.

My first time riding the X bus occurred during the spring of the sixth grade. My mom and I were en route to our new two-bedroom apartment at 1901 H Street Northeast. It was nighttime and a store on 6th and H Street Northeast had caught fire. From a distance, I could see smoke billowing from the burning building as fire trucks and other emergency vehicles were parked all around trying to deal with the blaze. Our bus turned off H Street and made its way through narrow side streets until we passed the fire and could safely get back on H Street.

H Street was bustling with all types of characters. There were drunks, bums, drug addicts, and rough-looking young thugs on almost every corner. The buildings were run-down, and the entire corridor was littered with carryout food places, liquor stores, and churches. Minus the prostitution, it reminded me of U Street.

Once we passed 15th Street, the bus made a slight right onto Benning Road. Hechinger Mall, a two-level shopping center under construction at the time, was on the left and the Pentacle Apartments were on our right. We rode the bus four more blocks and got off at 19th and Benning, then walked up a block to our apartment building.

Our two-bedroom apartment was located in an eight-unit building. Somehow my mom was able to get us two beds, a dresser, a cheap metal dining table with four plastic-covered chairs, and a television. We didn't have any living-room furniture, or a telephone. Of course, my mom rarely allowed visitors and she wasn't too keen on communicating with people in general. We did, however, have a radio like at Fort Totten. Sunday morning was her time for singing along to gospel songs.

I felt uneasy about the neighborhood. The Northeast and Southeast quadrants of the city were full of dangerous places. Just thinking about going there made me feel uneasy. I could now relate to how Frodo Baggins must have felt entering Mordor in *The Lord of the Rings*. The difference for me was the fact that I was living there.

Our neighborhood went by several names depending on how one was associated with the area. Carver Terrace was the name used by reporters and other outsiders, because most of the buildings were part of the Carver Terrace projects, even though the Langston Terrace Dwellings, another big housing project, was only a few blocks away.

Younger people in the neighborhood called the area The Hill, 21st, or Little Vietnam. The Hill tag came from the fact that Carver Terrace sloped up a hill, with Maryland Avenue running up the center. The corner of Maryland Avenue and 21st was at the heart of all the street activity. It was the hub for gambling, drugs, and violence. It wasn't wise for anyone to venture up there unless they knew people in that area. It was rumored that the Little Vietnam tag stemmed from veterans of that war being housed in the area after discharge. By the time I moved there, though, "Little Vietnam" stood for the violence that had become an ordinary occurrence.

The first boy I met was named Juan. He and his mother lived just around the corner on 19th Street, and they were the only Latin family in the neighborhood. We often hung out on his front steps or played in a grassy yard in the back of my building. Like me, Juan was about to finish the sixth grade. He attended Blow Pierce Elementary, a public school less than two blocks away on Benning Road. No one in the neighborhood messed with Juan, but he didn't have any friends. The fact that we had no one else to play with became our bond.

Right away, I noticed some troubling things about him. He was openly disrespectful to his mother, especially when he got angry. He'd curse and throw things at her. I'd never seen anything like that before. In Juan's case, his mother seemed helpless. My mom would've had my head if I acted like that.

My real introduction to Little Vietnam came through Tyrone "Red Ty" Owens. People called him Red Ty due to his light complexion. He was a few years older than Juan and me and also lived on 19th Street. Red Ty was a certified hoodlum. He always wore Izod or Polo shirts and expensive jeans with nice-sized cuffs at the bottom. His shoes were either the latest high-top Nikes or low-cut Adidas, and the slight dip in each step he took made it appear as if he was gliding up and down 19th Street. It was the coolest walk I'd seen, but he also gave off a menacing presence.

One afternoon he saw us playing in front of Juan's building and came over to us. He was wearing Calvin Klein jeans and black-striped, fish-head Adidas shoes; several thin silver chains hung around his neck.

"What's up, Juan?"

After they talked for a few minutes, Red Ty sized Juan up and declared, "Young'n, you alright." Then, he looked at me. "But you! I don't like you, you sucka-ass niggah!"

As he said this to me with a sneer, he gritted his teeth, looked down at my feet, and stepped off real cool-like.

My chest immediately tightened. I was thinking, *What have I done? Why doesn't he like me?* For the rest of the day I kept racking my brain trying to figure out what Red Ty could possibly have against me. Though I was scared as hell, my fear was mixed with a sense of admiration for how he presented himself.

Juan and I didn't say a word about the incident, but he started treating me differently. Perhaps after that he figured me as being soft or a chump. Those sudden and unpredictable outbursts that he used to direct toward his mother started being thrown in my direction.

We were playing on the grassy field behind my building some days later, when he got angry with me. Suddenly, he started flailing his arms at me and tried to get physical. Though I lacked confidence in fighting, I was pretty athletic, and by then I knew from all the playing we'd done together that Juan was uncoordinated, so I stood my ground. As we began circling each other, Kelly, a girl who lived with her aunt in my building, came outside to check out the action.

I kept my focus on Juan's face and upper body and readied myself for his next move. I noticed that he was inching over to his right for some reason. Kelly, who'd been intensely watching us, calmly walked over to where Juan was headed, picked up a broken brick that had been hiding in the tall grass, and tossed it over the fence into the alley. That's what Juan was trying to pick up, and I hadn't seen it.

Without the aid of that brick, Juan didn't want to fight any-more. Luckily, Kelly wanted to see us fight fair, or "head-up," as people in Little Vietnam called it. Juan and I never played together again. Sometime later, his mother started dating a man named Roy who lived in the building next to mine. Tensions between Juan and Roy caused Juan's mother to stand up to her son at last, and eventually Juan left, headed probably to either his father's home or a youth facility.

After Juan left, Roy and I became friends. I used to come over to Juan's mother's house and play checkers with him. Roy suffered from multiple sclerosis, which caused him to move slowly and walk with a cane. He always maintained an upbeat attitude, though. Every time he got me in a trap on the checkerboard, and I had no way out, he'd laugh and say in his scraggily voice, "Go head, take your jump; take your jump!"

He introduced me to the music of Stevie Wonder. I was look-ing through his albums and ran across Stevie's then-new *Journey Through "The Secret Life of Plants"* soundtrack LP. Just as with Earth, Wind & Fire, some of the lyrics were above my head, but the mel-odies and the sound of his voice provoked something inside me.

It was nice spending time with Roy, but I yearned to play with more kids my own age. I began venturing out to the 1800 block of Benning Road, where all the boys went to play pinball and video games at Sylvia's Records. It seemed like everyone except me loved Pac-Man, but my game was Crazy Climber, where you played a man trying to climb tall buildings in spite of closing windows, res-idents dropping plants, birds pooping doo-doo and gorillas tossing metal beams. I got pretty good playing pinball, too—my favorite was Meteor.

Kelly, the girl who helped me out when I was fighting Juan that day, had an older brother named Sean. He started coming over some-times, and as I had with the other Sean, we travelled to various parts of the city. The Downtown Movie Theatre, just past Chinatown, showed a lot of Bruce Lee and Chuck Norris films. It was Sean who took me on my lone fishing trip, to a spot near RFK Stadium. Using a makeshift fishing rod, he pulled a catfish out of the muddy Potomac River. Not wanting to eat it and having no place to keep it, he threw it back in the water.

Sean was streetwise and had a knack for getting in and out of sticky situations. This didn't rub off on me, though. We were coming back from watching another movie at the Downtown on a Saturday afternoon, when I saw Red Ty sitting on a curb drinking a beer with another boy, named Little Boo. When I got to the corner of my building, Red Ty called out to me, "Hey, Bernard. Hold up for a second."

I waited on the corner, compelled somehow by his stated dislike for me, as they approached—Sean, though, kept walking, and went into our building. As soon as they came up, Red Ty stepped around me, grabbed my arms, and locked them behind my back. I was a defenseless target for Little Boo, who hit me with a quick, one-handed two-punch combination to my left ribs and face. Then he reached in the pocket of my green khaki pants and grabbed all the money inside—50 cents. Red Ty let my arms go, but I was too scared to fight, so I just grabbed my face, crying, as I went home.

My mom called the police, but nothing came of it. The next day, she saw Red Ty near 19th Street and they exchanged words. No one knew my mom, but because she never left the house without carrying a wooden stick with two nails jutting out of one end, people in the neighborhood were aware of her. The next time I saw Red Ty, he had changed his tune, somewhat. He walked over to me and said, "We didn't jump you. After Little Boo hit you, I let go of your arms, so you could fight him head-up." I noticed that his palms were out and facing upward in a nonthreatening manner. I didn't argue with him. I was just happy that he wasn't trying to hurt me.

With Little Boo, it was a different matter. Despite the scowl he generally wore on his dark-brown face, he was small in size. Red Ty was the one I was really afraid of, and he'd just told me that he was okay with Little Boo and me going against each other.

I started envisioning myself getting back at Little Boo, the fists at the end of my longer arms finding his face over and over. He lived just half a block away, between H Street and Benning, so he wouldn't be hard to find. Getting by Juan didn't mean anything in Little Vietnam, but if I got out on Little Boo, that would garner me some real respect.

I didn't have to dream long. A few days later, I was walking to the stores on Benning when I saw Little Boo standing across the street from me in front of his family's house about fifteen or twenty row houses away from where I was. I stopped and stared at him, thinking, *I can do this.*

Little Boo wasn't looking in my direction at first, but after about 30 seconds of me just standing there, he noticed me. Once he realized that I was staring at him, he balled up his fists. He looked menacing and determined in spite of his small frame. He called out from the distance.

"What's up!"

This was my moment for redemption. No one else was out there, so I didn't have to worry about getting nervous from people looking on. But I just couldn't compel myself to step to him and fight. I didn't want any part of this guy, so I turned my head away, planted my eyes on the ground, and kept things moving toward Benning Road. With only a glare this time, Little Boo had defeated me again.

I later learned about the Napoleon complex in school. Little Boo may have had one, and it served him well in the streets, at least for a time. Ten years after my run-in with him, he'd become one of the most feared dudes around the area. He wouldn't hesitate to get down to business, gun in hand, at the slightest provocation.

In some cases, even if he squashed a beef with a guy, he'd kill him anyway.

Little Boo eventually went on a killing spree. Word on the street was he killed a guy from our neighborhood named Big Clayton and went on the run. One of his hanging spots was 18th and D Street Northeast. He was using a pay phone there when someone gunned him down. The triggerman had recently squashed a beef with him, but was aware of his reputation and didn't want to take any chances.

Periodically, I would see a group of boys playing touch football on H Place, a little side street half a block up from my apartment. Nestled between the busier H and I Streets, H Place had fewer moving and parked cars, so there was generally plenty of room in the street to play. One day I felt the need to be around people my own age. Fortunately, the boys there that day needed one more person, so I got picked to play. Loni, a boy who was a little shorter and a few years younger than me, was assigned to be my defender. As I ran my routes, he started pushing and grabbing me. I noticed that an older boy on his team named Don was encouraging Loni to rough me up. Before the game ended, Loni and I got into a brief scuffle, but fortunately my size served me well.

I felt good about how things went, so I started going to H Place every day. Loni and I became friendly, and I learned that the guys called him Doink-Doink because his head was supposedly so big. I also got to know Charles, Fat Butch, Bummy, Wayne Leander, Bobby, White-boy Tykee, and Fat Black Wills. Don, for whatever reason, was the only boy who didn't like me.

Of all the boys, Ricardo Perry, who lived in an apartment above Dot's Crab House and would sometimes hang out with us, had the most respect on our block. Guys from other groups in Little Vietnam admired him for being an all-around athlete. He was slim, slightly shorter than me, and played basketball well.

He was also an excellent football player and even boxed for a time. If a guy was known for fighting, he was called "thorough." Ricardo and another boy, Fish, were known as the two most thorough dudes at Blow Pierce Elementary.

It didn't take long for me to see why Ricardo had such a reputation. He got into a fight with a boy named Pop at the same spot where Loni and I had scuffled. When they squared off, Ricardo put up both of his hands in front of his face, with his left foot pointed toward Pop and his right foot at a 90-degree angle, about two feet behind his left foot. There was a slight bend in his knees, and he bounced on his toes while moving from side to side.

Almost as soon as Ricardo started moving to his left, he'd reverse himself and start moving to the right. This movement confused Pop, who was angrily lunging at Ricardo with his punches. Every one of those punches missed the target. Pop would get ready to punch but then have to reset himself, because Ricardo would move just enough to be out of range.

Then, Ricardo started using head fakes, which I later learned were called feints, to make Pop think he was about to throw a punch. And each time Pop momentarily paused to brace himself for the punch he thought was coming, Ricardo hesitated and threw it just after the pause. These right-hand punches were lightning-quick, straight, short, and pinpoint accurate. Everyone could see the punches land. I would have bet every coin in my pocket that Pop's face existed just to catch Ricardo's right hand. After each bop, Ricardo would glide out of the way before Pop could get his punches off. After a few minutes of this, Pop quit and walked away. I'd never witnessed anything like that. Most fights looked clumsy, with a bunch of grabbing, and wild punches. Watching Ricardo fight reminded me of a Bruce Lee movie. It was art in action.

My own status on H Place was still somewhat uncertain. Most of the guys looked up to Don, and he still hadn't accepted me. A disagreement over music gave him an opportunity to act on his dislike.

Even though I liked Chuck Brown's "Bustin' Loose," his hit song from a few years back, I couldn't embrace the DC-based music he created known as go-go. All that percussion sound was too much for me. It sounded like a bunch of noise, what with all the clanking from beating on cowbells, timbales, congas, and drums. But I was definitely in the minority on H Place and all over the rough areas of DC. Go-go was hot, and Rare Essence was the hottest band. Everyone was trying to imitate Funk and Little Benny, the two leaders of the group. Boys all around the city created little junkyard bands with fake instruments—buckets to serve as the drums, STP motor oil cans to fill in for the timbales, and a thick plastic cup or bottle to give off the sound of a cowbell.

The guys on H Place created their own little band, and they played in the wide alley behind H Place. It was an ideal place for it, because men usually left stuff there after working on cars. They were setting up to play one day while I leaned against a metal table, just watching them. When Don suggested that they use the same metal table I was on, the other guys agreed. But when Don came up to ask me to move, he was rude about it.

"Move!"

It was clear that Don didn't like me. But now he was being openly disrespectful, and I wasn't having it.

"Naw, I ain't movin'."

"Man, why don't you just move!"

I still refused.

Bam! Don punched me right in the face. It caught me off guard, and my head buzzed for a few moments. Once I got myself together, I stepped into the middle of the alley and threw my hands up to fight. Everyone else watched as we fought for more than a few minutes. During that time, I managed to hit him with my right hand.

The pace of the fight was slow, because I did more moving around than punching. Don couldn't get to me, so, after a while, he just extended his right hand to me and said, "You a'right." I shook his hand, and just like that I gained full acceptance into the group. Don and I became good friends, especially when we discovered that we shared a birthday—May 28. He was exactly one year older than me. Fighting Don, who was one of the group's most respected guys, garnered me a level of acceptance and respect I never had in Fort Totten. For the first time in my life, I didn't feel like an outsider.

Like me, everyone was pretty poor. And as far as my funny-behaving mom with her protection stick was concerned, she seemed to fit right in. Loni's grandmother used to hang her big underwear on some rubber cords in their backyard to let them dry. Wayne Leander had a mentally challenged brother who mumbled everything. Tykee had an oversized white mother. In DC, insulting someone for laughs was called "jonin'," and everyone had at least one thing we could all jone on each other about for a guaranteed laugh.

Fat Butch was one of the oldest, and easily the biggest guy in our group. None of us could do anything with him physically. He was actually chubbier than he was fat, but we took pleasure in emphasizing the latter word when saying his name, as a bit of payback for all the little irritating things he would often do to us.

Don, for some reason I didn't understand, would generally be the focus of Fat Butch's little games. One golden day in August, Don was on H Place enjoying a soda. It was too hot outside for him to be in a sharing mood, but Fat Butch didn't care.

"Don, let me get a sip! Come on Don, save me some!"

We could all see that Don wanted to finish off his drink, but he got tired of Fat Butch's pleading, so begrudgingly handed him the nearly empty bottle. As soon as Fat Butch got his hand on it, he poured out the contents and tossed the bottle in one of the cardboard boxes posing as a trash can that sat in the dirt next to a mangled fence. That move set Don off.

"Why the fuck you throw my soda away? I coulda drunk the rest of it."

"Man, you gave me so little, it wasn't gonna be enough to get a good taste. That was just gonna be a tease, so I threw it away."

"I hate your fat ass!"

Bummy, whose nickname always seemed totally illogical to me since he and Don were the best dressed in our group, greatly benefitted from the fact that the Oliver brothers, two highly respected dudes in Little Vietnam, were his cousins. He had a worry-free pass anywhere in the neighborhood. It also didn't hurt that he was pretty good at basketball.

He was also really good at jonin'. Every summer he would make a grand entrance on the block after spending time down South. No one could handle him in a jonin' contest, but one embarrassing family incident haunted him and always assured us at least one laugh.

White-boy Tykee was awarded his name from the fact that his mother was white (one of only two white people in Little Vietnam). His "good" hair, light complexion, lack of athleticism, and propensity to get under our skin brought him ridicule almost daily. Loni and he were among the youngest in the group, but instead of seeking a close bond with this other young group member, he would frequently dip his right palm in mud and leave handprints in Loni's grandmother's bloomers as they were drying on the clothesline behind her apartment.

On the other end of the color spectrum, Wills had the darkest complexion and, in the group's opinion, was plagued with the added burden of being chubby without the benefit of Butch's domineering size. He was shorter than all of us, and we called him Fat Black Wills so much that his last name nearly fell from memory.

Just as Butch seemed to take extra pleasure in messing with Don, Don, in turn, took advantage of every opportunity to deride Wills. After one of us discovered it was easy to access the electrical breaker to the apartment where Wills stayed with his parents, Don led the way as we cut the power to the place on several occasions. Afterward, we'd run out, stand underneath the front window of his apartment and loudly screech, "Wills!!!" He'd look out of the window in disgust, scramble downstairs to restore the power, and be forced to reset all the digital clocks before his folks arrived home from work.

When Wills naively confided in one of us about a summer lunch date he arranged at the apartment, we were incredulous. We just had to see who the girl was, so we popped in on him—only to discover she was a no-show. Wills looked defeated sitting at the little dining room table decorated with place mats and two plates topped with pork chops, potatoes, and veggies.

Despite everything we did to Wills, he possessed a natural coolness that kept him seemingly unfazed by our antics. He had a smooth walk and was always well groomed. On some hot days, he'd be hanging out on H Place with a damp facecloth draped over his left forearm, which would be used periodically to wipe away any sweat that appeared on his forehead. Wills was the first truly cool chubby guy I ever saw. Many years later, I became a huge fan of Cedric the Entertainer. His clever wit, deep appreciation for the nuances of black culture, and physical appearance were undeniably appealing. He reminded me of Wills.

I was too young to appreciate how differences in physical features, especially skin color, played such a significant role in our daily interactions. But I took note of the fact that anyone on the extreme ends of the color spectrum was tagged with some derogatory term. The psychological damage we probably caused each other over this and other perceived shortcomings is difficult to measure.

Becoming so deeply tied to the guys on H Place opened me up to embracing group ideas like never before. Even my feelings about go-go music changed. When a band called School Boys played at the Rosedale recreation center, it gave me an opportunity to hear the music live. I went down there with Don and Loni, who brought his little boom box to record it.

The basketball court was jam-packed with people. The music was real funky, and I could feel the percussion sounds from the drums, congas, timbales, and cowbells thumping right through my body. Everyone seemed possessed. People were shaking and dancing. Some dudes were just staring at the band like they were in a trance. The call and response between the band and the crowd was so intense that it seemed as if they were one.

That experience got me hooked and looking for more. The Washington Coliseum was the biggest go-go venue in the city, and concerts were held there regularly. Because of the violence that occurred at go-gos, most of the guys on H Place were afraid to travel outside of the neighborhood to hear the music. But Don and Loni were the most adventurous ones in the group, so I went with them to the next event at the Coliseum.

The Coliseum was located just a few blocks off of 3rd and H Street Northeast. The place drew thousands of people from all over the city, and even parts of Maryland. I'd never seen so many rough dudes in one place, and there were plenty of girls, too. When I went to the bathroom, there was a big crowd of at least 50 guys huddled up gambling. Two guys were shooting dice, while the others were placing side bets. Dollar bills were everywhere.

A long lineup of bands performed that night. The lesser-known bands performed first, then the established groups such as Trouble Funk and Experience Unlimited (EU) came on later. Rare Essence closed the show. Every band had a horn section, too. Whenever a band hit a real funky groove, people called that "crankin'."

The congas were my favorite instrument. I enjoyed the sound so much that I stood there watching Rare Essence's conga player, Tyrone "Jungle Boogie" Williams, licking the palms of his hands in between smacking those skins. He was wearing a sky-blue fisherman's hat and looked high as hell. Throughout the night, I could smell reefers and PCP all over the place.

The most startling discovery I made at the go-go that night was finding out how guys and girls danced together. Instead of dancing with girls face-to-face, dudes would approach them from behind. Whenever a dude saw a girl he liked, he'd make his presence known by dancing behind her and then placing his hands on her hips. She would sometimes turn around and look at the guy. If he was brave enough, he'd inch all the way up. If a girl didn't like a particular guy, wasn't in the mood to dance, or thought a dude was too freaky, she'd shove him off.

I immediately saw the potential benefits in this finding for myself. I could approach girls and be less fearful of getting rejected. A girl would let me know if she liked me or not without me having to risk embarrassing myself from nervously saying the wrong things. For a shy guy like me, who hadn't learned how to dance, it was perfect!

One day on Benning Road, I ran into Wayne Washington, my former classmate at St. Anthony's. He lived just three blocks from me on the other side of Benning Road in the Rosedale neighborhood. His mother and stepfather had moved into a single-family home on 19th Street. Wayne was finishing his sixth-grade year at Blow Pierce Elementary, which was just half a block away.

With St. Anthony's as a common connection, we started hanging out. Whenever it was slow on H Place, or I wanted to check out Rosedale, I would go to Wayne's house or catch him playing outside on Gale Street. He introduced me to his friends Shannon, Ernest, Otis, and Marlon—aka Slob Monster.

Although Wayne had respect among his peers, he wasn't a bully. He couldn't pull that off in a place like Rosedale or Vietnam. I learned that he had a gift for gab and used it to play the role of funnyman and practical joker. Wayne loved to jone on people, especially his friends. We were riding on the X bus one afternoon when he joned on this boy so bad that every passenger on the bus was laughing. The boy had had enough, so he pulled the cord to alert the bus driver and quietly exited out the back door at the next stop.

As funny as Wayne was, he had one major, ironic flaw—he suffered from an awful stuttering problem, which may have been the reason why he joned on other people so much. His stuttering was sometimes so bad that he used to stomp his feet as he walked in an effort to express himself clearly. If he couldn't say something simple like, "Let's go to the store man," he'd just point and say, "Store man, store." As a result, the rest of us joned on Wayne real bad.

Talking about girls was the favorite topic among the guys. No one talked about dating a girl or going out with her. Anytime someone mentioned that he was talking to a girl, someone would ask, "Did you fuck her?" If he wasn't gettin' that booty, then he got joned on. I was still too shy and lacking in confidence to enter into these conversations. I just kept my mouth shut and laughed at all the funny stuff the guys said.

I thought that fighting my way into the group and being accepted on H Place would solve my issue of being a new face in tough Little Vietnam. But, to my disappointment, our little crew on H Place was near the bottom of the food chain. Many of the other crews in the neighborhood had weight, which meant they were considered tough and, therefore, worthy of respect on the streets.

Some of these dudes were into more serious street activities. They would gamble, sell drugs, and rob people. Our activities were mainly playing football, sitting outside jonin' on each other, and doing little mischievous stuff like running from the police to make them chase us for fun.

Getting taken for bad, or "chumped" as it was called, became an almost daily thing for me. If I glanced at the wrong dude a split second too long, or ran across a rough guy in a bad mood, I ran the risk of getting chumped. One of my worst experiences happened when I was with my buddy Charles. He would sometimes go to the store for an old man who lived a few apartments down from his family. This man trusted Charles enough to give him money to purchase items from the grocery or liquor store, which in the early '80s commonly sold alcohol to minors. Once Charles returned, the man would tip him a dollar or two.

I was walking with Charles during one of these errands when we ran across two mean-looking dudes about our size. Charles was familiar with the meanest-looking one, but that didn't stop the guy from taking advantage of the situation. He saw a small paper bag of beer in Charles's hand, so he grabbed it. Charles pulled away from him, protesting, but the guy cracked him on the chin and took the bag. Charles did almost the exact same thing I had done when Little Boo hit me. He turned, walked away, and started whining, while I just stood there in fear, happy no one seemed to take any notice of me.

The old man wasn't too happy about Charles coming back empty-handed. Right in the middle of Charles's story, he walked to his closet and pulled out his shotgun. My eyes got big as he stood there yelling at us with that shotgun in his hand. Both Charles and I were stuck standing by the front door in this old man's upstairs apartment. Fortunately, he let us go with just an angry warning.

Two weeks later, I was standing in a fast-food place on Benning Road, waiting for an order of wings and fries, when in walked the dude who had cracked Charles on the chin. Seeing his familiar scowl gave me the shakes. While he was looking up at the overhead menu, my mind was racing for a way to secure my safety.

"You . . . you lookin' for Charles?" I stammered.

Now the dude's attention was squarely on me as a momentary question entered his mind.

"Yeah. Where that niggah at? Tell him I wanna see him."

Since I'd just given myself up, he confidently walked around me, patting each one of my empty pockets. As I endured this embarrassing probe, I noted that his left wrist had not one but two watches on it. *Damn, this dude just took someone's watch. He's that thorough.*

After completing his circle, he gave me what seemed like a meaningful glare. My food order and the money I'd given the guy on the other side of the thick plexiglass was the furthest thing from my mind, so I obediently darted from the carryout, walked three blocks straight up 19th Street, and knocked on Charles's front door. When there was no answer, I hurried back to the now-empty restaurant, and got my wings.

Who gets chumped as badly as I just had? From the safety of home, I took time to consider my plight. Being in the house with no one to talk to or play with wasn't an option, but being outside in Little Vietnam put me at risk without warning. What could I do?

In neighborhoods like Little Vietnam, being respected, which often came from being able to fight, was the most important thing for a young guy. It was like being able to speak the local language or having the proper credentials in order to get accepted into the best nightclubs. The better you could fight, the more exclusive clubs you belonged to and the more respect you garnered from your peers. One thing I noticed was that often, when the guys bragged about any dude walking through H Place who was known for fighting well, or "being sharp," as they called it, they'd often add, "He box for Ham AC." I kept hearing about this Ham Athletic Club, but I didn't know where it was. I soon found out that it was a boxing gym just beyond Rosedale in the basement of Eliot Junior High School, just blocks away from Southeast DC.

I wanted to check out Ham AC. I had to take into consideration, though, the fact that Ham AC was in a different neighborhood. Even though Wayne was from Rosedale and I knew a lot of his friends, I worried that it wouldn't be enough. Plus, I had this image of walking into a gym filled with dudes leaning against the wall, ready to pounce on anyone they perceived as being weak. I just couldn't go alone, so I asked Loni and he agreed to go with me.

Ham AC was run by Abraham "Ham" Johnson. Ham was short, very dark-skinned, bald, and pot-bellied. A cigar seemed to be sewed to his lips, and he loved talkin' shit all the time. He'd yell and scream all over the gym.

The gym was geared toward amateur boxers and was open weekdays after school and on some Saturdays. There was no ring, so fighters boxed or sparred on a large, gray padded mat. A few smaller mats were used for doing sit-ups, push-ups, and other exercises. There were also long, narrow mirrors, used by boxers who would watch themselves throwing punches and moving their heads to avoid oncoming blows, pretending to fight an imaginary opponent—shadowboxing. The gym didn't have a speed bag, but a heavy bag hung against the back wall in the equipment room. It was good for punching, but the fact that you couldn't hit it from all angles was a major drawback, as I later learned. Creating angles was an important part of becoming a good fighter.

The atmosphere at Ham AC was nothing like what I imagined. The fighters were actually encouraging, even fun-loving. As Loni and I started learning the basics, the more experienced guys gave us tips on technique. The training was hard, but we got used to the daily routine. Once we learned enough of the basics from shadowboxing and hitting the bag, Ham made Loni and me spar. We put on gloves, headgear, and mouthpieces, and spread Vaseline all over our faces to help prevent cuts.

Once we got comfortable sparring each other, Ham had us spar a more experienced guy named Lee Lee. Loni struggled against him but showed lots of heart. When my turn came, my size advantage helped me out, although Lee Lee landed punches on me from many different angles. I was more concerned with getting my own punches off than worrying about his stuff. I did well, and boxing him gave Loni and me that much more confidence.

I saw sparring, or puttin' in work, as an obligation. If someone asked me to spar, I never said no, even if it was a dude with much more experience. This self-imposed standard sometimes came at a pretty high cost. When Sam Jones from Valley Green, one of the worst housing projects in Southeast, asked me to spar, I said okay despite the fact that he had fought more than 100 amateur bouts. Ham wouldn't allow it, though, because I was too inexperienced. Neither Sam nor I would dare go against Ham's wishes, at least while he was awake. But he sometimes fell asleep during our work-outs. So, the next time we saw Ham bent over in his folding chair and snoring loudly, Sam and I got our gear on and put in some work. It wasn't like sparring against Lee Lee—Sam hit hard as hell. But I made it through the rounds.

Ham AC attracted boys from all over the city. Some were very dedicated to boxing. Guys like Charlie "Smitty" Smith, Andre Adams, and Ham's two sons, James Harris and Mark "Too Sharp" Johnson, were among the most serious fighters. Too Sharp eventually earned a spot in the International Boxing Hall of Fame by becoming a two-division world champion and the first and only black fighter to win a flyweight title. He was respected as one of the best pound-for-pound fighters during the prime of his career, when most of the top fighters in and around his weight class avoided him.

Some of the cats in the gym were mainly interested in developing their skills in order to build a reputation in the streets. Some were talented, but they didn't train consistently. Several came from Trinidad, a neighborhood near Little Vietnam on the other side of Hechinger Mall. The sharpest of these Trinidad guys was named Payton, but he was known as Ant Lee on the streets, and he would give James Harris, Ham's older son, all he could handle in the gym. Cliff Cobb was another Trinidad cat who was a very good boxer. He had a slim physique but was highly skilled. I got to know a

Trinidad dude named Pumpkin pretty well, and even though he was several years older and bigger than me, we boxed one time and I earned his respect.

I became familiar enough with Pumpkin and Sam Jones that they let me in on a little something. There was a pecking order in the gym as well as in the streets. Even dudes who could fight and had established reputations knew who not to mess with. Pumpkin refused to box Sam Jones. He straight up told me, "That niggah hit too hard." Funny thing was, Sam Jones said damn near the same thing about Andre Adams.

This opened my eyes to the fact that even thorough guys harbored fears. I felt better about the nervous feeling I got in the pit of my stomach every time I was about to fight or spar. Courage was not about being without fear but having the willingness to overcome it.

I started going to Ham AC in the summer before my eighth-grade year, and it was crucial in my development as a young boy growing up in the streets of DC. It gave me the confidence to defend myself if someone challenged me. If someone tried to intimidate or hurt me, they'd have to fight me. My willingness to face my fears enabled me to overcome my sense of helplessness.

Ham was so focused on certain fighters that he never asked Loni and me to fight in any amateur tournaments. We just continued building our skills in the gym and enjoying the newfound respect our friends on H Place started showing us.

Though Loni was his usual kind self, I noticed that the same fierceness he demonstrated while boxing in the gym would burst through his pleasant exterior if he felt wronged by someone. When Tykee, who always seemed to be nagging somebody, tried to snatch something out of Loni's hands, he got popped right on the chin. The next time someone brought out some boxing gloves I got a chance to show what I'd learned too. I popped Charles in the face with my jab so many times that he quit, mumbling something about me not fighting fair. Even Red Ty showed me a measure of respect whenever he came through H Place. He opened up to me and shared a story about his own brief time spent boxing.

My real test came in an unexpected fight with Ricardo. We were playing football in the grassy yard behind my building when we got into it. He felt that I was checking him too hard, so we knuckled up right there with our friends looking on.

I was nervous the entire time we fought. My mind kept thinking about the fact that this was the same dude I'd seen embarrass the hell out of Pop that day. I kept my cool and cautiously watched his every move. Fighting on grass instead of concrete probably helped me out as well, because he couldn't move as freely as he had against Pop. After we traded a few blows, the guys broke up the fight.

I didn't show it in front of everyone, but I was emotional inside. I went upstairs to my room and let it all out. My chest was heaving and my eyes got all watery. After calming down, I went back downstairs. Some of the guys were still there, and one of them told me that Ricardo had crushed a little Hot Wheels car I had left outside. Man, I was so happy to have held my own in a fight against a dude like Ricardo, I didn't give that car a second thought.

In a place like Little Vietnam, though, press releases weren't issued every time a cat gained more respect on his block or won a fight on the streets. News travelled by word of mouth, and only if it was noteworthy. What I'd accomplished since going down to Ham AC, despite being important to me, meant nothing outside of the small group of guys I hung out with. To all the other cats in Little Vietnam who had previously taken me for bad, I was still the same ol' weak-ass niggah.

Curtbone certainly felt that way. He was a cat with a King Kong reputation; a young legend in Little Vietnam I heard about long before I ever saw him. And when I did finally run across him before my days of going to Ham AC, he smoothly chumped me out of a quarter. What was different about the way Curtbone intimidated me was that he actually asked me for the quarter, but did it in such a way that I knew an ass-whipping would follow if I didn't oblige. I honored his request without hesitation.

Curtbone, a chubby, brown-skinned dude about my age, lived three blocks up from my building in the Langston Terrace Dwellings, a housing project designed by a black architect named Hilyard Robinson and built in the late 1930s. It was named after John Mercer Langston, a black congressman in the nineteenth century and uncle to poet Langston Hughes. By the 1980s, Langston Terrace was one of the roughest places in Little Vietnam. I rarely ventured up there.

Despite my best efforts to limit any interactions with dudes from off Langston, there was one winter night when fate just took over. I stepped outside into the cold weather sporting my favorite hat, a royal blue skullcap with a Lacoste gator sewn on. I couldn't afford any real Lacoste merchandise, but I had been lucky enough to come across a little gator that I had my mom sew onto a plain skullcap. The way I loved that hat, though, you couldn't tell me it wasn't real.

As I hit the corner to turn up 19th on my way to H Place, I saw my neighbor, little Maurice, walking toward our building. We teased each other all the time. So on this occasion, I lobbed a rock toward him. It was wide of the mark and happened to land near the feet of Curtbone, who was walking with two other dudes.

"Hey, slim, who were you throwin' that rock at?" he yelled.

"None of your damn business!" I replied.

I was confident in myself after my time at Ham AC, and the memory of the quarter he took from me was still on my mind.

Bam!

Maybe I was too confident, because I'd somehow allowed Curtbone to walk up and crack me on the chin.

We were standing near the corner of 19th and H place, so I stepped out into the street and yelled, "You bitch-ass niggah. I'm not afraid of you. Come on out here."

Part of me couldn't believe that I was saying these words to Curtbone, of all people. He calmly stepped into the street and threw up his hands. I caught him in the face with a right hand but kept my distance. Lucky for me, his two buddies just watched, so Curtbone and I could fight head-up. Some of the people I hung out with on H Place were outside, but they refused to come to the other end of the street where we were fighting. They could see it was Curtbone, and they knew of his reputation and didn't want to be associated with me, fearing for their future safety.

With no one to back me up, Curtbone's boys started shouting words of encouragement. One, named Black, said, "I like that gator hat you got on, niggah."

Knowing that Black wanted my hat, I pulled it down over my head and confidently did the same move he dared me to make. I used my quickness so Curtbone couldn't set his feet to punch. With the whole street behind me, I had plenty of room to move and strategically gave up ground. Curtbone was getting a bit frustrated from just plodding forward without landing any punches. His boys were getting impatient to get back to what they'd been doing, and let him know. Not being able to get to me, Curtbone walked away. My seeing him step away like that boosted my confidence. I threw insults at him as they walked away. The farther away they got, the louder I got. Curtbone didn't say a word in response.

A few weeks later, I was with Charles when I saw Curtbone walking by himself in front of one of the convenience stores on Benning Road. I was eager to get back in the mix with him and told him, "Let's finish this shit now, niggah!"

"Okay, let me just put my bag in the store," he replied.

Curtbone remained calm as he walked into the convenience

store. He came back out a minute later with the bag still in his hand and a dude walking behind him. Then, he bent down near the street curb and picked up a big rock. As soon as I saw this, I trotted up 19th Street, leaving Charles behind.

This became a recurring theme: every time we saw each other, Curtbone would pick up a stick or a rock, and I'd go in the other direction. One day, after seeing me playing a video game at the Safeway at Hechinger Mall, he doubled back outside and picked up part of a brick. Luckily, I happened to leave just before he came back in. Another time, on Benning Road, he grabbed another brick and chased me off the street, screaming, "I'm tired of your ass, niggah!"

Curtbone wasn't the only one tired. Our months-long dispute was wearing on me hard. Because of his reputation, no one gave me any support, and I had to watch my back at all times. The confidence I'd initially gained from holding my own against him was becoming a burden. To give myself a break, I started hanging in Rosedale with Wayne and his friends. I was with Wayne and four or five of his buddies at the Stadium Armory summer carnival when I saw Curtbone with his crew. This time, I had just as many guys with me as he had with him, and he had never seen me with these Rosedale cats.

I was surprised when he walked over and respectfully asked, "Can we talk for a minute?" We stepped aside and discussed what had taken place that winter night. Once he understood that I hadn't been throwing the rock at him, we squashed our beef with a handshake.

I immediately felt a big load fall off my shoulders. What I was learning at the gym hadn't prepared me for a dude like Curtbone. Boxing was not like fighting on the streets. There were no rules on the streets, and a guy like Curtbone understood how the game was played. He was in it to win it by any means necessary. Though I was going to Ham AC to learn how to defend myself on the streets, I wasn't a ruthless type of guy. I would defend myself, but I knew I couldn't do some of the things required to be feared on the streets.

My encounter with Curtbone also taught me something about my associations. Hanging with the dudes on H Place wasn't giving me the respect and support I needed. If I got into something with a guy who had a certain status on the streets, I couldn't rely on much support from the guys on H Place. I still went to Ham AC with Loni, but I began looking for opportunities to associate with guys who carried more weight.

In the less than two years since I'd moved to Little Vietnam, I had become accustomed to the neighborhood. Loni and I were becoming pretty tight. My social life was better here than it had ever been, and I was having much more fun and excitement at home than I ever had at school.

But I had one lingering problem. My mom had a parenting standard that was different than most of the other parents in the neighborhood. Besides Loni, I was the only kid from H Place who had a curfew, and my mom enforced it on the regular. This became embarrassing for me, because when I didn't hold to the curfew, she'd come looking for me at H Place with that stick in her hand.

It got to the point where all she generally had to do was come to the far end of H Place and simply wave or shake that stick. It never seemed to fail that one of my friends would see her first, and then say something like, "Look, there go Bernard's crazy-ass mother."

You couldn't miss her either, because she always wore red. She wore red so much that my friends nicknamed her the Red Baron. They teased me something terrible, too.

I wasn't the only guy from H Place who was rising through the ranks in Little Vietnam. My buddy Charles was doing his thing too. Red Ty had a buddy named Kenny Curl who used to chump Charles all the time. Eventually Charles got fed up, and they got into a fight on H Place. Charles banged Kenny out, and it was considered a major upset. I wasn't there for the fight, and when I came around everyone was talking about it.

Meanwhile, Kenny was quiet and sullen. His aura of superiority over us had been shattered. Personally, Kenny and I were cool. In fact, before I got into that fight with Curtbone, it was Kenny who had warned me that my mouth was going to get me into trouble. Now that he'd suffered a major upset, no one saw him around much.

On the evening of Tuesday, May 25, 1982, Loni, Ricardo, Fat Butch, and I were riding our bikes around H Place when Charles came rushing up. He had just come from the same Stadium Armory carnival where Curtbone and I would settle our differences later that summer. Some big dude who was with Kenny had just taken Charles's boom box, and he wanted us to go with him back to the carnival. Ricardo and I agreed to go with him, but Loni had a curfew. He'd just jumped off his bike and was walking it toward his apartment on H Place, because his mother forbade him to ride at nighttime, especially on a school night. But when Ricardo saw what Loni was doing, he said, "Loni, bring your ass on!"

After Loni got back on his bike, he and I took a different route to the carnival than Ricardo and Charles. Our route was quicker—there was no sign of them when we arrived. Being a little impatient, we rode through a section of the carnival, and I recognized someone, a girl in my grade at St. Anthony's. I had such a crush on this girl that seeing her always got me a little nervous.

I signaled for Loni that we should ride back out to the parking lot to wait for Ricardo and Charles to arrive. Loni zoomed off as I struggled to turn my bike around, distracted by the girl, I guess. Once I did, Loni was nowhere to be seen, so I just rode back out to the parking lot.

At the parking lot, I still didn't see Loni, but I could see Ricardo off in the distance. He was standing with his bike between his legs, looking down at something on the ground. I rode over. After getting closer, I could see that Ricardo was standing over someone just lying on his stomach with blood coming from the right side of his mouth. I looked at Ricardo and asked, "Who's that?"

"It's Loni."

Ricardo answered without taking his eyes off him. I looked again and realized it was true. Ricardo told me that he had seen a speeding car hit and drag Loni through the parking lot. Someone had called for an ambulance, but for a few minutes, Ricardo and I were the only people there. Soon, a crowd gathered in a large circle around us. Once the police and emergency people arrived, Ricardo and I were made to join the growing crowd of people. Eventually, a helicopter landed not too far from us; Loni was placed on board and flown to Children's Hospital.

I rode home and told my mom what happened. Then, I went to my room and wept. All of the other times I'd cried, it was from fear or because of some physical pain I was experiencing. This was different. These tears came from a place I'd never been to before.

I learned that Loni had been hit and dragged more than 30 feet by a stolen 1970 Ford LTD speeding through the parking lot. The stolen car was found abandoned later that night in Southeast. It'd been stolen from the Stadium parking lot by two guys and a girl who, in trying to make a quick getaway, accidentally hit Loni and kept going. Walter Terry, leader of the River Terrace 800 Crew in Northeast, was arrested and eventually convicted of the crime. Only sixteen at the time, he received a juvenile life sentence. He was released at eighteen, but I later heard he was killed during an attempted robbery of a police-owned jewelry store.

Loni died two days after the accident, on May 27, just a day before my fourteenth birthday. Loni had not even reached his twelfth birthday and was just about to graduate from Blow Pierce Elementary. I was shocked to discover that he was the valedictorian of his sixth-grade class, because we never talked about school.

In Loni's honor, the school created the Delonte Butler Award to be given to each year's valedictorian.

His mother, Tina, was only fifteen when she had Loni, but with support from her parents and sister, she did a good job raising him. I thought it was especially unfair that the only time Loni broke his mother's curfew, he paid for it with his life.

My mother never allowed any of my friends to come inside our house, but she made an exception for Loni's funeral. So, when several of them stopped by, she let them in until I finished getting dressed for the funeral. They stood patiently waiting in the living room, since we had no sofa or couch. The services were held at Peace Baptist Church in Rosedale, and all the schools in the neighborhood closed in Loni's honor. His father was escorted from jail that day in order to attend. He sat quietly in the front row in handcuffs with two police escorts. People were lined up on both sides of Benning Road for blocks as the funeral procession made its way from the church. I'd never seen so many people in the streets.

The day after the funeral all the guys were on H Place. When I showed up, they joned on me something terrible about my barren living room. Then they started talking about the Red Baron again. Fat Butch used to tease Loni and get on his nerves quite often, and he had an especially difficult time dealing with his death. For months afterward, he was plagued with nightmares. But he talked to some of us about it until the bad dreams went away. He eventually felt much better. On the other extreme, Charles disappeared the night Loni was hit. He also stopped coming around. I didn't see him again until nearly fifteen years later—he had a dead eye and appeared to be homeless. I gave him a ride to wherever he was going and put a few dollars in his hand.

My entire social life was caught up in the streets of Little Vietnam. I had no interest in sporting events or school activities, and even my relationships with Alfonso and Rick had tapered off. Two separate and opposing worlds were vying for my attention. The fast and exciting streets had outpaced whatever pleasure I'd previously derived from school life. Increasingly, school was just the place I had to go for nine months out of the year.

The discipline at St. Anthony's was no joke, especially for the seventh and eighth graders. If someone's grades became perilously low, the teachers would hold a conference with that student in the hallway right after lunch. It was the most embarrassing thing, because both the seventh- and eighth-grade classes were on hold while the four teachers gave you a loud scolding, which all the other students couldn't help but hear.

By the eighth grade I had established myself as one of the top students, and my previous poor performances were long in the past. Mr. Straight, who had been my sixth-grade teacher, had moved up to teach the eighth grade, and we were together again in homeroom and math class. As the school year progressed, though, my work began to suffer. I still never missed school, but my focus was elsewhere. I ended up in that hallway hot seat after lunch, standing in the middle of four big adults looking down sternly upon me.

Mr. Straight was the most upset. He told me that before my recent slump, whenever my answers on his math tests had differed from his answer sheet, he would double-check his work to ensure it was done correctly. He made it very clear how disappointed he was that he no longer had confidence in my work. Learning these things blew me away.

Humbled and ashamed, I picked up my performance, but somehow I managed to miss the graduation ceremony. It occurred just after Loni's funeral. I'd dressed for it but didn't really want to go. When there was some mix-up with my ride, I hurriedly took off my dress clothes and went down to Ham AC. While all my classmates were proudly receiving their graduation certificates with family members looking on, I was on that gray mat doling out and receiving punches to the head. The smell of leather, Vaseline, and sweat felt comforting to me. Perhaps, like Fat Butch and Charles, I was dealing with my own guilt over Loni's death. If my friend, who was Blow Pierce's valedictorian, couldn't graduate, then why should I? This wasn't a clear thought in my mind, but it showed itself in my behavior. It would take years before I understood how Loni's death had affected me.

My mother didn't seem to care too much about us missing the graduation ceremony. She was happy that I'd been accepted into a prestigious Jesuit high school in DC called Gonzaga. Perhaps it was a combination of my mostly good grades, recommendations from teachers, and a little of my mother's magic that got me in there. The school was quite expensive, and we were still living off my mother's Social Security checks, but somehow I was headed to another private Catholic school.

My mom was still running a tight ship too, especially when one particular relative came to our home. Uncle Atward was the only relative allowed to stay with us. He was always nice to me, but he talked really fast and was a little off, or touched.

One summer day, I was downtown with my mom and Uncle Atward. We stepped into a bank and my mom became upset with me over something. As all the other people were coming in and out of the bank, my mom slapped me hard across the face. I was stunned, especially since it had been a while since she'd put her hands on me. Considering that I'd been boxing, and that I'd been feeling more confident in myself in a physical sense, I felt violated. I broke away, ran outside, bummed a paper transfer from some-one standing on a downtown street, and caught the next bus back home. Without having a key to get in the house, I just stayed out-side with friends.

An hour or so later, I saw my mom walking up 19th Street with Uncle Atward. She looked over at me from across the street, gritted on me, and walked in the house. We never spoke about the incident, but her actions let me know that it was still her show, and she was still running it. Whenever she felt I'd gotten beside myself, she was gonna put my behind back in check.

After Loni's death, Don and I got real, real tight. We were starting to become preoccupied with girls, now that our teenage years were upon us. Don's light-skinned complexion, or being a "red niggah," as some people called it, drew a lot of attention from girls. They tended to like lighter-complexioned guys. Don dressed well too, because his mother bought him all the latest clothes—designer polo shirts, the latest jeans. When the new Timberland shoes first hit, he was the only one on H Place sportin' them.

I didn't have any particular strategy for meeting girls. My tendency was to follow Don's lead. If he started dating a girl, then I tried to go for her sister, cousin, or best friend. My confidence in meeting girls by myself was still shaky.

Eventually, I introduced Don to Wayne Washington, and we became a threesome. Wayne and Don got along so well that they became closer than I was to either of them. They bonded over their competitiveness regarding girls. Wayne and Don were pretty focused on meeting girls. They would take turns pretending to be a girl, so the other could work on his pick-up game. I tried it a few times, but they laughed at me before I could finish my lines. One of our favorite hangouts was Landover Mall in Prince George's County, Maryland. We'd take the subway and then the bus to get out there, decked out in our best gear.

Going out to Maryland to meet girls was the popular thing to do for DC dudes. Having a light-skinned girl who lived in a house in Maryland was considered something special. Most DC street dudes lived in the projects or a smaller apartment building, so we assumed that girls who lived in homes in Maryland came from better-off families. Wayne and Don talked about it all the time, saying things like, "Man, slim got a badass redbone from out Maryland!"

And for many of the Maryland girls, the feeling appeared to be mutual. DC dudes were considered tougher than guys from other areas, and the girls seemed to enjoy the attention.

My first sexual encounter happened when I was fourteen with a girl I didn't know. She attended Browne Junior High and would walk through H Street after school. Word got back to me, from one of my buddies, that the girl had spotted me several times, either hanging out in front of Bummy's house or on the corner of 18th and H Street. She wanted to meet me, so they arranged it. I had no idea who the girl was, but we met and talked for a few minutes the very next day after school.

I wasn't attracted to her, but there was a street code that had to be observed. A dude was never supposed to turn down sex being offered from a girl, unless he was willing to risk facing ridicule from his boys. If a girl was willing, you had to hit it.

I wasn't strong enough to let my buddies know how I really felt about the girl, so I went along with their plan. They'd already made arrangements for me and this girl to have sex at Bummy's house. His parents didn't get home until 5:30 or 6:00, which would give us plenty of time, since we planned to hook up around 3:15.

The next day, the girl came to Bummy's house at the appointed time. I was sitting in the living room getting coached by Bummy, Don, and a few others. When the girl came in, we barely said two words to each other before going upstairs to Bummy's room.

Without saying much of anything to each other, we took off our clothes. She lay down on Bummy's bed, and then I got on top of her and tried to enter her. After a few uncomfortable moments, she tried to assist me. The problem was my penis; it was too soft. I played it cool and tried to hide my embarrassment. After a few minutes, I told her to wait a minute as I put some clothes back on and went downstairs.

After consulting with my coaching staff, I went back upstairs and asked the girl to rub my lower back. She gently rubbed her fingers over that area, but there was still no erection. I went through the motions of trying to enter her again but couldn't. *Damn, what's going on?* I thought to myself.

I put my clothes on again and slowly walked back downstairs, feeling defeated. None of my friends laughed or teased me, but one of them said, "I guess the music wasn't playing for you."

The girl put her clothes back on and left the house. I never saw or heard from her again; I don't even remember her name.

The pressure I felt to perform sexually stemmed from the conversations and stories I'd heard from my peers. Neither my mom nor anyone in my family ever talked about sex, and it wasn't a topic that was discussed at St. Anthony's or Gonzaga. Everything I heard about sex came from the streets, and I felt compelled to try and live up to the standard that was being set by what I heard there.

The first time I remember hearing about sex, a dude was standing on H Street saying to several of us, "I was having sex with this girl, and had just finished bustin' three nuts when her mother came home. I had to sneak out her damn house." I accepted everything the dude was saying without question.

Fat Wills had a cousin named Marsha who I eventually started dating. Considered a real catch, she lived with her parents and sisters in a nice townhouse in Fort Lincoln Northeast. Her cute face, tan complexion, shapely figure, and the fact that she was a year older than me caused some of my friends to ask, "Can you handle that, my man?"

On top of all the things my friends were focusing on, Marsha was very nice. But, there was one major problem: I didn't have a phone at home. In spite of all the things guys said about girls on the streets, I somehow realized that Marsha was the type of girl a guy needed to spend quality time with. And at our young age, this meant talking on the phone daily.

I made my best effort to develop a relationship with Marsha. As often as possible, I tried to use Bummy's or Wills's phone before their parents came home from work. I caught the bus out to Fort Lincoln Northeast on several occasions to see her and meet her family. We even went on a double date to the movies with Don and his girlfriend.

Sadly, this just wasn't enough. Not having a phone or access to a ride to see her more often meant that we spoke and saw each other so infrequently that the relationship fizzled. After several months of not seeing each other, we mutually agreed to break up. I was fifteen at the time.

At that point in my life, my sexual experience was still limited, compared to my peers. I'd done some kissing and made one failed attempt at having sex. Still being a virgin was becoming more and more embarrassing to me. Looking at girls and laughing with the guys about them was enjoyable, but a sense of uneasiness started growing within me. The more I heard about how good sex was, the more fearful I became of it. Being shy helped with my discomfort about sex. Whenever the guys talked about girls, they rarely asked for my input.

My attending Gonzaga was a big deal for my mom. Before I started as a freshman, she handed me $75 to purchase some new clothes. This was more money than she'd ever given me, enough to buy a few different outfits. Gonzaga had a dress code: our pants had to be blue and either khakis, corduroys, or slacks, and our shirts had to be white and have collars. No jeans, sweats, or tennis shoes.

Downtown was the place for shopping. Woodward & Lothrop and Hecht's department stores were only a short ride away on the X bus. I asked Wayne and Don to go with me. After I had purchased my first two items, Wayne asked us to ride farther uptown to 14th and U so he could get some money from his father. From there, we would come back downtown, so I could finish my shopping.

We caught the bus and got up there fairly quickly. Don and I waited for Wayne as he went to cop $10 from his father. The bustling U Street atmosphere was no different than it had been when I was staying at the Pitts Hotel. Uptown was still the place in the city where street people went to make money.

Oftentimes, certain metro buses were just an extension of what was going on uptown. Dudes gambled in the back of the bus on the regular, and I never saw any bus driver make an issue of it. On our bus ride back downtown, there was a dude dealing three-card monte on the floor of the bus. If you're not familiar with it, this was a game played with three cards, two black and one red. The dealer would show them face up, then turn them over and shuffle them around. A person would bet money that they could select the red card after the dealer finished shuffling.

There was a woman betting against the dude, and she was winning. Then he started coming back and took all her money, at least what she was willing to gamble away. Wayne stepped up and put his $10 down. After the dude finished shuffling the cards, Wayne picked a black card and lost his money.

I noticed that the red card, over the course of all the shuffling, had gotten a slight bend in one of its corners. The dude didn't seem to notice, so I put down a $20 bill. As the cards were being shuffled, I kept my eyes on the bent card. The woman who had lost her money tapped me on the shoulder. She had slid over to the seat just behind mine and was leaning over my right shoulder giving me some pointers. I glanced at her a few times but kept focusing on the cards.

As soon as the dude finished shuffling, I quickly and confidently reached down and flipped over the bent card. It was black! Everyone sitting in the back of the bus gave a hushed gasp. *What? How is this possible?* I thought. I quickly put down my last $20 bill, determined to get back my first $20. But I got the same result as before.

My chest was pounding and my breathing short. I was desperate. All I had was $3. *I can work my way back with this. Just win a few games*, I told myself.

"Let's bet $3."

"I really don't play for small amounts like that, shorty."

"Come on, man; let's play for $3, $3, man. Gimme a chance!"

"Okay."

After the dude relented with a shrug of his shoulders, I eagerly put down my $3. He took that too, adding my last three dollar bills to the biggest wad of money I'd ever seen.

I was delirious. Everyone on the back of the bus was quiet. The woman got off the bus several stops later, and the dude got off at the very next stop. I watched his every step.

After that, a man who had been watching the whole thing broke it down for me. He explained that the woman and the dude were a team. The bent card was a kind of feint move to bait me into betting my money. The woman's job was to distract me, so the dude could swiftly unbend the red card and bend a black one without me noticing—a sleight of hand. Man, I felt so stupid.

With no money to finish shopping, we caught the X bus back to Little Vietnam. Wayne and Don laughed during the entire bus ride. Wayne kept mocking me—*$3, man, $3!*—and I just sat there in silence and pain. When we reached our bus stop, Wayne and Don literally fell off the bus laughing. What was I gonna tell my mom? The walk from there up 19th Street to my house was one of the longest of my life.

"Mom, I got robbed."

"You got robbed?"

"Yeah."

Before she started asking me for details, I said something else to take her mind away from the lost money.

"Mom, I need a job."

To my surprise, two weeks later my mom told me to go see a woman named Lucille Mahoney. She was the manager at Holly Farms, a fast-food restaurant in the Trinidad neighborhood. I tried to speak to Ms. Mahoney, but every time I went to see her, she was busy. Finally, on my fourth try, she came out from the back to speak to me. But the first thing she said was, "I'm sorry. I really don't have time to talk to you right now. You'll have to come back." All I could think was, *What! This is my fourth time down here. I'm tired of this shit!*

"Are you gonna hire me or what?" I blurted. I was frustrated as hell.

A week later, I started working as a Holly Farms cook. My shifts were from 7:00 a.m. to 3:00 p.m., every Saturday and Sunday, and my hourly wage was $3.35. Lucille and the other staff liked my work so much that I also started working on the cash register.

When I found out the company paid double-time for working holidays, I became the go-to guy for working Christmas and every other major holiday. When a reporter from the *Washington Times* interviewed me for a story about people who worked on Christmas, I was quoted in the article as saying, "Christmas is just another day."

I never thought working at Holly Farms would be so fun and exciting. Like Little Vietnam, Trinidad was a very colorful place. The bus stop directly in front of Holly Farms was on the B bus route, which ran from St. Elizabeths, a psychiatric hospital in Southeast. Many of the patients who got out would catch the B52 bus and ride it to Holly Farms. Fights frequently broke out in and around the restaurant. Sometimes, we were even robbed by people from the neighborhood.

On one occasion, a guy pulled a gun on me and demanded the money from the register. I gave him all the bills, but not the coinage. I didn't think he'd want it, since there were only nickels in the till.

After taking the bills I handed him, he noticed the till full of nickels, looked at me, cocked his head to the side, and said in an irritated voice, "The change too; the change too."

In one scoop, I managed to cup every nickel in my hand and place them in one of his hands. He walked out of the restaurant without dropping a single coin. Then, after my shift, I saw the thief on the street, a block from my house! He said to me, "Sorry about that, shorty. It was nothing with you. I just had to do what I had to do."

Another illegal, or at least inappropriate, activity that took place at Holly Farms was drinking on the job. Lucille would buy six-packs of Schlitz Malt Liquor Bull and try to hide them in one of the freezers. Since I knew she wasn't supposed to drink at work, I'd clip off a beer or two.

To hide what I was drinking from everyone, I'd get a Holly Farms cup, fill it with ice, and pour the beer in there. People thought I was simply enjoying a fountain drink, but I'd be sipping, smiling, and getting real nice. Whenever Lucille went to her stash and found a beer missing, she'd know it was me, but couldn't really say much. It became our little unspoken ritual.

At the time, I had no idea it was illegal for a fourteen-year-old to work without a permit. Regardless of what the law said, though, I was one of the best workers Lucille had. Working at Holly Farms was the renewal of a love affair that started when I was hustling bags at the grocery store. I enjoyed working, and earning my own money gave me a sense of pride.

I never asked my mother for money again.

Gonzaga was a completely different world compared to my life in Little Vietnam. The school was located at the edge of downtown on North Capitol Street, a main thoroughfare that separated the eastern and western sections of the city. Gonzaga was considered a college preparatory school, because more than 95 percent of its graduates attended college.

I rarely saw white people in Little Vietnam, but at Gonzaga they were everywhere. All the teachers and administrators, except for two coaches, one teacher, a dean of students, the guy who ran the food service, and the security guard, were white. The over-whelming majority of the student body was white. Blacks made up less than 10 percent of the school's student body.

I didn't have any ill feelings toward white people—but I didn't understand how and why they got to run everything. I couldn't help but notice that they lacked style, in spite of their better financial standing. The white boys at school didn't seem to care about what they wore. Their pants were never ironed, they wore corduroys year-round, their loafers were flat and ugly, and they seemed to be allergic to wearing socks, even in cold weather.

Being a student at Gonzaga came with a lot of culture shock for me. The two worlds I started shuffling between at St. Anthony's were pulled even further apart by my being in this predominantly white school. I had a difficult time adjusting to the environment and would act out. I didn't find the schoolwork difficult, but I did have a few disciplinary problems. During the first few weeks I got into several altercations with classmates and was sent to the headmaster's office each time. When the office secretary, who was tired of seeing me, gave me a frustrated look, I felt a tinge of embarrassment, so I asked her sheepishly, "I guess I keep causing trouble?"

"No, you just keep getting into trouble," she replied.

I calmed down, but not before being tagged as the class hoodlum. It was a label I wore proudly. I felt I was representing the streets, and being cast as a rebel suited me. When a black classmate named Kevin White, who was a talented running back, asked me to consider going out for the football team, I dismissed it, even though I liked football. For me, life at the time was all about working for money and trying to build my reputation in the streets. The streets still meant more to me than anything that was happening at school. And for a guy who saw things the way I did, there was no better sport than boxing.

Sometime after Loni's death, I stopped boxing at Ham AC. A year or so later, though, I met an older street dude known for fighting, and he told me about Finley's Boxing Gym located on 10th and Maryland Avenue Northeast, so I went down there to watch him work out. I joined the gym soon after, the same place where my cousin Brother used to box.

Finley's was located above a car repair shop. Old fight posters lined both sides of the staircase. The entire room was carpeted. A small boxing ring was situated in front of the left-side wall and two speed bags hung from the right-side wall. In the middle of the floor were three heavy bags, a double-end bag, and a space with two mirrors on the wall for jumping rope and performing exercises. There were more fight posters adorning the walls.

Finley's catered to professional fighters but also had a small amateur program. I eventually came under the tutelage of Ken Stribling. Everyone called him Cap. He was an ex-military guy who had been the captain of the guard at Lorton Reformatory, a prison in Virginia, before retiring. Besides driving a cab, he dedicated much of his time to teaching the sweet science.

He was the veteran of nearly 50 professional fights between 1940 and 1951. During that time, he went toe-to-toe with some of DC's best fighters—men like Smuggy Hursey, whom he bested, and the legendary Holly Mims, whom he fought to a draw. Cap's biggest fight was against the great middleweight champion, Jake LaMotta, of *Raging Bull* fame, who knocked Cap out in the fifth round.

Cap had the respect of everyone in that gym. He was like a father figure to many of us, especially those who had spent time in the streets and prison. At Lorton, he had coached the prison boxing team and trained many of those guys when they fought professionally after their release.

Cap was both a tough disciplinarian and a master storyteller. He always stressed that there were three basic punches in boxing: the jab, the right hand, and the left hook. To him, the jab was the most effective punch in boxing because everything worked off of it. The boxers who worked with him spent months shadowboxing, working on the heavy bag, and watching him show us the proper way to deliver punches.

Whenever we made mistakes he snapped at us. These verbal lashings were an essential part of his training, and he often told us, "If you can't handle what I have to say then you certainly can't be no fighter." Unlike Ham, Cap gave us intense scrutiny. This was the most attention any man had ever shown me.

Cap's stories were usually cautionary tales. He told us numerous stories about fighters who had taken what they'd learned from him to the streets to build a reputation there. A few of them lost their lives when they ran across guys who chose to pull triggers rather than throw punches. Cap knew that those same streets were calling out to us on a daily basis, and his stories were designed to encourage us to resist those calls.

One summer day, a call from the streets came to me right at Finley's, when a dude walked in and checked me out as I was hitting the double-end bag.

"What's up babes!" he said. He had an exaggerated bounce in his step. In between rounds, he extended his hand to me and said, "I'm Lawrence from Trinidad."

Every Saturday and Sunday morning on my way to Holly Farms, I walked past the words "Trinidad Trouble Makers" spray-painted on the wall of a Sears parking lot just beyond Hechinger Mall. It was as if those words marked the entry point into a new and exciting world.

Little Vietnam and Trinidad were not on the best of terms. Tensions had recently been sparked by a full-scale brawl because two well-connected brothers from Little Vietnam, known as the Love Twins, almost got jumped in Trinidad while visiting a girl named Shauna. Their older brother, Ricky, gathered up some of Little Vietnam's roughest troops and ran up in Trinidad. A day or two after the battle, it seemed like everyone in Vietnam was talking about it.

The simmering tensions were felt throughout both territories for some time after the incident. I got an uneasy feeling every time a Trinidad cat was in my presence. It wasn't just because of the big brawl. I'd had my own run-ins with Trinidad dudes. Before I started boxing at Ham AC, a guy named Rodney from Trinidad chumped me bad at Hechinger Mall. Dudes from Trinidad were generally easy to identify, because many of them, like Rodney, wore a high-top fade haircut, also known as a philly. Due to the upkeep that cut required, I frequently ran into Trinidad cats at Jake's Barbershop on 14th and H Street, which had some of the best barbers in the area.

After spending some time at Ham AC, I ran across Rodney at Hechinger Mall again. When he saw me, his eyes widened as he began coming toward me. This time I was ready for him. But, it didn't come to that, because someone from his crew stuck out his forearm to stop Rodney's forward progress.

It was Pumpkin, my former stablemate from Ham AC, and he was pointing at me to let Rodney know I was off limits. "That's my man right there," Pumpkin said, and he walked over and shook my hand. Rodney's mood turned sullen, and it was clear from his reaction that Pumpkin was the leader of their group. My willingness to box anyone at Ham AC had paid dividends. Because I was never afraid to box in the gym, I didn't have to prove myself as much on the street. What happened that day at the mall became a fairly common occurrence.

Now, meeting Lawrence at Finley's brought Trinidad into my everyday life. After I finished training at the gym the day I met Lawrence, he invited me to his neighborhood, and I accepted, putting aside any reservations. He took me to some of Trinidad's most popular spots. We hung out on 16th and Meigs Street, at Trinidad playground (where I saw Pumpkin walking around like a made mafioso), and the upper part of Montello Avenue, the hood's main street, which had dudes chilling on nearly every corner. Unlike Little Vietnam, Trinidad didn't have any intimidating-looking housing projects like Carver and Langston Terrace. Instead, it mainly consisted of row houses and two-story apartment buildings.

As in Philadelphia and other cities on the East Coast, dudes in DC prided themselves on being able to use their hands to resolve disputes. Ant Lee and Cliff Cobb, both of whom I'd met at Ham AC, had earned a high level of respect in Trinidad, as well as other parts of DC, due to their fighting skills. They were able to build upon this due to their involvement in the drug trade.

Ant Lee was a little guy, who a lot of bigger guys feared because of his hands. He was so good that Cliff wouldn't confront Ant Lee if he intimidated one of the young guys who worked for him. Cliff, being no slouch himself, would travel around sections of Northeast with a bag full of boxing gear to challenge dudes on the street. He also had a trigger-happy brother named Roy, and their squad became the most well-known and respected group from Trinidad. They were making money, sporting Fila tennis gear and cruising in Jaguars before most street dudes in DC even heard about those brands.

Lawrence introduced me to numerous dudes with unique names like Dirty Lee, Milk, Black Smurf, Spark Ears, Tank, and Cheese. However, the two I eventually got to know best shared a fairly common name, Raymond. To distinguish between the two, everyone referred to them by their last names, Singleton and Underdue. I'd previously met Singleton through Fat Wills, because they went to school together at Brown Junior High. Underdue was an intimidating-looking guy with a big philly, who I'd frequently seen at Jake's. The three of us became fast friends, and I started spending more time with them than with Lawrence.

Singleton's personality was much different from Underdue's. Singleton was dark-skinned, reserved, and had a short fade, while Underdue was tan-complexioned, sported a huge high-top philly, and was talkative—the most outgoing person I'd ever been around. He liked to draw attention to himself without seeming to care for what people thought. It was impossible not to know when he was around. Underdue had a way of dealing with people that made them feel special. He was fond of saying things like, "That's my main apple scrapple." In general, Trinidad dudes had a unique way of expressing themselves. It was like they had created a distinct dialect, different from other hoods. Everybody greeted each other as Joe or Moe: "What's up, Joe?" "Ain't nuthin, Moe."

Other times, guys would greet each other with a military-style salute and say, "What's up, soldier!""

Whenever a dude strongly disagreed with a point someone was trying to make, he'd slowly shake his head sideways, contort his face, wave his hand, real cool like, down by his waist and say, "Dry, Joe, dry!"

Thanks to boxing and Lawrence, I was being offered an opportunity to start fresh in a different hood. Coming into Trinidad the way I did connected me with the type of respected dudes who wouldn't deal with me in Little Vietnam due to my association with lowly H Place. These Trinidad cats had style. They were respected and could hold their own against any hood. Being part of a group like this gave me a feeling of respect on the streets. This meant almost everything to a dude like me trying to make his way.

Being with Underdue, who was so well-liked and respected, allowed me to meet and be around some of Trinidad's most respected cats. Lawrence, I quickly discovered, was not well liked, because he often displayed odd behavior.

The first time I noticed this was when Lawrence, Underdue, and I were hanging on 16th and Meigs Street snapping photos. A chubby dude nicknamed Jazzy Fats was standing off to the side just checking us out. For some reason, Lawrence got into a verbal dispute with him for simply being there.

Jazzy Fats tried to calm Lawrence down so things wouldn't escalate, but our buddy wasn't having it. He cracked Jazzy Fats on the chin right near an alley just off 16th, and they got to rumbling.

That surprise punch gave Lawrence the early advantage, but Jazzy Fats gathered himself and starting gaining some momentum. As he continued landing retaliatory blows, the tide shifted. Jazzy Fats got so confident that he began rocking from side to side, then suddenly announced,

"*Now, I'ma show you why they call me Fats.*"

He launched a big, looping right-hand (we called it a dough blow) that caught Lawrence on the left side of his chin, buckling his knees. Jazzy Fats didn't start the fight, but he sure as hell was finishing it. We'd seen enough, so Underdue stepped in and put a stop to it. We all knew that Lawrence was out of line for pressing the fight like that, but none of use spoke about what happened that day. That incident was only the first in a recurring series of strange episodes with Lawrence. The funny thing was, every time I saw Jazzy Fats after that day he'd ask me, with a big grin on his face, "Where your boy Lawrence at?"

While I was having an exciting time in Trinidad, I experienced some slippage in the gym. Since Cap didn't allow new fighters training under him to spar until he felt they understood how he wanted his guys to fight, it'd been some time since I'd actually boxed someone. By the time my opportunity came, Lawrence had started training there, and Cap put us in against each other since we were nearly identical in size.

It was my first time boxing a left-handed fighter. Lawrence's left hand looked like it was coming from the right, and his right hand looked like it was coming from the left. In the confusion, I forgot to move my head. His right jabs and left hands were snapping my head back so much that Cap waved off the sparring session before we made it out of the first round. Cap was so impressed with Lawrence's performance that he put him in with the best young fighter in the gym, a guy named Tony Standard, aka Taterbug. Lawrence performed well enough in the sparring session that Cap invited him to fight in an upcoming tournament. Everyone in the gym was excited about his potential, but the amount of time Lawrence spent in the streets kept him out of the gym after that first fight.

Getting passed over because of my poor sparring session didn't discourage me from coming to the gym. When the next sparring opportunity came around, I showed vast improvement. Before long, I was the guy staring across the ring at Taterbug. He was short but real fast and very athletic. Everything he did was precise, and it seemed as if his movements were effortless. I really learned how to fight when I began serving as his primary sparring partner. He made me miss so much that at times it felt like I was shadow-boxing. I always did my best work whenever Taterbug got tired and laid on the ropes. I cherished those rare occasions when, in between rounds, Cap would tell me, "That was a perfect round right there, son."

When Cap left Finley's with one of the assistant trainers to start a new gym called Neutral Corner, Taterbug and I were the only amateurs who followed him. We had to catch the bus out to Marlboro Pike in Maryland, but to be up under Cap it was more than worth it.

Cap trained all of us in a professional style. We were allowed to fight in some tournaments, with one of the gym's assistant trainers in the corner. I won my first bout by decision in a tournament at Hines Junior High School in Southeast, against a guy from Ham AC. My next bout went even better when I scored a second-round TKO. I was so hyped about the victory that I committed a bamma move by wearing my winner's medal outside on Benning Road a few times. The fake-gold-plated metal glistened in the moonlight as I strutted up and down the block pining for attention.

In my third bout, I was thrown in against Kelvin Daley, who was in the semi-pro division and had more than 50 fights under his belt. The tournament took place at the Takoma Park Recreation Center, where he trained. The hometown factor and Kelvin's ring experience affected my confidence. He came out punching hard and fast. The blows weren't hurting me, but the referee stopped the fight when I failed to punch back enough.

After we got dressed, that "wish I would have done more" feeling came down on me hard. Kelvin was standing front and center in the main hallway, sportin' his Timberland boots and a fancy light-gray sweat suit. Two cute honeys were in his face, and other well-wishers were crowded around like he was going to be the next Sugar Ray Leonard. And I'd certainly done my part to make it look that way. Everyone on our team lost that night, but I was the only one who hadn't given a full effort.

As high as I'd been from my previous TKO victory, that's how low my spirits were after suffering the loss. I was mad at myself for not fighting back. I even stopped going to the gym for a time.

In the '80s, DC was notorious for its street gangs. These weren't organized groups with rules and structure—more like just a bunch of guys and sometimes girls from the projects or a particular hood who liked causing trouble. The police referred to them as "loosely knit crews."

Young people from tough neighborhoods all over the city took pride in representing their turf. Coming from a place with a strong reputation gave them a sense of being someone important. I once heard a girl bragging to some people while riding on the bus, "I live in Simple City Southeast, where a niggah gets shot *every day.*"

Washington DC was and is divided into four quadrants: Southeast, Northeast, Northwest, and Southwest. Southeast, which had the highest concentration of poor black people, boasted the worst reputation. There were more projects in that part of town than any other. Any dude living in Barry Farms, Valley Green, or Condon Terrace generally got a measure of respect just for being from there. In Southeast, cats were known more for robbing and shooting people. Big Bad Southeast, as some people called it, was about that strong-arm game. Northeast was also rough, with hoods like Little Vietnam, Trinidad, Clay Terrace, Paradise, and Montana Terrace.

Northwest, or Uptown, as it was often referred to, had the U Street area, Sursum Corda, Clifton Terrace, 7th and T Street, and Georgia Avenue. Dudes from Uptown conducted themselves more like businessmen, taking pride in their ability to make fast money. The dope and heroin game was big up there. Southwest, the smallest of the four quadrants, had only a few rough areas.

Aside from the neighborhood crews, the mid-1980s also saw the growth of new gangs that attracted people from all over DC and Maryland. Deriving their names from TV programs, the A-Team and the Gangster Chronicles were the most popular. They weren't as rough as the other groups, but travelled in large numbers to go-gos and a few other places.

The guys I'd gotten to know in Trinidad helped me feel more confident navigating the tougher places and people I encountered in the DC of that time. Underdue and I became even tighter than I'd been with Don. Like Don, he was slightly older, lighter complexioned, and naturally drew more attention from people, especially girls. I was like the younger brother, who observed and learned things as we went on various adventures.

Underdue was a natural ambassador in Trinidad. He was welcomed on every corner of the neighborhood. Guys from opposing factions wanted his attention, and he rarely spoke ill of one person to another. He'd let me know his real feelings about a person or situation once we were alone.

When guys were smoking marijuana or PCP, they'd see Underdue and say, "Underdue, come hit this with me."

He'd step off to smoke with them, but he never asked me to come with him. I'd just wait patiently until he returned. Sometimes, we'd be among a group of guys hanging outside or huddled up in a hallway of an apartment building. One of the guys would pull out a joint and pass it around. Right before the joint reached me, Underdue would tell everyone, "He don't smoke, y'all."

And without fail, if one or several of the guys didn't know me, at least one of them would shake my hand in admiration.

Singleton was supportive of me in that way as well. On one occasion, I was with Underdue, Singleton, and another guy when they bought some PCP. The other guy wasn't aware that I didn't smoke, and when I told him, he was disappointed. "Man, you gotta hit this, so we can all have fun."

Before I could respond, Singleton told him, "He ain't gotta hit shit!"

Despite Singleton and Underdue's drug use, they always supported my non-use. Amazingly, they never asked me why I didn't smoke drugs. I never had to explain that all the coughing from smoking joints simply to get a high never appealed to me. Plus, when I considered the side effects, like how smoking marijuana made you *hungry*, it all seemed impractical. At least when it came to drinking alcohol, which we did on occasion, you could quench your thirst and spend less money.

It was Underdue who helped me with my shyness concerning girls. He was the epitome of a hood lover. He was good-looking in a tough sort of way and could charm almost any girl. He also didn't "give a fuck about 'em," as he sometimes told me, which somehow made him more appealing. There were times when he'd sleep with three girls in a day. He was never possessive or concerned about whether a girl was dealing with another guy. He'd often tell me, "Never get mad about a bitch messin' with another niggah, 'cause you can't stop that. But you can always find another girl."

Though he wasn't always the nicest guy to certain girls, he never encouraged me to mistreat girls. He accepted that I was different in certain ways and never seemed to judge me for it. Like with smoking, we never talked about those differences. He would ask me to go with him to other neighborhoods in DC and Maryland to see this girl or that one. It was during one of these trips that I met China Stewart.

China was the leader of a gang called the Lady Chronicles, the female version of the Gangster Chronicles. They were based in the DC Shrimp Boat area of East Capitol Street Northeast. Underdue and I went over there to see a girl he was dating, and China, being one of the girl's close friends, was also there among a large group of other girls. We didn't meet that night, but she sent word through her friend that she wanted to see me.

I wasn't so excited about seeing China, because she had looked a little rough that night. But when we actually met, I was pleasantly surprised. It was like she was a different person. Her hair was nicely done, and she was sexy as hell in a street sort of way. She also had a fun-loving personality. The first day we met she gave me a nickname, "Bernie Baby."

I was thrown off and somewhat overwhelmed, because I was thinking she was all street, but she had this sweetness about her that was very attractive. It was like some person who was hiding inside of her had snuck up on me. Being around a girl like China, who showed such confidence and openness in liking me, was something I'd never experienced and didn't quite know how to handle.

I happened to run into her one Saturday while Don and I were shopping in Georgetown. She was standing in front of a mirror, admiring how she looked in a brown, waist-length leather jacket. When I tapped Don, so he could also enjoy the view, China caught me peeping. She laughed and said, "Stop looking at the cookies, stop looking at the cooookies, Bernie Baby!"

Not long after that day, we were kissing and cuddling at her parents' place near 58th and East Capitol Street. Singleton and Underdue were hanging outside, waiting for me. Unlike the time at Bummy's house, I was into China. And yet, the same thing happened again. There was no music again. I didn't embarrass myself any further by trying to ask China to rub my back or anything like that. I just put my clothes back on and accepted defeat. She didn't get upset or say anything to make me feel bad.

When I stepped out onto 58th, Singleton and Underdue were waiting on me, but I had nothing to tell them. The uneasiness I felt over my nonperformance, and the fact that I was still a virgin, was something I wanted to keep in the dark. My hope was that by taking a silent approach, they'd assume that I'd handled my business with China. I didn't have to think about it for long. As we were leaving off 58th, people started running from the sounds of gunshots. We scattered too.

What happened up on 58th was too embarrassing for me to continue seeing China. I didn't dwell on it too long, because Underdue kept me busy roaming around to so many different places and meeting so many different people, which is how we met Sandra Jenkins and her friend Irlene. Underdue and Irlene dated for a little bit, but Sandra and I started seeing each other nearly every day. If the guys had thought Wills's cousin, Marsha, was a catch for me, dating Sandra took that to a whole different level. She was a redbone with green, catlike eyes. On Saturdays, when I worked at Holly Farms, she'd come an hour early and wait in the lobby until my shift ended.

Since Sandra lived out in Maryland and my mom wouldn't allow any girls over at our place, we hung out over in Huntwood Northeast, where Don's mother had recently moved. It was the only way we could spend quality time together. Going out with Sandra was my first serious relationship, and my mom wasn't pleased about it. We finally had a phone at home by then, and Sandra and I talked so much that my mom would sometimes pick up the other receiver and tell both of us to get off. Sandra wasn't having it, so she would sometimes argue with my mom. I thought she was crazy, but, to my surprise, my mom actually started liking her.

All of Sandra's friends were telling us how much in love we were. There was even talk about us one day getting married, which

I liked. During all this time, my fear of failing in bed again kept me from trying to have sex with her. I simply took pleasure in being around her.

I noticed that Sandra didn't talk much about her family or life at home. One time, we got stranded at a Metro station in Maryland after seeing a late-night movie with friends. When we dropped her off at home in Maryland early the next morning, she didn't mention anything about a worried mom or dad. It seemed as if she could go wherever she pleased. Oftentimes, she stayed with Irlene's tight-knit family weeks at a time.

This was the summer after my sixteenth birthday, and it was one of the best times of my young life. But as fall approached, things between Sandra and me began to peter out. Instead of arriving early to wait for me in the Holly Farms lobby, she started coming just as I got off. Before much longer, I was getting off work and having to wait for her.

When I pulled her up about it, she apologized, but the late arrivals didn't stop. I was furious and let her know that I wasn't going to tolerate it. The next Saturday, I waited for more than an hour after I got off work, but Sandra didn't show. She'd spoken with her actions, and I was left with nothing but my bold words. But I was so caught up with being her boyfriend that I couldn't hold the line, and I called her a few days later.

After that, we still talked, but things were different between us. She didn't seem to have much time for me anymore. Then, Lawrence told me that he'd heard Sandra was back to seeing her old boyfriend, another Trinidad cat. I didn't want to accept it, but before I could even verify it, she started seeing another dude, from nearby Wylie Street.

By fall, the disappointment of no longer being with Sandra was causing me a pain I'd never felt before. I was in a daze. Luther Vandross's *Busy Body* album was out, and his "Superstar/Until You Come Back to Me" became my theme song. I thrust myself into my work. By then, I was one of Lucille's most trusted employees, so I convinced her to hire a few of my friends out of loyalty. She hired Don, Lawrence, and Pop at various times, but none of them panned out. Don worked for one day and didn't come back. Pop got caught stealing money out the register. Lawrence just never showed up.

By the time I suggested Underdue to Lucille, my credibility was nearly spent. Reluctantly, she gave him a chance, and he shocked us both by working out well. He even worked harder than me, so hard that the district manager heard about him. He was so impressed that he gave Underdue a raise and transferred him to another location. He ended up working that Holly Farms job until the company went out of business. Years later, he got his commercial driver's license and became one of the main drivers in his cousin's business, Goode Trash Removal.

I left Holly Farms before it closed down and began working in food services at Gonzaga. Dan Boone, who was the first legitimate black entrepreneur I ever met, ran the school's food and catering service. He paid well but cracked a mean whip. If he caught someone slacking, he'd fire him on the spot. I worked with him in the mornings before school, during lunch, and on the weekends at the rectory where the school's Jesuit teachers and staff lived. I also picked up extra money whenever Mr. Boone had to cater any school functions.

Mr. Boone paid attention to everything and always preached against being wasteful. Every time he saw me coming out of the walk-in freezer with the light still on, he'd tell me, "That could be your raise right there." Another of his favorite sayings was, "Work your job; don't let your job work you."

Working at Gonzaga was definitely a step up from Holly Farms. The money was much better, and the food we served was of a higher quality. Mr. Boone seemed to be doing well for himself financially. Every year, I learned he'd be pushing a new Cadillac, and seeing him in action piqued my interest in finding out how a business was run.

Aside from the quality of the education (which meant very little to me at that point in my life), and the opportunity to earn better wages and develop my interest in entrepreneurship, Gonzaga offered me something else of great value at the time: the Academy of Notre Dame, a nearly all-black private school for girls, was connected to our school. Seeing the girls walking up North Capitol Street in the morning was quite an event. I wasn't the only black student who was posted up out there like an NBA forward, trying to score a look at the pretty girls in their plaid skirts.

My heart was still healing from Sandra, but I lucked up one morning and met a brown-skinned cutie I saw walking along North Capitol Street. She was toting an oversized purple corduroy bag, and I saw a way in.

"What you doing with that big bag over your shoulder," I asked, "running away from home?"

A smile came over her face and she slowed up her pace, giving me the confidence to take things further.

Robin Smith and I were the same age, and she lived several blocks off 6th and H Street Northeast. I started walking her home after school. When we got there, we watched cartoons and talked for hours. We messed around some, but she was a fairly popular girl and there were a lot of other guys calling and stopping by to see her. Some of the things Underdue had taught me helped me not to get jealous. What Robin offered me was very unique and special: a hanging buddy who also happened to be a pretty girl I enjoyed kissing. For almost two years, Robin was the primary girl in my life.

By senior year, though, I wanted a serious girlfriend. There was an attractive and stylish sophomore at Notre Dame named Delida, but she wasn't interested in me. But when Underdue came up to Gonzaga to meet me one afternoon, I introduced them to each other and a match was made.

I'd never seen Underdue spend so much time with one girl. Delida lived just a few blocks from Hechinger Mall, and they became inseparable. He was over at her house nearly every day and even got really close to her parents.

I'd lost my hanging buddy. But Delida made up for it by introducing me to her equally stylish friend, Cindy Blake. There was one immediate hurdle though, and it came from Cindy's mother, who made it known that if I wanted to date her daughter, then I would have to go over there and meet her.

I wanted to date Cindy, so I caught two buses over to Stanton Road Southeast to put myself under a mother's scrutiny. Ms. Blake, who was very attractive, explained that she had only been a teenager herself when Cindy was born and was determined to do everything she could so that her own daughter wouldn't have a child at such a young age. She kept us under her watchful eyes. On Fridays, I was allowed to come over to watch music videos with Cindy on their living room couch where we'd have to sneak smooches. Cindy was pleasant, quiet, and inexperienced, while I was shy, fearful, and trying to put up a good front. We never got close, and our relationship was boring—nothing like what Underdue and Delida had. They went to performances by Patti LaBelle and Maze featuring Frankie Beverly, or they went out shopping together. Their relationship was like a new Porsche cruising down the highway, while Cindy and I puttered down the road in our old station wagon.

My relationship with Ms. Blake, on the other hand, blossomed. She had a caring attitude, and her sternness reminded me of my own mom. Sometimes I'd ride with her over to Cindy's grandmother's house, and she'd talk about living life responsibly. Once, in her car, she pointed to a guy hanging out and said, "See that guy right there? He did something and went away to jail for five years. Think about that; he put his life on hold for all that time."

When I opened up to her about not knowing who my father was, she shared a story from her own experience: "Growing up, I'd never seen my father, too. Eventually, a family member told me where he lived. I travelled to where it was and watched from a distance. When I saw him come out the house, he looked so poor and downtrodden that I no longer saw a man who had abandoned his daughter and family, but a man who was simply struggling to make it through life. All of the anger and negative feelings I'd been holding onto about him turned to compassion for his state in life. See? You don't know what your father's circumstances are."

My own mom never talked to me about such things. Her entire focus was on me doing well in school and staying away from people who were a bad influence. This is why my mom didn't like Underdue, who had dropped out. Every time Underdue knocked on our door, she never showed him any courtesy. He'd have to stand in the hallway as she yelled out to me, "That damn Raymond is here," but despite that, he was always courteous to her.

Underdue and I were close, but that wasn't enough to stop me from wanting something he had. One spring afternoon, I was sitting near the back of the X bus on my way home from school, and I kept dozing off in my seat. The bus stopped in front of the Pentacle Apartments, and I was suddenly awakened by the feeling of something falling down my chest.

It was my fourteen-karat gold chain, and it'd just been snatched off my neck!

The thief was short and stocky. I woke up just in time to see him dart out the back door. I jumped up and gave chase. He whipped through the Pentacle Apartments complex and zoomed through an alley. Thinking I wasn't going to be able to catch the dude, I turned around and ran home. When I got inside, I went straight to my little hiding place and pulled out the .22 caliber pistol I'd recently bought from someone in Trinidad for $60. After I had my little burner properly concealed, I gave my mom an excuse and went back outside.

I felt violated, desperate, and embarrassed. People on that bus had seen what happened to me, and just thinking about that was enough to push me forward. Once I got to the Pentacle Apartments, there was no one around. I walked around for a while but couldn't find the dude.

Up until that point, there had never been a situation where I felt I needed to use a gun. DC was still more about using your fists to resolve disputes, but more and more guys were buying guns, so I simply followed suit by getting one for myself, and I wanted that chain back. I had to risk going into an area where the dude probably had a whole crew behind him, and I didn't have time to get Underdue or anyone else. My burner was just what I needed for the situation.

All of these emotions were running through me, yet I had no way of getting them out. I thought about Delida. She only lived a few blocks away, so I stopped by her house. I knew I could talk to her, because our conversations were always pleasant and unforced, nothing like the ones I had with Cindy. Delida often called me when she was looking for Underdue or wanted to share certain concerns, and we'd developed a close friendship.

Delida's parents knew me pretty well by then, so when I knocked on their door, they just told me to go downstairs. She was on the couch, relaxing in her school uniform. I sat down next to her and explained what had happened. She listened with real concern as self-pity and a sense of helplessness brought out my emotions. All of the conversations we'd had to that point, sometimes on a daily basis, made it easy and comfortable for me to open up to her. I laid my head on her lap, and her willingness to allow me to be so open gave me the confidence to act on an urge for something I realized I had been harboring deep within me.

This chain-snatching incident presented me with an unexpected opportunity. Here I was, alone with the only person I felt truly at ease talking to about my vulnerabilities. Cindy and I were distant.

As far as my boys were concerned, there was an unspoken code—you could never share certain parts of yourself, even if you wanted to.

When I looked down at Delida's pretty legs, they spoke to that urge inside of me. I began gently caressing her right calf, hoping this would lead somewhere else. An excitement welled up in me. With this one act, I was stepping over two friendship lines, but my desire for sensual pleasure didn't care about the essential role I'd played in bringing Delida and Underdue together, or the fact that Underdue was my man and Delida was his girl. My urge was forcing me to dishonor what they had—what I didn't have with Cindy. I was asking Delida, without saying a word, to give me a piece of what Underdue enjoyed by being with her.

But her response wasn't what I had hoped for. Instead, she calmly got up, walked over toward the other side of the room, and looked at me, then said, "You a trip."

Those three simple words, and the dismissive expression on her face, were all it took to put me back in place. All of my hope and desire immediately turned to shame and embarrassment. The place I'd come to for comfort and solace was no longer a fitting place for me to be. I left Delida's house without another word.

Delida and I never spoke about the incident; Underdue never came to me with his fists balled up, ready to fight. For my part, I didn't mention what I'd done to anyone and eventually tucked the incident away in my mind. To my surprise, Delida helped me out by treating me as if the incident never happened. Though I didn't know why she did this, and didn't dare ask, I definitely appreciated it.

That entire afternoon, from getting my chain snatched to embarrassing myself at Delida's, taught me something invaluable about envy and forgiveness, all for the price of a $300 gold chain.

The night of Wednesday, October 31, 1984, Lawrence, Underdue, Singleton, and I, along with several other dudes, were on the G2 bus travelling from Trinidad to Georgetown for the annual Halloween street festival. Georgetown was the place to go on Halloween night, because thousands of people from all over the city walked up and down M Street and Wisconsin Avenue decked out in costume to celebrate the holiday.

Several white students from Gallaudet University, a private school for the deaf and hard of hearing, were on the bus. The university was on the edge of Trinidad, and dudes from surrounding neighborhoods would taunt, harass, and even rob students on the regular.

This night was no different. As soon as we noticed hearing aids in those students' ears, some of the fellas started in on 'em. They got to mumbling loudly and pointing at the female students. A few of the guys began making crude hand and mouth gestures. The girls turned their heads away or started looking at the floor, and the other passengers just looked ahead with straight faces, trying to hide their disgust at our behavior.

Singleton and I were the only two who didn't participate in the taunting. Always quiet and observant, Singleton's dislike for public displays always kept him from acting out in any way. He never seemed to get caught up in the moment. By then, I had also recognized that he was not only trustworthy, but also quite capable in a dangerous sort of way. It was these qualities that garnered him respect, and made him sought after by some of the most well-known dudes in Trinidad. For my part, I never picked up the habit of openly teasing people. I was still shy. I never acquired any real skill when it came to jonin' and didn't have any urge to try gaining confidence by picking on easy marks.

When we reached Georgetown, people everywhere were in a festive mood. But without warning, we were suddenly thrust into a stare-down with a group of guys from the Uptown Crew. Their leader, Alley Cat Jenkins, was out in front of a group of about fifteen dudes, and his gaze was squarely on Underdue. Whatever the reason, we were outnumbered by a group about six feet away and these guys were ready to get in the mix.

Lawrence, who was standing off to the side of our little stare-down, stepped into the space separating both groups and said coolly, "I'm just lettin' y'all know, somebody gonna take a fall if one of you jump."

By this time, Lawrence was heavy into selling drugs, so he always carried a burner. His threat was enough to get Alley Cat and his crew to step off.

A few minutes later, a fight broke out about 20 yards ahead of me. There were so many people that it was hard to see, but once the crowd dispersed, I could see Underdue skirmishing with a group of guys from the Uptown Crew. Singleton ran up and cracked a dude square in the face with a right hand, sending him falling back on his heels.

Underdue got up from the scuffle and joined us as we came up. The guys from the Uptown Crew stood their ground but didn't come forward. Perhaps they were still concerned about Lawrence's threat, even though now he was nowhere in sight. Both groups went their separate ways.

Underdue and another guy—the main two who'd been taunting the Gallaudet students, as it turned out—got the worst of the Uptown Crew's surprise attack. The incident ruined our night. All of the fun and excitement were gone, and the bus ride back to Trinidad was quiet and respectful.

It was after midnight when we got back to Trinidad. I had been talking to Underdue about buying one of his leather jackets, so we headed to my house to get my money. After passing through Hechinger Mall, instead of staying on the sidewalk, we, as was our habit, walked in the street next to the cars parked along H Street, between 17th and 18th. We saw two dudes to our right in skull caps walking on the sidewalk in the opposite direction, toward 17th Street, as the cab that had just dropped them off drove slowly by us.

We continued walking in the street and came upon a body lying on the ground directly in front of us. It was a white man lying motionless on his left side with a bullet hole just below his ear. I had seen two other people shot before, but they were alive at the time.

Just as we started to walk away, Mann, a guy who lived on the block, came running to us from across the street. He told us that he and his father had heard some gunshots and called the police. Underdue and I left Mann standing there as we continued on to my house.

Underdue and I realized that we'd just missed the cab driver getting robbed and shot. We figured that the two guys in skull caps walking up the street were part of a three-man team, and the third guy was the one driving the cab. They must have robbed the cab driver, shot him, and then pushed his body out before we walked up. The driver probably picked the other two back up somewhere around the corner before going across town and ditching the cab.

After we reached my house, I gave Underdue the money for the jacket and walked him to the edge of Trinidad, making sure to take a different route there in order to avoid the police. We didn't want to get blamed or accused of anything. On my way home I walked along I Street and looked down 17th and 18th streets from the top of the hill. I could see the police everywhere, the lights flashing from their cruisers and yellow incident tape spread around the scene.

I later discovered that the cab driver's name was Walter Hardesty, and he was actually still alive when we had seen him lying on the ground. In my view at the time, he was just some unfortunate white man who'd been shot in Little Vietnam. His death was just another violent and senseless act of the kind I was accustomed to hearing about, or had seen on several occasions. His whiteness disconnected me from his humanity; I didn't see him as a family man with a wife and two children at home in Northwest DC. Nor was I aware of the fact that earlier that evening he had taken his son and daughter trick-or-treating in Georgetown, where my friends and I had been.

Mr. Hardesty wasn't only a cabdriver. According to news reports, he had been close to obtaining his PhD in clinical psychology at George Washington University. Driving a cab was his way of earning extra money for his degree. He died at DC General Hospital four hours after we discovered him lying on the ground that Halloween night.

The Washington Coliseum was not just the premier place for seeing live go-go in the city. Black people from all over the area came in order to resolve disputes that had started in the streets. If you had a beef with someone, you figured they'd eventually show up at the Coliseum.

The area surrounding the Coliseum was controlled by the 8th & H Street Crew. They were highly respected in the city, and their territory stretched along H Street Northeast from 3rd to 14th and from Florida Avenue to Maryland Avenue.

Fortunately, Trinidad and 8th & H were like family. I'd become pretty cool with a coworker at Holly Farms named Reggie. He was from the Brentwood projects in Northeast. We were both proud of our hoods, and I wanted him to see how strong Trinidad and 8th & H were, so I invited him to go with me to an upcoming concert at the Coliseum.

When Reggie and I stepped into the Coliseum, it was packed as usual. The seats were filled with people, and the floor was so congested that you had to squeeze through people to get anywhere. I was moving around so excitedly that Reggie had problems keeping up with me. I kept losing him in the crowd. By the time I ran into Singleton on the Coliseum floor, I was by myself.

We were making small talk when somebody bumped my left shoulder from behind, real hard. That type of bump could damage one's reputation if people were around to witness it and you did nothing about it. I turned around and glared at a dark-skinned dude. He turned around, glared right back, and said, "What's up?"

"What's up?" I replied.

As soon as I'd spoken, a line of guys came up behind him, single file. There were about fifteen of them, and a real big dude, who was black as night, brought up the rear.

"What's up?" the big dude said in a deep, slow voice. My heart dropped to my feet.

"You ain't got nuthin' to do with it," Singleton responded, and my heart bounced back up. But then it went right back down again when two little boys, who must have snuck into the Coliseum through a side door, ran up and gave the big dude and another guy some blades.

I broke off running to the left. As I pushed through a crowd of people, punches began landing on the back of my head. I quickly planted my feet, turned, and threw a desperation jab, but someone yanked the hood of my New Balance sweat-suit jacket, causing my arm to go straight up into the air and my balance to falter. As my left palm touched the ground, the thought of getting kicked and stomped on the dance floor flashed through my mind. Some dudes wore boots to the Coliseum for that very purpose.

I stumbled along the floor and managed to regain my balance. At the point where I reached the edge of the dance floor, I turned around and got popped with a punch from the dude who had first bumped me. We started fighting in a tight clinch. My fists were moving fast as I struggled to keep the dude at bay. From the corner of my eye, I noticed a security guard standing nearby just watching us get it in.

I'd more than held my own, so the dude backed off and stepped away through the crowd. Taterbug, my stablemate from Finley's Gym who must have been watching from the stands, came down to me as I was catching my breath and said, "That was good work there."

After Taterbug and I talked briefly, I managed to catch up with Singleton. He'd stumbled on someone's foot and fallen on the ground with the big dude coming down on him hard. Luckily, he was saved when a guy from the Uptown Crew, who knew both of them, came over and broke it up as Singleton was using his legs to keep big dude from stabbing him.

The big dude's name was Big Black, and their crew was from 7th and T Street Northwest; a well-respected group from Uptown. In order for us to get back at them, we needed help from 8th & H, so we caught up with Chrissy and Hollywood, two of the crew's leaders, up in the stands. They were 25 or 30 dudes deep and told us they'd "get them niggahs."

We joined in and started making our way around the Coliseum. I ran into Reggie, told him what had happened, and asked him to come with us.

"Man, you hot!" he said with a dejected look on his face.

I'm hot? *Damn, Reggie just tagged me as a troublemaking-type dude*, I thought to myself. He joined us but seemed hesitant about it, and as we kept searching for the 7th and T Street dudes, Reggie hit me with a duff move and disappeared. It was the last time we ever hung out together.

When we didn't see any of the guys from 7th and T, Singleton and I ventured off by ourselves. Rare Essence had just started groovin' to close the show, so we peeped out two cuties to dance with. Just as we settled in, people around us started scattering. I turned around and recognized the dudes from 7th and T approaching me and Singleton, waving blades from side to side. They were smiling and bobbing their heads up and down, saying, "Uh-huh, uh-huh, uh-huh."

We slipped away into the crowd and headed toward the exit. Once we left, Underdue, Lawrence, and another cat named Brandon were standing outside. Lawrence had his burner, and Singleton ran to retrieve his from wherever he stashed it before going into the

Coliseum. As usual, my gun was at home, and Underdue had never gotten a weapon.

Near the corner of 3rd and Florida Avenue, we spotted Big Black squared off against another guy in the middle of the street. A crowd had gathered as both of them threw up their hands. This was the perfect opportunity to catch Big Black preoccupied, so we quickly ran up into a wooded, hilly area that looked down onto the street.

Once we concealed ourselves in the woods, Lawrence and Singleton slowly pulled out their burners. Over to Lawrence's left, I could see a grimy-looking dude, who was lying low just a little ways behind us. As Lawrence and Singleton were aiming, the guy pointed to his left and called to us in a hushed voiced, "Look over there."

We stopped, looked over, and saw about ten police cruisers sitting in the parking lot of the Roy Rogers fast-food restaurant on Florida Avenue, facing 3rd Street. Many of the officers were standing next to their cars. Lawrence and Singleton quickly put their burners away, and we blended in with the crowd on the street. After the fight was broken up, we tried to follow Big Black and a few of his crew, but there were too many police floating around.

Three years passed before we saw Big Black again. Singleton and I were standing in front of the Metro Club, a small go-go venue in Northeast where Rare Essence played weekly. As people were coming out of the concert, Big Black was lying on the ground, suffering from a stab wound. A police officer was standing over him trying to get information, but Big Black was uncooperative. Even in his condition, he was sticking to the code of the street of not talking to police.

"Well fuck you then," the officer told him, walking away.

That night at the Coliseum brought Singleton and me closer together. He looked out for me, and I, in turn, looked out for him. When I had established credibility after working at Gonzaga for a while, I recommended Singleton for a job at the school's rectory on the weekends, and Dan Boone hired him.

My exposure to drugs while hanging on H Place had been limited to beer and cheap wine. Sometimes, I'd drink Olde English 800 and Wild Irish Rose with Don and Bummy. On one memorable occasion when I was just fourteen, we got drunk and went to Wheaton, Maryland, where I got into a fight with an adult man. He came into the McDonald's claiming I had disrespected his girl, so we stepped out into the parking lot.

Even though I was drunk, I managed to hurt the guy with a right hand, but it didn't end well for me. At least that's what Don and Bummy told me after they helped me home. I had gotten knocked out. I was too drunk to remember anything. That experience taught me a lesson about being drunk in public.

When I began hanging in Trinidad, even though I still didn't use any drugs myself, I eventually became involved with selling some illicit substances. All of the dudes I hung around with were dealing with drugs on some level. Marijuana, and especially PCP, were the popular drugs in our hood. PCP had been called "angel dust" in the '70s, but now had a new name: "love boat," or simply "boat."

Boat was on the streets with a new vigor. It was such a dangerous drug because you never knew what affect it would have on a person. One dude might get extra strong after smoking it. Another would hit a joint and then go out and kill someone. And it was absolute comedy whenever a dude got high off it and stripped down butterball naked. In fact, some people started calling PCP "butt naked."

Lawrence told me about a Trinidad dude named Mad Dog who smoked some boat, shot a mailman, and got killed by the police. Pumpkin, my old stablemate from Ham AC, started smoking boat heavily and began distancing himself from everyone. He'd walk through Meigs Place and Montello Avenue without speaking to anyone. Several months later, he drowned in his own bathtub. Underdue liked smoking boat too, but for me the idea of spending $10 or $15 for two or three joints didn't make much sense—not when we could buy a 32-ounce beer for $2 and get a nice buzz off that.

Seeing Lawrence pick up those quick dollars on Montello Avenue selling PCP got me into it. Working was still my main thing, but I saw hustling as an opportunity to make some good side money. The top side of Montello Avenue had such a festive and family-oriented atmosphere; the risk of selling drugs receded to the back of my mind.

Lawrence had a slick little marketing technique. Every time he got new product, he'd give a free sack of boat to an old-head drug addict, who spread the news that Lawrence had that "good shit." Lawrence would then usually be sold out by nighttime. Sometimes he'd give away his last sack if it stayed on him too long, from fear that the jump-out police might nab him while he was standing on the corner trying to service customers.

I didn't have the same connections in Trinidad as Lawrence, so it was a struggle for me to get rid of my product. I also wasn't a very aggressive street peddler. I always had in the back of my head the words of that administrator at Gonzaga who had told our incoming class that 95 percent of the school's graduates go on to college. Regardless of my financial situation, I assumed that I'd be a part of that majority percentage; I never wanted to jeopardize that opportunity by taking too many risks on the streets.

In spite of the risks involved in selling drugs and owning a gun, I never saw these things as something beyond my ability to manage. I was in the streets; this is what dudes did out here. Besides, I wasn't a go-hard dude. I never jumped or robbed anyone. My overriding concern was making that extra money.

Even though I didn't make a lot of money selling PCP, Lawrence and Brandon approached me with an idea to start selling larger quantities, known as weight. In order to accomplish this, we'd have to put our money together and purchase a bottle of water. Both of them had earned enough money from selling drugs, but in order to take part, I needed to throw in some of my work money to come up with my share.

I was keenly aware that selling weight was a move up the drug-selling chain, and the monies coming in could significantly increase. The risks involved, though, would be less in some ways— we'd be selling to other drug dealers instead of standing outside on street corners peddling $10 and $15 bags. I didn't care about extra attention or gaining higher status in the streets; my thoughts were on making extra cheese.

I saw my role in this new venture as more of an investor who entrusted Lawrence and Brandon to handle everything, since most of my time was devoted either to school or my job. They bought a pound of marijuana and the bottle of water, which contained embalming fluid, among other substances, to wet the reefers down. They found a place to store the product in a freezer so that it would maintain its potency.

But something went wrong. At least, that's what they told me. Somehow, they said, they'd ruined the product in trying to stretch it with different additives, and they had to destroy all of it. Of course, I was furious, since I'd lost all my money—and I hadn't seen what had actually happened, or any of the ruined product.

Lawrence got so fed up with all my questions that he stepped off the corner, leaving me there in a heated argument with Brandon. It wasn't a secret to any of my friends that I worked a lot, and that going to college was now my primary focus. Making it in the streets didn't mean as much to me as it meant to them. Even though I couldn't prove it, I suspected that Lawrence and Brandon had used my nearly $400 investment to get to the next level in the drug game, and now they were cutting me out.

NEVER STOP

I was disillusioned by the experience, but I wasn't quite ready to throw in the towel on the drug game. I started selling marijuana at Gonzaga and made a deal with Don's older brother, Big Mike, to sell PCP for me in Huntwood. It was my senior year at Gonzaga, so I had a good idea by now who was into smoking. I purchased a pound of weed for about $500 from one of Curtbone's boys and set up shop.

I don't remember to whom I first offered a nickel bag at school, but the student I did approach was eager to buy. He put me on to a few more people. There wasn't a lot of money in selling nickel bags to a limited clientele, but I knew it was important to keep things on the low at school. I felt a tinge of uneasiness with every transaction, but I enjoyed the satisfaction of handling my own money. Most of my sales took place in the mornings and at lunch. I got so cool with certain pot-loving white boys at school that they rode me over to Trinidad to see Underdue. He chuckled when I pulled up in front of his house on Oates Street with two white boys and an Asian in a convertible pumping go-go music.

My hopes for making real money rested on Big Mike. He needed money to supplement his work income, was well connected in the neighborhood, and knew a person who could get us some high-quality drugs. I caught the bus over there and dropped some bread on him to get things started.

A few weeks later, I checked up on his progress, hoping to hear that it was time to come collect my money, but Big Mike gave me some bad news. The guy he trusted to cop the PCP had run off with the money. My hard-earned cash was gone again, but this time, Big Mike promised to pay me back in installments from his work income. And true to his word, he did. Every other Friday when he got paid, I was on the X bus to Huntwood to collect my money. The day I rode over there to pick up my last installment was a happy day for me. When Big Mike placed those bills in my hand, a weight was lifted off my shoulders.

As the X bus travelled down Nannie Helen Burroughs Avenue, the thought of leaving the drug game comforted me. The losses I'd taken in Trinidad and Huntwood gave me an even greater appreciation for earning money through honest work. My heart was no longer weighted down from knowing I was doing something wrong. I'd freed myself of a burden. For the first time, I made Gonzaga's dean's list that semester. Despite the appeal of being in the streets, deep down I knew that this was a temporary thing, a phase for me. I was always conscious of the possibility of living a different type of life; the type of life college could offer me.

And though I'd made a personal breakthrough, I wasn't aware of how my involvement in drugs affected my mom. In spite of my best efforts to keep her from knowing what I was doing, she was aware.

For my part, by the time I turned sixteen, I was aware of why we'd been evicted from our apartment in Fort Totten years earlier. My mom's mental state was the cause. She'd had a number of other episodes since we'd moved to Little Vietnam. During those times, she'd tell me she wasn't paying the rent. The problem was that she'd only admit this after the resident manager for our building would inform me that the rent hadn't been paid for several months. He could see that my mom had some issues, and he knew I'd been working for several years, so he went out of his way to let me know when we were behind in rent.

Every time he pulled me aside, I'd hurriedly approach my mom, take whatever money she had left, and add some of my money to it to pay up the rent.

But there was one episode where my mom told me she wasn't paying rent—and then said that she intended to shoot the resident manager. *Shoot the resident manager?* Then it hit me—I ran to my hiding space in the closet only to discover the little .22 pistol was gone. I had to talk my mom down from her threat and convince her to give me the gun back.

By the time I was in my last years at Gonzaga, the roles my mom and I played at home had begun to reverse themselves. My mom stopped being the authoritative, butt-tapping type of mother, and the money I was making allowed me to assume more of an adult role in the house. I never asked her for money anymore, and I would step in from time to time to cover certain monthly expenses for the household. We established a tacit agreement: she didn't say anything about what I was doing, and I managed to stay out of serious trouble.

When it came to my mom's habit of smoking cigarettes, I was definitely the parent. I hated cigarettes. Every time I discovered an unflushed cigarette butt in the toilet, I searched the house until the hidden pack of Kools was found and thrown away. She couldn't say one word about this, either, because she agreed that smoking was dangerous, and she had promised me many times that she'd stop.

While I put the drug game to rest, Lawrence and Brandon became more deeply entrenched in it. Lawrence bought a car and a new wardrobe. Brandon's ambition and toughness caused him to break away from his former mentor to join with Cliff, my stablemate from Ham AC, and his brother's crew. Their squad controlled much of the drug game in Trinidad, and Brandon became their rising young star.

I still hung out with Lawrence from time to time, and I happened to be with him and several other Trinidad dudes the day Levy, Snotrag, Lamont, and a few others from the 8th & H Street Crew came to visit. They spent some time with us on Montello Avenue, and then Lamont invited Lawrence, Underdue, and me over to Wylie Street, one of the most drug-infested and violent streets in Northeast, where he lived. Underdue opted out, but Lawrence and I went along with the members of 8th & H.

Lawrence and Lamont were pretty tight. There was so much dialogue going on between them that they stepped away to Lamont's house. Nighttime was still a few hours away, but Wylie Street was filled with people hanging out. Besides Lawrence, though, I didn't know anyone too well. When Lawrence didn't come out after a while, I decided to head home.

As I was walking along Florida Avenue, someone called out to me. It was Lamont, but Lawrence was nowhere in sight. He was trotting toward me, and asked, "Hey, can I get that class ring again?"

Lamont had borrowed one of the many class rings I owned one night at the Coliseum, and had just returned it to me earlier that day when we'd all been in Trinidad. We used class rings like brass knuckles, which meant wearing three or four on each hand. I had a thing for class rings, so whenever a dude was selling one on the streets I'd buy it.

I hadn't had a problem lending Lamont the ring the first time, but something didn't feel right this time. Before, he'd been respectful, but he seemed more aggressive now. Then I looked over and saw Snotrag skip-walking toward us with a pair of brass knuckles on his hand. I didn't feel too confident about coming out of this situation without getting hurt. Lamont was several years older than me, at least a few inches taller, and had a larger build. Snotrag, a full-grown man at 26, was 8th & H's oldest member. I actually looked up to these guys; now they were getting ready to put a beatdown on me.

As if things weren't bad enough, Levy, who was 8th & H's foremost leader, walked up, and asked, "What's going on?"

"Lamont wants to use my class ring," I told Levy as he walked up to me.

"Man, let me have the damn class ring!" Lamont said, walking up aggressively.

"Naw you ain't. Let me hold it for you, shorty. I'll make sure you get it back." Levy said to me reassuringly.

I took the ring off my finger and gave it to Levy. As he was walking away, Lamont followed behind, like a whining child, begging him for the ring.

A few days later, Underdue and I went to Levy's house, and he gave me back the ring, and added, "Shorty, let me know if anyone gives you any other problems."

When I told Underdue about what had happened, he wasn't surprised. The day of the incident, he'd overheard Lawrence telling Lamont that I wasn't family, because I was from Little Vietnam. Some dudes from up there had recently tried to jump Lamont, so he made up his mind to try and take my ring as get-back.

I never would have thought Lawrence would turn on me like that. When I first started hanging in Trinidad, I was concerned about how dudes from Little Vietnam might react to me once they found out, but I never thought my living in Little Vietnam would be a problem for the dudes I hung with in Trinidad.

I already knew that Lawrence was a strange dude, and I already thought that he'd cut me out of that drug deal with him and Brandon. Underdue and Singleton both had experienced some bad stuff with Lawrence too, and had already started distancing themselves from him. I did what I should've done long before; I stopped dealing with him altogether.

On the evening of October 1, 1984, during the fall of my junior year at Gonzaga, a married mother of six named Catherine Fuller was robbed near the corner of 8th Street, dragged to an abandoned garage, and murdered. The details were grisly. The authorities were calling the incident one of the most brutal murders in the city's history.

Days after the murder, the police issued the first of numerous arrest warrants. During the investigation, more than 400 people were called downtown for questioning, and Underdue was one of them. I went with him and sat in the waiting area while he was questioned. As I sat waiting, a detective came out and asked where I lived, but I refused to tell him. When Underdue came out, he told me that they had asked him where I lived, and he told them. The detective talking to Underdue wondered whether I knew anything about the murder of a cabdriver that had occurred two blocks away from my house. Unbeknownst to that detective, this was the same cabdriver Underdue and I happened upon that Halloween night. Though we hadn't seen the shooting or recognized the killers, talking to the police about what little we did know was too scary a proposition.

Nine months after Mrs. Fuller's murder, seventeen people were arrested. Among them were Levy Rouse, Kelvin Smith aka Hollywood, Christopher Turner aka Chrissy, and Timothy Catlett aka Snotrag: the leaders of the 8th & H Street Crew.

Underdue was dating Hollywood's sister, Tonya, at the time, so we went to the DC jail in Southeast to visit him and Chrissy. Both of them claimed they were innocent. By the time the trial started, just over a year after the murder, ten members of the 8th & H Street Crew were tried; two others had already pleaded guilty and were testifying against their former crewmembers.

Toward the end of 1985, the first semester of my senior year, Underdue and I went down to DC Superior Court twice to watch the proceedings. Though I knew nothing about the law, the public defenders didn't seem to be doing a good job for the members of 8th & H; it was like they were just going through the motions.

The community was horrified by the murder, and the politicians and police wanted to respond quickly. The 8th & H Street Crew was a convenient target. They were known for fighting and robbing people in the neighborhood. I myself had witnessed them doing this several times, but the victims were always dudes about our age.

Levy, Hollywood, Chrissy, Snotrag, and four others were convicted of the crime, and the other two defendants were found innocent. Of the group, five received 35 years to life, while Chrissy received a slightly lesser sentence of 27.5 years. He was the only one from the group with a high-school diploma and a steady job—a job that had ended the Friday before the murder. If the company Chrissy was working for hadn't closed down that Friday, he probably wouldn't have been hanging around H Street when Mrs. Fuller was killed.

Levy and Snotrag got 40 years to life. Levy was very charismatic and a natural leader. The police and the court were fearful of his ability to sway young men in the community, it was reported, so the judge tacked on five extra years for him. Snotrag's propensity for violence earned him the added time, even though the joke on the street was he got five years extra for his nickname.

I couldn't accept that the 8th & H Street Crew killed Mrs. Fuller. What Levy had done for me near Wylie Street the day Lamont and Snotrag tried to jump me was something he didn't have to do. I just couldn't see this same guy doing something so vicious to an older woman, or even allowing it to be done by a group of guys he had so much influence over. But I was just a seventeen-year-old kid at the time. No one cared what I thought.

The convictions made the 8th & H Street Crew notorious in DC, but it also completely wiped the group out. Despite what the authorities and most other people may have thought about them, I still felt connected to the group. When it came time to order our senior class rings at Gonzaga, I had *8th & H* inscribed on mine. To me they represented strength, something with which I was proud to be associated. There was nothing about my family or school life that could offer me, at that age, anything close to this. My time on the streets, however, was coming to a close. Though I didn't openly talk about it to my friends, going to college was shaping up as my escape route. Despite the fact that I was enjoying my time hanging out, I wasn't willing to deviate from Gonzaga's standard of academic achievement. Without knowing how I would get there, I just assumed that college was in my immediate future. I applied to three schools: Syracuse University in upstate New York was my first choice, while Mount St. Mary's University in Emmitsburg, Maryland and St. Joseph's University in Philadelphia were recommended by my high-school counselor, Mary Freburger.

Mrs. Freburger was very honest; she told me that the likelihood of my getting into Syracuse was slim. She really liked Mount

St. Mary's for me because of its small size and the opportunity for exposure to a different environment that wasn't too far from home. Emmitsburg was only 75 miles from DC; away from the city but close enough for me to get back quickly if I ever needed to do so.

I knew Mrs. Freburger was telling the truth. My grades weren't the best. I made the dean's list my final two semesters, but my academic performance from the previous three years was closer to average. I was pretty smart, but my strong dislike for carrying books hindered my studies. Being cool was very important to me, so travelling light was my style. Some of my classmates wondered how I managed to get decent grades when they rarely saw me carrying books. They didn't know that I was studying in the library during my free period and other down times.

I wanted to apply to Georgetown University but didn't, because I felt that my academic record wasn't strong enough. Aside from my grades, standardized testing wasn't a strong point for me. The colleges with the strongest academic reputations were looking for students with a bare minimum SAT score of 1,000, but I didn't meet that mark.

When I got a rejection letter from Syracuse, Mrs. Freburger arranged for me to visit Mount St. Mary's and St. Joseph's. Fr. George Quickley, who was the only black Jesuit priest teaching at Gonzaga, had become something of a mentor to me, and he offered to drive me to both schools.

On our way to Mount St. Mary's, Fr. Quickley and I slipped into one of our typical conversations. There were always a lot of questions in my head about life and its purpose, and I didn't feel comfortable talking to any of my buddies about such things. My discussions with Fr. Quickley offered me an outlet to explore these deeper concerns. After some of our talks, he would point out that I was very inquisitive.

During our trip, I asked for his opinion on what I should study in school. His response surprised me: "You should study philosophy."

Philosophy? Socrates, Plato, and the other philosophers we studied at Gonzaga were well off, or at least had access to resources. They had leisure time! I'm too poor to do that, I thought. But I didn't want to discuss this with Fr. Quickley, so I offered no response to his suggestion.

We arrived at Mount St. Mary's, affectionately known as the Mount, and were greeted by an administrator named Lou Grillo, who talked to us about the school and gave us a tour of the campus. Something about the Mount just felt right. I told Fr. Quickley just before we left that my mind was made up; the Mount was my choice.

My graduation ceremony from Gonzaga was approaching, but I wanted to skip it. Aside from a handful of friends and the time I'd spent working for Dan Boone, I didn't feel any real connection to the school. It was simply the other world I had to deal with before rushing back to the excitement of the streets. But my mom was so excited about my graduating that I felt obligated to attend.

Our graduation ceremony took place inside of St. Aloysius Church next door to the school. We were all decked out in white tuxedo jackets with black pants and matching bowties. As individual awards were being handed to those students who had achieved special accomplishments, I was surprised when my name was called. The school presented me with an award for "academic ability and confidence in pursuing academic excellence."

As I sat in my seat looking at the actual award, there was another surprise. The award was from Georgetown University and the school's president had signed it. Just then, a tinge of regret entered my thoughts. Gonzaga and Georgetown are both Jesuit schools. Obviously, they're connected. If I would have just applied, whoever somehow realized my academic potential might have been able to help me get into Georgetown.

When I saw my mom outside, she was beaming like the sun. Underdue, Delida, and Cindy were there too. Singleton couldn't be there, because he was serving a little time in jail for beating up another Trinidad dude.

During the school year, when I was still trying to figure what colleges I would apply to, I had attended a Mount recruiting function, where I met an alumnus of the school named Joseph Horning. He and his brother, Larry, owned a very successful local real estate company called Horning Brothers. Mr. Horning promised me a job if I decided to come to the Mount, so after I committed to go there, I contacted him.

Mr. Horning set me up to work as a construction laborer on a few job sites. My hourly wage was the highest I'd ever earned, but the work was very hard. My final summer assignment was an apartment complex in Northeast near St. Anthony's called the Cloisters. The supervisor was mean as hell. He fired someone nearly every payday.

Making matters worse, he had this butt-kissing black foreman named Robert, who enjoyed harassing us for no apparent reason. When I got Underdue a job there, the two of them bumped heads constantly. Underdue finally cracked Robert on the chin so hard one day that he wobbled from the front doorway of one apartment to the other. All the other workers were happy, especially because Robert shut his mouth for the rest of the summer.

Working construction was the perfect motivator for entering college. Doing that kind of hard manual labor made going to school that much more appealing, and I was as determined as ever to use my mind to provide for myself.

During my spare time, I hung out with Underdue and Singleton, who got released from jail during the summer. We had fun hanging around the neighborhood and going to go-gos whenever Underdue could drive his brother-in-law's Nissan Maxima. My relationship with Cindy had pretty much fizzled out. It was generally difficult to gauge how she felt about me and our relationship, but I sensed that it wasn't too positive. An incident a few months prior, more or less, confirmed my suspicion. Since Cindy was a snazzy dresser, I knew I had to come strong for her birthday in April. I'd bought a $250 navy and gray Fila sweat suit from Georgetown for her special day. I'd never spent that much money on one item, even for myself.

As my birthday approached the following month, I got a little nosy and asked what she had in store for mine. When she let me know that my birthday hadn't really been on her mind, I was peeved. I didn't know whether I was more upset over what she said or how quickly and nonchalantly she said it. I spoke to my gym teacher, Coach Jackson, who was one of my mentors at the time, about the whole thing. He told me to chalk it up to experience, but I couldn't go the gentleman route. I asked for the Fila sweat suit back, and she obliged. We both sensed our relationship wasn't going to survive beyond the summer.

My conversations with Underdue and Singleton that summer were more personal than they'd ever been. I was shocked when both of them, on separate occasions, told me they weren't too confident about how life would turn out for them in the future. I looked up to both of these guys. Underdue was like my big brother, and Singleton was a shining example of physical courage. Being their friend had brought me the acceptance and companionship I had most desired. Being around them boosted my confidence in the streets, no matter what was going on around me. I valued these things, but they valued something different—where *my* life appeared to be heading. In their eyes, opportunities appeared open for me that they might never see.

What they saw for themselves was only what appeared right in front of them. Underdue had seen a lot of dysfunction in his own family—but, there was some hope. He had a great work ethic and a girlfriend who he really liked. Sometimes he spoke of having a stable life away from the streets.

Singleton, though, had a deeper connection to the streets. He and Brandon had become close, and their relationship offered him an avenue to advance himself in the drug trade, which was starting to boom. Outside of working at Gonzaga's rectory for a time, the money Singleton made came from the streets. He felt comfortable there. When I decided it was time to get rid of my little .22, it was Singleton who bought it from me.

Through all of this, I was still involved in boxing. Cap had moved to a new gym on Kenilworth Avenue Northeast called M-PAC. Many of the pros I trained with at the gym fought on a series of local cards held at St. Benedict the Moor Catholic Church in River Terrace Northeast. The church had a small auditorium next to the chapel where a boxing ring was set up, surrounded by metal bleachers and foldout chairs near ringside. It was a nice, intimate setting for fans to see up-and-coming fighters.

One of Cap's best fighters was Louis "Heidi" Curtis, who had boxed alongside Sugar Ray Leonard and the Spinks brothers at the 1976 Olympic Games. Heidi's career took a detour when he spent some time in Lorton Reformatory. There, he came under the tutelage of Cap, who became his trainer upon his release. Heidi, campaigning as a bantamweight, fought in the main event on one of St. Benedict's cards. My seat was pretty close to ringside, and when I sat down and looked over, Curtbone, my former nemesis, was in the seat right next to me.

Since we'd squashed our beef years before, he had become one of the most respected and well-known dudes in the streets of DC. He'd somehow hooked up with Rayful Edmond, the city's biggest drug dealer, and was making big papers on the street. The energy between us seemed good. He even shared a story about his month-long suspension from Spingarn High School.

"Me and this dude named Eric Carter from the Orleans Crew, who I never got along with, got into it at a home football game. I dropped him and they suspended both of us for two weeks. When the suspension was over, both our mothers brought us back up to the school to get readmitted. Man, right there in the principal's office, me and the dude get into it, I dropped him again, and they gave me another two weeks!"

We had a good laugh about it.

When the main event kicked off, Heidi had the whole place on its feet throughout the entire fight. If there was any lingering tension between me and Curtbone, Heidi's performance probably wiped it away. He looked so good in the ring that Curtbone and I were falling over and slapping hands like old friends. I was relieved that our little run-in had happened before he became the person everyone in and around Little Vietnam knew he was going to become.

Curtbone was a hard-core street dude, who had done and was willing to do things I couldn't bring myself to do. For much of my six years living in Little Vietnam, I was infatuated with the streets, but instinctively I knew it wasn't the place for me. I'd learned how to defend myself, but I wasn't a go-hard street dude. And in just a few years, I'd find out whether that was a good thing.

Education

MOUNT ST. MARY'S UNIVERSITY, AKA THE MOUNT, WAS founded in 1808 as the country's first independent Catholic college, at the base of a mountainous region in the town of Emmitsburg, just fifteen miles south of Gettysburg, Pennsylvania. I arrived on the Mount's small campus in the summer of 1986. This was my first time living so close to nature. Besides my infrequent trips to North Carolina to visit family, my exposure to any sort of natural scenery had been limited to DC parks and the filthy Anacostia River near RFK Stadium.

Nothing I'd been around before came close to the beauty of the Mount's scenery. Every time I rode from DC in a car along Route 15, the tallest mountain I'd ever seen—I hadn't seen many— jumped out from a distance as we rounded a bend on our way to the school. This mountain stood next to some smaller ones, and they were all adorned with trees. I was a city boy who, for the first time, was constantly surrounded by grassy fields, trees, and open space instead of asphalt, concrete, housing projects, and office buildings. I could feel the presence of the mountain almost everywhere I went on campus, as if it was always peeping over my shoulder.

Nearly all of the freshmen were housed in either Sheridan or

Pangborn halls, two coed dorms. Since girls, who had only been admitted since the '70s, now made up the majority of the student body, the guys lived on the first floor while the ladies occupied the two upper levels. I stayed in Sheridan with a white boy named Jess.

There were only two other black guys on my floor, and only one of them, a guy named Cliff Warren, who had been recruited to play point guard for the basketball team, seemed interested in hanging out with other blacks. Of slightly more than 1,500 students, fewer than 100 of us were black, and there was no X bus or any other way for me to escape living in a predominantly white environment.

More important to me than the beauty of the Mount's campus was the beauty of the female students. I looked at the black girls first, but there were so few of them, and it seemed as though the handful of pretty ones were already spoken for. I'd had a few dates with a white girl in high school but had never seriously considered a relationship with a girl who wasn't black.

At the Mount, though, pretty much all there was were white girls, so I began peepin' them out, and much of what I saw shattered the image of white girls I'd been holding onto since the fifth grade. Most of the women at my grade school, St. Anthony's, wore robes, but my fifth-grade teacher, Mrs. Phillips, wore slacks nearly every day, and her butt was as flat as an ironing board. My sixth-grade teacher, though, Ms. Hathaway, was black, and she had the biggest butt I'd ever seen.

Us boys used to talk about her butt so much that one day she overheard us outside her window after school. Looking at her all year reinforced my belief that flat butts belonged to white women, and big butts mainly belonged to black women.

But at the Mount, some of these white girls had butts that could've given Ms. Hathaway all she could want. Every day, I saw attractive white girls on campus. The problem was that I didn't know how to get their attention. In DC, my Fila sweat suit, New Balance shoes, and fresh low-cut fade would attract the girls, but at the Mount these white girls didn't seem to notice me at all. The black guys on the basketball team were the only ones who seemed to have a way of getting white girls. During my first week, I was with some of them at a nearly all-white beer party in the Towers, which housed juniors and seniors, and one of the guys whispered in my ear, "See all these white girls? There's a lot of pussy walking around here tonight. You better get you one." As we went from party to party, some of the players pointed out girls they'd slept with. In every case, the girl was so drunk that she couldn't stand up straight. The ballplayers' method was to catch white girls during the weekend when they were drunk and easier to approach, but they'd barely speak to each other during the week.

I befriended a short, blonde-haired white girl in my early morning math class who was nice and seemed approachable. She lived in Sheridan too, and we started talking, even sometimes continuing our conversations in my room after class. By the time I built up the courage to express a romantic interest in her, she was already fielding offers from two black guys on the basketball team. Being rebuffed after stepping across the racial line like that didn't sit well, but the girl that interested me most was Shelley Logan. She was a cute biology major who played field hockey. We didn't share any classes, but she also lived in Sheridan, so I saw her almost daily. I decided to play it slick by leaving a message on her door board, without knocking, to give her the impression that I'd stopped by. When a message from her appeared on my door board the next day, I was thrilled. Later that day, I left another message on her door board. She came by my room a second time but missed me again. But that was okay, because I figured it was only a matter of time before we'd finally have a real conversation.

Unfortunately, the dreams floating around in my head about Shelley didn't last long. That Friday night, I was headed to my room when I saw Shelley was making out with a white-boy freshman at a party on Sheridan's first floor. Everybody else at the party was inside drinking and talking, but the two of them were in a hallway corner getting it in. It didn't stop there, either; they started dating seriously.

I'd failed to truly pursue Shelley; I couldn't admit to myself that I was afraid of being rejected by her. To open up and let her know my true feelings was frightening, so I made assumptions about her to justify not doing it. And since she was a white girl who, I assumed, hadn't spent much time around black people, it was easy for me to use her whiteness as the reason why we could never be together.

My race consciousness grew stronger as a reaction to the Mount's predominantly white environment. Like most black students on campus, I joined OSCA, the Organization for Student Cultural Awareness, which was mainly a social club. OSCA sponsored trips and activities that catered to the interests of black students.

Our first event was a trip to the Kings Dominion theme park. A group of us travelled there in a van provided by the Mount. When Teresa Grillo, a black freshman who happened to be the niece of Lou Grillo, the Mount administrator I met during my initial visit, kept hearing me refer to girls as bitches, she objected, asking, "Why we gotta be bitches all the time?"

Her question was posed in a very matter-of-fact tone with no anger or attitude attached to it, and for the first time since I'd begun using the term, I had to grapple with my own gender bias. I'd picked the term up from hanging in Trinidad and being around Underdue. If he was upset about something a girl did, he'd call her a "skank-ass bitch." If he didn't think much of a girl, he'd call her a "dingbat bitch." If the girl looked good, he'd double-up on the term for emphasis: "Man, that's a baaaddd-ass bitch right there, Joe! Bad-ass bitch!"

Using the term felt harmless, like calling your boy "niggah" or someone else "Joe" or "Moe." But, in my gut I knew Teresa was right, and the trip to Kings Dominion allowed me to deal with myself about it.

We arrived at Kings Dominion and had a good time getting on rides, acting silly, and even making an old-school R&B recording in one of the amusement park's make-believe studios. After that day, I stopped using the term bitch when referring to girls.

Before I left for the Mount, several older black people gave me unsolicited advice about dealing with racism on campus. No one expressed any concern about blatant or overt racism. Based on their own years of intimate dealings with white people, they talked to me about the emotional and psychological impact of racism. Fr. Quickley thought attending a predominantly white school would further my education about the white world, and this was the general sentiment of the others as well. Implicit in their words was the idea that I needed something white folks had. "You have to go after it," they encouraged. "You'll have to be twice as good as they are, if you're going be accepted," they warned.

I didn't adopt this view when I arrived at the Mount. Because I'd gone to Gonzaga, going to college felt more like a right than a privilege to me. I felt the streets of DC had been the toughest thing I'd faced, and that nothing white folks could ever throw at me would match up. I didn't find the academics at the Mount difficult—in part because there was so little going on socially to distract me.

I set my own standards to follow while on campus. One of these was adopting a no-nonsense approach to whatever I perceived as racism, whether overt or subtle. Perhaps it was my way of dealing with living in a predominantly white environment without being able to run to the comfort of my friends in the streets. Just as I had during my first semester at Gonzaga, I reacted strongly to any perceived slight from a white person.

I developed a platonic friendship with a white freshman named Beth, who also lived in Sheridan. We started talking almost daily. I was surprised that even though she lived outside of DC in Potomac, Maryland, she was unfamiliar with the city aside from Georgetown. She was just as surprised that I didn't know anything about Potomac. When she gave me a ride home one Friday, she was awestruck by Little Vietnam.

A few weeks later, Underdue, Singleton, and Earl Harrington from Wylie Street came to visit me at the Mount. From my vantage point, they were representing quite well. Earl, who was making good money on the streets, was flossing in a long black trench coat. Since Beth and I were developing a friendship, I wanted her to meet my friends. So, after we finished walking around campus, I took them up to Beth's room. Underdue, who did most of the talking, was his normal flirty self. He talked Beth's ears off about all types of stuff. She seemed a bit uneasy but was very polite during our visit.

About a week before our very first midterm break, Beth told me about a party she planned to have at her house while school was out. She wanted me to come but not with my buddies. I felt slighted by her request and was quite upset about it. I considered my friends to be like family, and by taking the time to introduce them to her I had shared a part of myself. The way I saw it, if she couldn't accept my friends then she couldn't accept me. We didn't have a conversation about it, though. I just didn't talk to her anymore, and we stopped being friends.

Things were much worse when I got into it in the middle of class with a white girl named Tracy who started making fun of the way I talked. Our writing teacher, Dr. William Lawbaugh, tried to quiet us down, but I was too far gone. "You can go get any of those white boys you know. I guarantee you that I'll fuck them up," I fumed.

Tracy got quiet, and class resumed with no further incidents or outbursts. Once class ended, Dr. Lawbaugh pulled Tracy and me out into the hallway. "What was going on in there?" he asked. "She teased me about my diction, and nobody should ever tease me about the way that I talk," I replied. I pointed my finger toward Tracy's chest as I spoke. Then I just walked off, leaving the two of them standing there.

The next day, Dr. Lawbaugh reached out to me by phone. It was a few hours before lunch, and he wanted me to stop by his office as soon as I could. I came right away. His office was a small room with a desk, mounted with stacks of papers, a few pictures on the walls and two wooden chairs facing his leather seat. I sat in one of the chairs.

"I understand what happened yesterday, and I'm prepared to support you in filing a claim against Tracy for racism," he began.

"File a claim? I don't want to do that. I'm not interested in getting her in any trouble like that," I replied.

"Well, okay. That's admirable, but I must say that even Dr. King wouldn't have handled things the way you seem to be trying to."

I didn't know what to say to that, so I just sat there. Then he asked me if I had ever heard of a book called *Soul on Ice*.

A few days passed before I went to the Phillips Library to check out *Soul on Ice*, written by Eldridge Cleaver, who had spent time in prison before writing for *Ramparts*, a radical political and literary magazine. He later went on to become the national spokesperson for the Black Panther Party for Self-Defense. Largely a collection of essays written during the time Cleaver was locked up in three different prisons, *Soul on Ice* discussed his anger with white people, and how raping white women was his way of getting even. He eventually ended up at Folsom Prison, where he joined the Nation of Islam, and he wrote about its spokesman, Malcolm X. This was the first time I had ever encountered that name.

As Malcolm had when he was in prison, Cleaver studied the dictionary while he was locked up, and this had an immediate impact on me. As I continued reading through the book, I began placing parentheses around all the words I didn't know—words like *iconoclast, putrid, impunity, axiomatic, eunuchs, vitiated,* and *mitosis.* Then I ran to the dictionary and wrote down the definitions next to the words.

I was saddened by what I learned about Malcolm's assassination, and how the rise in Malcolm's popularity in Folsom almost caused a war between his supporters and those who supported the Nation of Islam's leader, Elijah Muhammad. Later in the book, Cleaver attacked the writer James Baldwin for being gay and (supposedly) uncomfortable with black masculinity. Toward the end of the book, Cleaver laid out his theory of how white men control America by using intergroup conflict to keep certain groups apart, while pitting other groups against one another. What white men fear most, he suggested, is that black men, who they believe are mentally weak but physically strong, will eventually find a way to build greater mental strength.

I found the book very interesting, but most of all, I was captivated by what it had to say about Malcolm X. I immediately read his autobiography, and eventually I did a paper in Dr. Lawbaugh's class on Malcolm's views on the civil rights struggle compared to those of Dr. King.

What I discovered about Malcolm helped me with my transition from the streets to my predominantly white college. Malcolm was intelligent and learned, but he was also cool. I admired him for never losing his connection to poor people, no matter what environment he ventured into. Even as he debated the country's leading intellectuals, Malcolm maintained his street sensibility. I sought out film and video of his speeches and interviews, and I'd never heard anyone speak like him: the clarity, the profundity, and the simplicity. Listening to him speak about the conditions of inner-city black life was mesmerizing. I could also relate to certain aspects of Malcolm's upbringing. Like him, I hadn't grown up with a father, and our mothers had both had mental-health issues. The poverty, violence, and crime of our surroundings were similar as well. I was in awe of how he had been able to rise out of those circumstances.

Malcolm assumed a role in my life that, up to that point, no other man, living or dead, had been able to fill. I'd never met, or even read about, an adult man I wanted to model myself after. With Malcolm, I felt an immediate, intimate connection with his journey and what he sought to accomplish for black people. Once I grasped his mission and purpose, I wanted to take up the mantle of his cause.

Embracing Malcolm as a model this way led me to focus on school work as I never had before. My best class was accounting principles, in part because I'd taken an accounting class at nearby Notre Dame High School during my senior year. My motive for taking that class had been to meet girls, but what I'd learned was paying off at the Mount. I was busting As on every test in that class. Cliff was also in the class, and he was amazed when he saw the grades coming my way.

Word of how well I was doing in accounting class got around to a few people. My friend Alex Morris told me that a white girl in my class wondered how I kept getting such good grades, so she started watching me during tests to see how I was cheating. After she watched me several times without seeing me pull any slick moves, she finally accepted that I was smart. "That's messed up," Alex told me.

But I didn't care. What that girl thought didn't matter to me. I began to feel that I didn't have anything to prove to white people. I got good grades for me, because it made me feel good to excel at something.

In writing class, Dr. Lawbaugh required us to keep a daily journal, and I started looking forward to writing in it. Every evening I got the opportunity to document my private feelings without being interrupted by music or television. My last journal entry of the semester was directed to Dr. Lawbaugh.

December 8, 1986

Just in case I didn't get a chance to talk with you.

I often talk to a priest, Fr. Quickley, from my high school. We've become very close and I often get advice from him. He helps me realize the important aspects in my road of life. These aspects have often been overlooked by me.

I realize my experience with Tracy may be more helpful and more important than all the English classes or any other class I'll ever take. I learned something from my experience. You helped me turn my anger, frustration, and rage into a form of motivation and achievement. You were an ally to me. You saw what was going on in that classroom, and you knew how to handle the situation. I realize these types of occurrences will probably happen again, and the next time I might not have an ally or a person capable of handling or communicating as well as you. I hope and pray I can handle the next situation correctly.

Maybe Tracy learned from this experience also?

By the spring of '87, Tracy and I had patched things up. We even ended up riding together to a venue just outside of DC to watch Sugar Ray Leonard win a controversial split decision over the reigning middleweight champion, the great Marvelous Marvin Hagler, on closed-circuit TV.

My freshman year at the Mount was uneventful romantically but ended well academically. During the fall semester, my grades were just good enough to earn a spot on the dean's list, and my performance was even better in the spring, which helped me earn a cumulative GPA of 3.66 for that year. I'd chosen business as my major, but when my accounting teacher told me that I shouldn't go through the Mount without at least getting a minor in accounting, I decided to add that on as a second major.

I wanted to do a sport at the Mount, but unfortunately boxing was out, at least for the time being. In 1960, a Wisconsin student boxer had died as the result of injuries suffered during a match in April of that year. The resulting fallout caused the NCAA to stop sanctioning the sport of boxing. As a way to reintroduce boxing back into collegiate life, at least as an intramural sport, the National Collegiate Boxing Association (NCBA) was created in 1976, but it was limited to only 30 or so colleges by the time I graduated from Gonzaga, and the Mount was not one of those schools.

Since running was an essential part of boxing, I figured it would be good to get into track or cross-country. I'd done some running, or "roadwork" as we called it in boxing, a number of times with other fighters or on my own. So at the beginning of my freshman year, I showed up for cross-country practice. Since I'd never run cross-country before, Jim Hartnett, who was the coach, told me to go out with the other runners for two miles and then run back to campus, for an easy four-mile run, while some of the more experienced runners would go eight miles. About fifteen of us started out running at a very relaxed pace. I was the only black guy in the group, but the team captain, Anibal Gonzales, was a Hispanic guy from New York. Everyone was joking around, and a few guys started teasing me by asking if I knew where the Mount's infirmary was located. Then they told me that if I made it back okay, I'd be accepted as a full team member. I just smiled thinking, *At the pace we're running, I can hang with you guys all day long*. I went by the two-mile mark feeling fine.

When the team reached a three-mile water break, Coach Hartnett, who had been following us in his truck, told me to turn around and head back to the starting point. But I felt so good that I convinced him to let me continue on with the group. I even refused to drink from the water hose when one of the runners passed it to me. Anibal and his girlfriend, who was captain of the women's team, led the pack by about 50 yards, and I felt so confident that I sped up to run with them.

As we were on the fourth mile, I noticed the joking and talking had stopped. The sky was clear and the weather quite pleasant. When I looked to either side of me, I saw farmland and grazing cows. Everyone was completely silent; the panting of our breath and the pounding of our feet on the hard pavement were the only sounds.

During the fifth mile, the intensity of our pace began taking a toll on me. The ambition I'd started out with turned to doubt. By the six-mile mark, my confidence was fading fast and I wanted to quit. My body was hurting, my legs were getting stiff, and I had no idea where we were. To give myself some relief, I fell back from the front group and managed to hang on with the others until we unexpectedly reached another rest stop.

While we stood there, Anibal came over and reached his hand toward me, saying, "Congratulations! You didn't quit. You must be a pretty good runner to have made it this far on your first day."

His words encouraged me to bear down and finish the final mile and a half of the run, which seemed like it took forever. Coach Hartnett was impressed that I'd lasted the entire eight miles, and he informed me that I'd earned a place on the team. It was a gratifying day for me.

Our training regimen for cross-country required us to run at least five days a week, regardless of weather. The running was grueling; my legs hurt like never before, and the pounding on my feet caused several of my toenails to fall off. Coach Hartnett and a few of the veteran team members stressed the importance of stretching our leg muscles before and after every run, something I never did consistently enough. Stretching was something else I'd never learned about before, and I didn't fully understand how important it was to maintain my flexibility as a way to improve my running.

Despite the pounding, the pain, and the ugly toes I was developing, running cross-country was worth it. I loved the exposure to the beautiful mountains, pastures, and farmland; being in such excellent physical condition felt wonderful; and my mind became more meditative with every run. Everything seemed to slow down as I looked out across the vast fields during our six-to-eleven-mile daily runs. Running became a new constant in my life.

After I started training on the cross-country team, another student told me about a punching bag located in a small gym above the student activity center directly behind Pangborn Hall. Every day after cross-country practice, I started adding five or six hard rounds of heavy bag training to my workout schedule, and I kept up the consistent bag workouts throughout the school year.

Contrary to my earlier assumption, I learned that I wasn't the only black on the cross-country team. Two Kenyan brothers named Kip and Charles Cheruiyot were 1500-meter runners who had competed in the 1984 Olympics and now attended the Mount. They ran cross-country merely to stay in shape, as they were training for the upcoming 1988 Olympics in Seoul, South Korea. One of the track coaches at the Mount had some really strong connections that enabled him to attract a lot of top foreign athletes to the Mount.

The Cheruiyot brothers were my introduction to the great tradition of Kenyan running. Though we were all teammates, the Cheruiyot brothers were much too advanced to run with the rest of the team. After meeting them, I started paying more attention to long-distance racing. It seemed like every time the results of the Boston Marathon or some other major long-distance event came in, a Kenyan was the winner. Running was incredibly popular in Kenya, and the high altitudes in certain parts of the country helped Kenyan runners develop great lung capacity.

Since our races took place on Saturday mornings, all the runners had to go to bed early on Friday, which was my favorite day of the week. I was generally in bed by 9:00 p.m., which left me with no time for any social activity. I could hear folks running up and down the hallway until I managed to fall asleep.

Our cross-country meets took place mostly against other NCAA Division II schools in Pennsylvania and Maryland. Our races were either five-mile or ten-kilometer races, and the Cheruiyot brothers won every one that they entered. For them, it wasn't even a true competition. During one race, a white boy from an opposing team broke down crying when he heard Kip whistling as he ran. Though the races may not have been much for the Cheruiyot brothers, it certainly helped our team place higher in the division rankings.

My performance in races was decent but nothing special. The funny thing was, some of the white boys from other teams thought I was Kenyan, because I'd often be the only other black racing besides the Cheruiyot brothers. At the starting line for one particular race, a white boy standing beside me looked over and said to me, "Intimidating!"

I said to myself, *I guess he and anyone else who thinks I'm a Kenyan will find out once they see what place I finish in.*

May 21, 1987

I've started my summer at home. I've started working, and I'm adjusting to my job very well. This job is definitely what I need. I've seemed to mature much, much more from my experiences at school. I'm trying to respect and appreciate all the wonderful things my mom has done and consistently does for me. Up to this point, I haven't really been out, but starting this weekend I'll make up for a lot of that.

I plan to stay in boxing, even though it's the hardest thing I've ever done. I get butterflies in my stomach, my workday is totally different, and I'm quiet, always thinking. Boxing is definitely a good experience for me. I'm pretty sure it's what I want to do for the summer. I listen to the dreams all the young guys have in the gym and the beauty of it all. Today Milton "Iceman" McCrory, the former WBC welterweight champion who is from Detroit, came down M-PAC. It picked my spirits way up. I no longer hang in the streets. I talked to Alfonso yesterday and his road has become a little rocky, but I'm sure he'll overcome it. I often think of Loni and a lot of my old friends. I'm glad to be from the ghetto. I realize that I'll always be from the ghetto, but from this point on I'll never be of the ghetto.

I kept myself busy during the summer after my freshman year by working at Horning Brothers, boxing, and training for the next cross-country season. I used my good academic performance at the Mount to secure a job at the Horning Brothers main office in downtown DuPont Circle Northwest. My primary responsibility was to create and maintain Excel spreadsheets for the accounting and property-management divisions of the company. The work was much easier than being a construction laborer, and the pay, which was at least a $2 per hour increase, was the most I'd ever made.

Joe Horning also helped move my mom and me out of Little Vietnam to the Azeeze Bates Apartments located on the other side of Benning Road, near the Rosedale neighborhood. We were still in the same general area, but our apartment was nicer and the rent was $200 less per month; because it was Section 8 housing, the rent was based on a percentage of my mom's Social Security income. My mom was thrilled with the move, and it brought me a great sense of satisfaction to play an important role in moving us to a better place.

The material and financial gains my mom and I received that summer didn't improve our interactions at home, however. While I was away at the Mount, we had only talked on the phone a handful of times, and now that I was back home, we were once again living as distantly as two people could in the same house. She was proud of my accomplishments and still concerned about my development, but our daily routine consisted of asking each other how our days were, without saying much else to each other. My mom preferred speaking to whomever the person was in her own mind. She also watched soap operas and the local news on TV, while I liked to watch football or boxing, or else read up on black consciousness.

I began training at M-PAC with Cap, who was now the gym's head trainer. The three owners were rumored to be former bank robbers turned drug dealers. Despite all the shady affairs that appeared to be going on around the gym, Cap seemed able to maintain a healthy distance from it.

Cap had a new crop of talented young fighters, some of the sharpest dudes coming out of DC at the time. The two best young fighters were Bernard Barnes and Leon "Smitty" Smith. Bernard was a short, stocky pressure fighter, while Smitty was slimmer, slicker, and quick. Both were pretty close to turning professional.

After a few weeks of shadowboxing, hitting the heavy bag, and jumping rope, Cap put me in the ring with a seventeen-year-old named Antonio, who people in the gym had been raving about. He was physically bigger and slightly taller than me. In our second round of sparring, Antonio caught me with a nice one-two combination that buckled my knees. Fortunately, he failed to throw a follow-up left hook and left himself open for a counterpunch. I caught him with a right hand and didn't realize he was hurt until Cap screamed, "Go get him!"

I went into attack mode, but the sparring session was abruptly stopped when Antonio complained about his right hand hurting.

The next day, Cap pointed at Antonio and me as he was talking to one of the owners, who had missed the previous day's sparring, saying, "Man, you missed something yesterday. These two hit each other on the chin like they owned each other."

Later during training, Cap walked near me as I was shadow-boxing in the ring and said, "Boy, there sure ain't nuthin' wrong with your heart."

His words meant a lot. Cap rarely gave direct compliments. I'd spent enough time in the gym to know that his yells, sharp remarks, and put-downs were his way of trying to make his fighters better and more prepared for what happened in the ring. For me, and for many of the other fighters, he was the closest thing we had to a father figure. Every second of every minute in the gym, I was conscious of his critical, probing eyes.

After a month of training, Cap put me in against the gym's best young fighters. Smitty's hands were so fast that he caught me with two quick left hooks in the first round. I had to adjust to his speed, but once I did, I was able to time his movements and get in some of my own punches.

When one of the assistant trainers, Keith Harrison, first told me I'd be sparring a big, strong dude named Barksdale, I was a little anxious. When I came to the gym the next day, Keith was standing next to a heavy bag grinning at me. "I thought you were gonna duck this work," he said.

Keith figured I wouldn't show up to face the thick-necked Barksdale. He didn't know that I never ducked work. I kept my distance and used a stiff jab and side-to-side movement to keep Barksdale at bay. He was so confident in his punching power that he kept cocking his right hand back before letting the punch go. In boxing, this was known as "telegraphing," or loading up on your punches, and it let me know what he was intending to throw. At one point, he got me against the ropes, but when he telegraphed his right hand, it gave me enough time to pop him with my own quick right to his head and then slide off to my left to avoid his punch. Keith liked the move, and called out, "See, Barksdale, you keep trying to load up on him, and he snuck one in on ya."

The fact that Barksdale was stronger than me didn't mean much if he couldn't land his punches. I'd boxed him intelligently enough to make his power a nonfactor. Boxing was more about being smarter than being stronger. After our sparring session had ended, the admiring look of Keith let me know I'd earned his respect.

I was also adhering to Coach Hartnett's cross-country summer training schedule. All team members were required to run 40 miles a week in June, 50 miles in July, and 60 miles in August. To keep things simple, I did a ten-mile run that started off at Hechinger Mall, went down Maryland Avenue to the Capitol, then onto the Washington Monument, which I circled four times before running back to the starting point. With each new month, I just added another day of running for the week.

Music was an important part of my training. My old friend Bummy was big on Maze featuring Frankie Beverly. During freshman year, I fell in love with their *We Are One* album. Maze's music, more than anything else, carried me through summer training. When I was in a good running stride, and the music was in a nice groove, it felt like I was moving through the air without my body. One of Chuck Brown's lyrics often came to mind: *When your body is strong and your wind is long/Just carry on/You can't do no wrong/ Sure you're right!*

My summer went beautifully until near its end, when I received a phone call from my friend Keith Johnson concerning another friend, Rick Gardner, who we knew from St. Anthony's. He'd just died of AIDS, contracted from intravenous drug use. According to Keith and another friend, named Troy, Rick had gotten heavily involved with using drugs and chasing girls. I'd certainly heard about AIDS, mainly due to the news of Rock Hudson's death, but until Rick I hadn't known anyone who'd died from it. The last time

Rick and I hung out was during the spring of our senior year in high school. We spent the entire day together, but the main thing on Rick's mind was getting high. This wasn't so unusual to me, because many of my street buddies got high so often. Our night ended with my taking him down Wylie Street to buy some drugs before parting ways.

After Rick's funeral service, I accompanied Keith and Troy to a gathering at a house just off upper 16th Street Northwest, an area divided into neighborhoods known as the Gold and Platinum Coasts. Most of the city's affluent blacks lived there, and the parents of the girl who was hosting the gathering were very successful professionals.

Their house was spacious and had a beautiful backyard. When I spotted a particularly cute girl out back, I told Keith and Troy that I was interested in meeting her. So they passed word to Karen, the girl hosting the event, and she signaled me over to where the girl was and introduced us. The girl didn't seem too interested though; she was cordial as we talked for a bit but refused to give me her phone number. Instead, she asked me to give my number to Karen, so she could get it from her later. I took that to mean she wasn't interested. When Karen asked me how things went with her friend, I simply thanked her for making the introduction. At least I'd met a very nice host and got the chance to spend time in her parents' wonderful house.

Being at the Mount kept me away from what was going on in the streets of DC. When I sold my gun and left for school, my timing was good. One night, when I was home during a summer break from school, Singleton and I rode uptown to see his attorney about an upcoming court appearance. Singleton was being charged with attempted murder.

When I saw the big-bellied attorney step out of Faces, an old-school club on Georgia Avenue, he looked disgusting to me.

He was also the attorney for Brandon's brother, Little Gary Terrell, and it was obvious to me from the way this man spoke and behaved that he was on the take. Since Little Gary's girlfriend lived nearby, and he was spending most of his time over there, Singleton and I stopped by to see him. As we were standing outside near Kennedy Street Northwest, they were talking about their attorney and Singleton's upcoming attempted murder case. At one point, Little Gary looked at me and said, "You should think about getting yourself a good lawyer too."

Little Gary and I weren't close, so maybe he assumed I was still dabbling in the game. Maybe Brandon had told him about my involvement with him and Lawrence from a few years back. And I was tight with Singleton, who always seemed to stay in trouble. In my heart, though, I knew I would never again do anything to put myself in a position to need an attorney—despite all the money Little Gary and others were making on the streets. When Lawrence and Brandon cut me out of that drug deal back in high school, I realized, it had been a blessing.

Brandon was dead by then. He had come a long way since the days of being shooed away from us by Lawrence for being too little and too young. He had gone to work for the Cobb brothers, bought himself an SUV, and started his own little drug house uptown. Lawrence, who had grown increasingly jealous of his former protégé's climb, had the tables turned on him when Brandon beat him down right on Montello Avenue. His standing got a big boost when word spread that he gunned down Ant Lee, one of the most feared dudes in Trinidad—and my former stablemate at Ham AC.

Brandon's growing reputation brought him to the attention of Rayful Edmond, the biggest drug dealer in DC. Rayful, who came up on nearby Orleans Place Northeast, was always looking for strong soldiers for his crew, and he fronted Brandon some drugs at the behest of Columbus "Little Nut" Daniels, a Trinidad dude who was now one of his trigger men. Things took a tragic turn one night at the Chapter III nightclub in Southeast, when Brandon not only refused to pay for the drugs but also called Rayful a "bitch-ass niggah." Rayful didn't take kindly to the public slight, and Little Nut was angry and probably embarrassed by his friend's disrespect.

Michael Frey, a well-known and respected Uptown drug dealer from Kennedy Street, made a futile attempt to calm things down. As the club was letting out, however, Little Nut ran around Frey and gunned down Brandon in front of hundreds of partygoers. According to some bystanders, Little Nut pumped several more into his body as he stood over him to ensure the job was done. Only eighteen, Brandon, the young tiger, was no more.

The old rivalry between Trinidad and Orleans had gone from fist fighting to a deadly level. Singleton, who had developed a close connection to Brandon, was in jail again on a drug distribution charge at the time of his friend's killing. By the time he got out, shortly after Brandon's murder, the two crews had somehow worked out a war truce. But there was one member of the Trinidad Crew who was unhappy with the peace. Little Gary had been following in Brandon's footsteps. The Cobb brothers encouraged Singleton to talk to him, but Little Gary was determined to exact revenge, so he enlisted the help of a friend who his associates didn't know.

This mystery man shot Little Nut while he, Rayful, and others from the Orleans Crew were at the B&B barbershop on 19th and Benning Road Northeast, just two blocks from my old apartment in Little Vietnam. Little Nut was getting his hair cut when the mystery man opened the front door, fired three shots, and hit him in the chest, spine, and abdomen.

A few weeks later, while recovering from his gunshot wounds at DC General Hospital, Little Nut was arrested by the police for Brandon's murder. He ended up being paralyzed for a long time as a result of the shooting. Little Gary had gained a measure of revenge for his brother's murder, and now the feud between the two crews was reignited.

The days of scrapping with a dude and living to fight another day were becoming a thing of the past. And it wasn't just about shooting someone. If a dude liked using burners, then he had to go to a dude's head. Before the movie *Scarface* came out in the mid-1980s, a dude got big respect on the street if he was known to have shot someone. But after everyone saw the scene in the movie where Al Pacino splattered this guy's brains all over a car window, dudes felt they could only get respect if they shot someone to the head.

By the end of 1988, 369 people had been murdered in DC, a 64 percent increase from the year before. The fall of the 8th & H Street Crew had failed to bring about less crime in the area. The police speculated that some former members of 8th & H had become part of Rayful's crew. Robbing people didn't bring money like selling drugs did, and the demand for PCP and cocaine was high. In spite of the drug feud between Trinidad and Orleans, Rayful was making a ton of money.

Curtbone, my former nemesis from Langston Terrace, was tight with Rayful as well. Rayful became his drug supplier, which quickly made Curtbone the biggest dealer in Little Vietnam. Rayful had other worries besides violence: the FBI, the DEA, and the DC police were investigating him and, after two years, they were on the verge of making their move. On the night of April 15, 1989, Rayful, his partner from Uptown, Tony Lewis, Curtbone, and many others were arrested in a major drug sweep throughout the city and surrounding area. The Rayful Edmond trial was such big news in DC and throughout the country that it knocked the Oliver North/Iran-Contra scandal trial off the front page of the *Washington Post*. The jury eventually convicted Rayful of a kingpin charge for running a continuing criminal enterprise and sentenced him to life in prison without parole. As it turned out, even though Rayful's crew was believed to have committed as many as 300 murders, the killing of Brandon Terrell was the only murder the police were able to connect directly to Rayful.

Curtbone caught a break. The authorities, in their haste to take down Rayful, had failed to record Curtbone's real name, so his high-priced attorney was able to get the most serious charges against him dropped. But since Curtbone was only 21 and didn't have a job, yet had hundreds of thousands of dollars in cash, he had to cop to a money laundering charge. For all of his involvement, instead of serving 35 years to life, he spent just four and a half years in jail.

Meanwhile, Little Gary had already started branching out on his own. He and Singleton grew closer due to their mutual connection to Brandon. Little Gary started renting limousines for trips up to New York to purchase kilos of cocaine. Up there, the prices were lower, which meant more profits for him. Over the next few years, he got involved deeper and deeper in some tangled and violent relations among dealers seeking to expand territory from New York into DC after Rayful's imprisonment. On October 23, 1991, while riding in a car along 16th Street Northwest, Little Gary was shot in the head by someone sitting in the rear seat. His dead body was dumped in nearby Rock Creek Park. Word on the street was that his former partners, a New York dude named Alpo and the notorious DC hitman Wayne Perry, did him in.

I'd just spoken to Little Gary less than a month before at a fight card at the DC Convention Center. I knew Gary's death would be hard on Singleton, who at the time was back in jail again after being charged with attempted murder and copping out on a plea deal. Now, both of the Terrell brothers were dead, and he hadn't been around to help them or seek revenge on their behalf. I wrote Singleton a letter encouraging him to let things ride and not seek revenge.

Everything was different for me at the Mount. My second year, I shared a room on the Terrace with two other sophomores, both of whom were athletic, handsome, and well liked by the ladies. Lee Hicks, a black guy from Hagerstown Maryland, was a rising star on the basketball team and Mel Morris, a white boy from Ellicott City, Maryland, had just transferred from a Division I soccer team at East Carolina University to play at the Mount. All of us got along well.

Lee was a light-skinned fella who drew the attention of not only the black girls but many of the white girls too. But despite having more options than most black guys on campus, he "kept it in the family," as we called it, by dating a black senior from New York named Angela Murdock. Most weekends, he'd go to his nearby hometown of Hagerstown. And after he suffered a broken arm, which kept him from playing or practicing with the basketball team, he started missing classes.

Most of the other black students spent nearly every weekend looking like sad puppy dogs watching the white students party and have fun. We had our occasional get-togethers, but they always seemed lame compared to the white students, who were getting buck wild. There was an unspoken feeling among the blacks that it wouldn't be smart for us to party like that ourselves, so our main get-back was to talk about the white students. Every time we'd see a white student drunk and stumbling all over the place, we mocked them. Of course, even though we laughed at the white students when they got discombobulated, there were times when we wanted to experience more of the fun they seemed to be having.

Despite being in a funk about my social life, there were opportunities right in front of me to establish relationships that I either failed to pursue or didn't see. During that first semester of my sophomore year, Shelley, the white girl I really liked, stopped by the dorm to visit Mel. Shelley and Mel had recently become friends, but I was the only one there at the time, so we talked for a bit.

As we were conversing, she picked up a framed picture from my dresser that was taken at a prom I'd escorted a girl to the previous spring. I tried to be cool and nonchalant, but that's not how I really felt. I mishandled the situation, telling her that I didn't think much of the girl in the picture and of relationships in general, and Shelley left not long after. The truth was that I just wanted to be in a relationship with someone I liked, and I liked Shelley. I just didn't have the confidence to tell her how I really felt. But her unexpected presence in my dorm room, of all places, caught me off guard, which led me to panic.

What was true was that I didn't really like the girl in the picture. She had asked me to take her to her high school prom, so I obliged and received the photo for my efforts. When I came back to the Mount with no real prospects, I found Mel, in a committed relationship with a girl back home, and Lee, with girls seemingly waiting in line. I'd just put the prom picture on my dresser, so I wouldn't look so left out.

I had my doubts about Mel's commitment to his long-distance girlfriend because of all the attention he got from girls at the Mount. Despite that, though, I never saw Mel messing around with any other girls. He told me and Lee that regardless of what anyone else thought, in his mind, his lady was the prettiest girl in the world. There was conviction in his eyes as he said it. I got the impression that whoever Mel's girlfriend was, even though she may not have won the Miss America pageant, that was only because Mel wasn't the judge. I had never heard a guy speak like that about a girl. I'd heard plenty of dudes talk about how fine a female was, or how good she was in bed. But Mel was into his girl for more than just those things. I did eventually meet her and thought they were a great couple.

Mel and I became real tight. I'd heard him stand up for me one night when he and another friend of his, a junior female student, were talking about me when they thought I was asleep in our room. The girl asked Mel what he thought about me, and I could tell just by the tone of her voice that she wanted to lay into me. Perhaps it was a racial thing, but I could tell she wasn't sure how Mel felt about me, so had thrown out a soft pitch to feel him out. Mel replied instantly, "I think he's cool as shit."

I smiled to myself, because that probably wasn't the answer the girl was expecting. They changed the subject, and I eventually drifted off to sleep with that big smile on my face.

My relationship with Mel, though, grew in direct contradiction to my growing black militancy. I had gone deeper into exploring Black Nationalist and Pan-Africanist ideas. Besides Malcolm's speeches, I was listening to Dr. Frances Cress Welsing, a psychiatrist from Chicago who lived in DC and was advancing a new theory concerning the supposed genetic inferiority of whites due to their being the offspring of melanin-deficient African albinos. She would later document this theory in a book called *The Isis Papers*.

I got so into reading black literature that closing out a chapter or finishing up a book became more important than doing my schoolwork.

Academically, school wasn't much of a challenge. Most of what I was learning in the classroom was rote. I had developed a study technique where, a few days before an exam, I rewrote all of my class notes and anything else I could remember from the professor's lectures. When exam time came, I just spewed it all back out. This method kept my name on the dean's list.

I had started my sophomore year in tip-top shape for cross-country, but then someone gave me the idea of starting a boxing club on campus. I decided to focus on boxing and quit the cross-country team before our first race. Fr. Forker, a priest who taught at the Mount, agreed to be my sponsor, and we put in an application with the Student Government Association (SGA), of which I'd recently become a member. Once the funds for the club came in, I immediately started recruiting members. We started practicing in the old gymnasium, but moved to the Knott Arena once a heavy bag was placed over there. The school also set up a speed bag in an adjoining workout room.

We had a small but dedicated group. A few of the members planned to go into law enforcement after graduating, and wanted to use boxing to prepare themselves. The club gave me the opportunity to work with a number of students, nearly all of them white. They weren't the most skillful or athletic, but they possessed a lot of heart, and I came to respect them immensely.

During one of my visits with Fr. Forker, we had a very serious conversation about boxing. Though he had willingly agreed to sponsor my idea for a boxing club, he seemed intent on tempering my enthusiasm for the sweet science. He gave me an article on boxing and morality along with a few words of warning: "Always be in control of boxing; never let it control you."

While I was keeping busy to fill up the space from my almost nonexistent social life, Lee was spending less and less time at the Mount and more back home during our sophomore year. Hagerstown had become popular for New York dudes who wanted to ply the drug trade outside of their city. Eventually, Lee stopped going to class, and even seeing him on campus became a rarity.

His girlfriend, Angie, and the assistant basketball coaches were always asking Mel and me about Lee's whereabouts, but we had no information. The coaches had high expectations for Lee's basketball career and wanted him to fulfill that promise. Angie's interest in finding Lee was decidedly more important: she was pregnant with their child.

If Angie's hope was that the pregnancy would bring them closer together, it was a hollow one. By the time she graduated in May, Lee had dropped out of school and was firmly rooted in another relationship. Angie and I, though, stayed friends. On September 24, 1988, Jasmine Murdock Hicks was born. Several years later, after Jasmine's godfather died, Angie asked me to fill that role.

My romantic life finally began to show a bit of promise over the Christmas break that year. I spent some time with Brenda, my old flame from Notre Dame High School. I still liked her, and in the year and a half since we'd last seen each other, she looked better than ever, and her disposition was just as sweet. I wanted Brenda to be my girlfriend, and this time I made sure she knew it. Like always, there were other suitors, but I felt good about my chances. Before she travelled back to North Carolina A&T State University for the spring semester, I gave her my coveted gold rope to wear around her neck, although we weren't quite official yet.

As it turned out, a guy named Jason Scott, a friend I'd first met through Brenda, transferred to the Mount that spring semester. I'd first met Jason during our final year of high school, when we were both visiting Brenda at the same time. Instead of butting heads over our common love interest, we had a friendly conversation.

From time to time I'd ask Brenda about Jason, and during one such conversation in the fall semester, she told me that he'd encountered some difficulty at his college and dropped out. Brenda told me that Jason had been a good athlete in track and basketball in high school, and I told one of the track coaches at the Mount about him. In the end, the Mount offered Jason a scholarship.

On the first night of the new spring semester, Jason and I were hanging and talking. Another student inquired about what had happened to the gold rope everyone at the school had become accustomed to seeing me wear. Jason sat there silently listening as I told the student a little bit about Brenda.

When Jason and I got back to my room, his mood became serious, and he told me more about their relationship. I already knew from Brenda that Jason had been the first person she slept with—but I didn't know that she'd been sleeping with him the entire time he had been dating someone else. It was disappointing to hear Jason talk about how willing she'd been to play second fiddle; I felt even worse when he told me how many times they'd had sex.

When I told him about one occasion when I had been speaking to Brenda on the phone and asked her where she'd been the night before, and her response was that she'd gone over to Jason's house for pancakes before they went to see a movie, he looked at me in disbelief. Jason made it clear that pancakes and a movie hadn't been involved. I was so inexperienced and immature where women were involved, that news like this crushed my hopes for a relationship with Brenda. It was bad enough that Jason had broken her virginity, but the thought of him having sex with her over and over and over again was too much for me to bear. I felt like a fool for giving Brenda my gold rope.

My disappointment pushed me further into my school activities. Since I was now a double major, I was taking six classes a semester. And with my extra reading, the boxing club, and my involvement in the SGA, I was busy. My sophomore year ended with two more trips to the dean's list.

In the late 1980s, "African American" started to become the preferred term for people of African descent in the United States. I was very intrigued by this shift. During my junior year, I became more interested in Africa.

I had a good rapport with a senior named Dave Lishebo, an Olympic hurdler from Zambia. We had trained together a few times, so when I saw him on the Mount's track one day I excitedly mentioned the new term to him, hoping he'd be impressed by it. Instead, he offered up a viewpoint I didn't expect: "Some people feel as if all black people might as well just call themselves African."

His suggestion struck me as so radical at the time, I couldn't give him a response.

In addition to my interest in the motherland, I wanted to experience something more of black college life. In the fall semester of my junior year, I drafted an internship program that would allow me and other students to attend one of the historically black colleges and universities (HBCUs) for a semester. The Mount administration had never done anything like that, but they were open to the idea. So, during the spring semester, I lived at home with my mom and took three classes at Howard University (HU).

The quality of the education I received at HU was at least on par with what the Mount offered, especially in the business school, where I took classes on auditing and taxation. My auditing teacher was a partner at one of the large and prestigious CPA firms, and my tax teacher had worked at the Internal Revenue Service. Both of them incorporated their work experience into their lectures, which resulted in some important practical advice.

In addition to the quality of the education, HU's campus was full of beautiful women. But I felt hampered because I didn't live on campus, I wasn't outgoing enough to approach girls in or around the classroom, and I never ate in the school cafeteria. There just didn't seem to be an easy way for me to meet people. My lack of confidence in approaching women was becoming quite debilitating. One day I spotted Kamiya, a girl from my auditing class, standing at a bus stop in front of the business school. I desperately wanted to strike up a conversation with her in the hope of asking her out, but I just couldn't bring myself to do it. I told myself that I'd catch her in class, but never followed through on it. My romantic disappointments once again translated into academic success. During the fall semester of my junior year I earned a 4.0, and I did almost as well at HU in the spring.

Over the summer, my mom and I moved away from the Little Vietnam area entirely, to another of the Section 8 properties owned by Horning Brothers, called Franklin Commons. Our new apartment was a two-bedroom duplex located at 117 Franklin Street, right across from Trinity College and a block and a half from the Cloisters apartments, where I used to work as a construction laborer. Franklin Commons was definitely a more peaceful environment, and the rent was even lower. The only troubling thing about living there, for some people at least, was the fact that it was so close to Glenwood Cemetery. Some of the residents nicknamed the complex "the Poltergeist," after the 1982 horror film where an idyllic suburban neighborhood was discovered to have been built over a cemetery. Aside from any potential haunting by angry spirits, there were very few disturbances among the residents of Franklin Commons.

At the start of my senior year, I began a part-time job organizing books and manuals at the Federal Emergency Management Agency (FEMA) in Emmitsburg. One of Shelley's roommates, a girl named Shannon, also worked there, and she would give me rides back to campus in her little gray Nissan Z-28 after we got off work. Every time I finished my shift, like clockwork, I'd meet Shannon at our designated space. One evening I got off work and jumped in Shannon's car, only to find out that she wasn't behind the wheel. It was Shelley! She smiled and said, "Shannon didn't have to go to work today, so I offered to drive over here and pick you up."

As we pulled off, the car started jerking, and it was quite obvious that she didn't really know how to drive a stick shift. With an embarrassed look on her face, she told me, "I guess I'm a little nervous." At least she was willing to admit her feelings—something I still couldn't bring myself to do. Being alone in the car with her seemed almost unreal. I was as stiff as a board sitting in my seat, and when we got back to campus all I could do was politely thank her for the ride, letting another opportunity pass on by.

During the semester, I became close with a student named Thomas, who was in one of my classes at HU and had just transferred to the Mount to run track. We both had a deep interest in black consciousness and become fast friends and hanging buddies. Cliff, who had been my roommate since junior year, even agreed to allow Thomas to move in with us after our other roommate finished his classes in the fall.

I also lucked up on a girl—a very attractive one, too. Leslie was a student at Hood College, a mostly women's school located about 25 miles south of the Mount in Frederick, Maryland. Whenever Hood's Black Students Association (BSA) sponsored events on campus, black students from the Mount would try to attend. I had first encountered Leslie the previous school year while attending a BSA event at Hood. She was, hands down, the best-looking black girl I'd ever seen at Hood or the Mount. But when I tried talking to her, she ignored me. I tried again in the fall when I saw her at the Mount. This time she was much more approachable, and we quickly developed a relationship.

Even though I felt lucky to be seeing such a pretty girl, something kept me from getting into a committed relationship with her. Leslie was pretty and blessed with a gorgeous body, but something I didn't understand was holding me back. In spite of this, one night in her dorm room, toward the end of fall semester, things went to the ultimate level, sexually. It had now been seven years since my initial failed sexual encounter, and Leslie was the most physically attractive girl I'd ever been seriously intimate with. Yet the result was still the same as during the previous two occasions: my penis let me down once again.

Leslie was disappointed, but she rubbed me gently and compassionately without saying a word. We never talked about what happened that night. For my part, my embarrassment pushed me away from her. We still talked, but the thought of being intimate with her was too much to consider. I was a senior now, and there was a beautiful woman right in front of me that I was certainly attracted to, and none of my buddies were around complicating things. Yet I still couldn't get the music playing.

Here I was, a dude making it through an impoverished upbringing, who had delivered himself from the streets, who was consistently on the dean's list and a student leader in college, but who couldn't go all the way with a woman. I'd done my best to put my other two high-school sexual fiascos behind me. This time, my failure was too devastating for me to ignore. I had to investigate whether I had some kind of problem.

The whole thing was confusing, because I'd had wet dreams, I'd briefly masturbated, and my penis had no problem getting hard.

I'd never had any sex education classes in school. My mom never came close to talking about such things, and what I'd picked up on the streets didn't offer me any kind of insight. I didn't understand what was going on and I felt really embarrassed about it. I needed to solve this mystery.

I visited a doctor's office on 5th and H Street Northeast during a break from the Mount. A male doctor checked me out, and he informed me that I had no physical problem. I was so relieved to hear this that I didn't even question him about the prescription he wrote me for some pills. I simply got the prescription filled before heading back to the Mount.

After closing out fall semester with another strong academic performance, I went to a party with my buddies Keith and Troy, who used to hang out with Rick Gardner, at one of the apartments in the recently built HU Towers. The host was Karen, a junior at HU and the girl who lived in the beautiful house on the Platinum Coast. I'd developed a fondness for Karen since the memorial ceremony she'd hosted for Rick. We'd been around each other a few more times after that and I'd even given her my phone number, but she never made use of it. Not long before, I'd seen her working as a hostess at the Uno's Pizzeria at Union Station and I'd kidded her about never calling me.

Now I was beholding Karen standing in her kitchen, decked out in a beautiful blue blouse and skirt with matching hosiery and high-heeled shoes, and she looked better than I'd ever seen her. I posted up in the kitchen for almost the entire night as Karen was serving up food for all the party guests. I only had eyes for her. As people started clearing out, Karen and I took our conversation to her room, where we talked for hours. The only problem was that Keith and Troy kept bursting into the room at the most inopportune moments. It was approaching daylight by the time I finally leaned in and began kissing Karen. Those kisses formed the beginning of my first real committed adult relationship.

I soon learned that what had happened with Karen and me that night was all a setup. Karen had bet my two buddies that she could get me to kiss her before the party ended. Every time Keith and Troy barged in on us, they were attempting to prevent the kiss from happening. I thought the whole thing was terrifically flattering.

There was something unexplainable about Karen that drew me to her. Just as I couldn't understand what had kept me from committing myself to Leslie, I couldn't understand why it was so easy to connect with Karen. What I did know is that she was the nicest and most intelligent girl I'd had the pleasure of really getting to know. She and I spent nearly every day together over the holidays, and when the spring semester started she began coming to the Mount on the weekends.

Things got really intimate between us one Friday evening in the room Thomas and I shared. While my roommates were in the living room, Karen and I were getting heavy back in the bedroom. Swiftly, and unexpectedly, she pulled my sweatpants down and slid my hardened penis inside of her. Just as my eyes grew as big as tennis balls, Karen whispered in my ear, "You haven't been up here sleepin' with these white girls, have you?"

All I could do was to shake my head no as I thought, *Wow, this is what all the talk has been about.*

Karen, by doing what she'd done, didn't give me an opportunity to be intimidated by the big, scary vagina monster. She'd simply slid my penis inside her, and I was suddenly having the most pleasurable physical experience of my life. We stopped before either of us reached a climax, but she'd given me enough of a taste to get me hooked.

Every weekend after that, the two of us primarily hung out in my room and had sex like rabbits. I was wide open! We were doing some serious catching up, or at least I was. I told her about my penis problem and that I'd been a virgin until she came along.

None of this surprised her, because she'd done some research after noticing the bottle of prescription pills on my desk.

Even though I'd taken the pills a few times, I didn't care what they were and never bothered to ask. It was such a delight to finally be a part of the club that the other aspects of intimacy were lost on me at that time. No longer being a virgin was more important than seeing the beauty of knowing that I could only give myself to someone who was special to me.

Being with Karen so much left me little time for hanging out with Thomas. When Leslie and I had been spending time together in the fall, we had introduced Thomas to one of her freshman classmates, and those two were still talking after things had cooled off between Leslie and me. During one of Karen's visits, we were holed up in my room, as usual, when I received an uninvited guest: Leslie, who'd come over with a few of her friends to visit our apartment. To my dismay, I walked out into the living room to find a group of them sitting out there. After a few minutes, Karen came out of the bedroom, wearing a pair of my sweatpants, and innocently spoke to everyone before heading back to my room.

Karen didn't know anything about Leslie, because I didn't feel there was a need to tell her. Leslie and I had never been in a committed relationship—plus, I'd avoided her after my failed sexual performance. In fact, I hadn't spoken to her at all since the end of the fall semester.

After Karen went back to my room, Leslie slid over beside me and asked in a low voice as everyone else were engaged in conversation, "Who's that girl?"

"That's my new girlfriend, Karen," I admitted reluctantly.

The disheartened look on Leslie's face caused all of my earlier rationalizations for not talking to her, and telling her about Karen, to fall by the wayside. I didn't know how to explain to her about what was happening between Karen and me, so I had just avoided telling her. But I would have never wanted her to find out like this.

Before long, I was being accused of staging the entire incident as a punkish and mean-spirited way of letting Leslie know about Karen. I didn't know what or who had caused the incident to go down like it did, and even though I was shocked by the accusation, I found myself having to accept it as the price to be paid for not telling Leslie about Karen. Leslie's pain and embarrassment turned to anger and a demand for me to return some beautiful photos of her that she'd given me. I didn't want to give her the photos back, and we got into a little back-and-forth over them when she stopped by unexpectedly. At the very end of it, I didn't have any pictures in my photo album to remember her by, and a few of her girlfriends compelled me to apologize for my unwillingness to readily comply with Leslie's demand.

I was so into Karen, though, that the incident with Leslie was only a minor hiccup in the magic carpet ride that was my new relationship. What I had earlier fantasized about having with Robin and later Shelley became real with Karen. I'd never spent so much time around a girl, and there was a comfort level unlike anything I'd ever experienced with someone else. For the first time, I had stumbled into a friendship with a woman that rivaled what I had with Underdue and Singleton. Karen's gray Peugeot helped us get away from our respective campuses as often as possible. For a guy accustomed to visiting girls at their homes and going on a few movie dates, this was front-page stuff.

Karen was very affectionate and quite uninhibited sexually, and she broke me in real good. Before long, I was asking for sex so frequently that she had to teach me more about the fine art of masturbation. I'd always tried to avoid masturbating. The few times I'd done it before had been momentary and unplanned, and I immediately felt guilty after. I didn't want to embrace the enjoyment I'd just experienced, because a dude would get joned up and down a very long street if other guys thought he was into that. In Karen's mind though, there was no negative stigma attached to something that brought you so much pleasure.

During spring break, a friend and I were riding up the escalator of the DuPont Circle Metro station. I was on my way to work at Horning Brothers, and we were having a discussion about Malcolm X. As we stepped off the escalator, a brown-skinned, slender man who had passed us on the way up was standing just to the side. He approached me and politely asked, "I overheard you mention the name Malcolm. Was there, by chance, an X at the end of that?"

His name was Eric Peterson, and he was a member of the African Development Organization (ADO), a DC-based group started by him and two other students from UDC. In DC and other major cities, there was a small resurgence of the kind of black radical activity that had been prevalent during the civil rights and black power eras, although it was mainly theoretical in nature. ADO was one of many Black Nationalist and Pan-African groups that were spawned from what I was hearing generally referred to as the African-centered movement.

ADO and its close to 20 members participated in three primary programs. Alternative Study Groups (ASGs) were held weekly at a member's home, where the group discussed books written by scholars such as John Henrik Clarke, Ivan Van Sertima, or Chancellor Williams would be selected for group discussion. ADO also assisted in setting up public lectures with scholars like these in DC. The Youth Program (YP) sought out schools in DC that would allow ADO members to come into the classroom to speak to students about the importance of African history to developing healthy self-esteem. And the Continuous Food Program (CFP) sought out food donations in order to supply meals to needy families on major holidays.

Shortly after speaking with Eric, I invited ADO to the Mount to speak to the black students. During the previous semester, I had started holding Thursday evening classroom discussions on black history, so that venue offered an excellent opportunity to have ADO come in as guest speakers. Eric came with a few other members, and the students received them warmly. Shortly after their visit to the Mount, I accepted Eric's invitation to become a member of ADO.

Everything in my life was pointing me back to DC after graduation. My mom and our home were there. Karen was just finishing up her junior year at HU. And I had just accepted a job as an auditor at Ernst & Young, one of the biggest public accounting firms in the country.

I initially balked at working for Ernst & Young. They had offered me $26,400 a year to start there in September, but I had it in mind that if I was going to accept a job in the "establishment," despite my increasingly radical black ideology, I wanted to start off earning at least $30,000. But I got some advice from a mentor at Horning Brothers, who told me not to get hung up over a few thousand dollars, and I decided to accept the job offer.

As graduation was nearing, though, I got embroiled in some unpleasant rumors. I was approached by a black female student who said that my roommate Thomas had been telling people that he'd slept with her. She also told me that Thomas was saying similar things about other black girls on campus—and that my name was mixed up in it, too, though she never made clear in what way. I promptly went to speak with the other girls involved, and they confirmed that Thomas was telling people he'd slept with them. They were very upset, and I was shocked by the extent of the lies he was spreading. I gathered all of this information before I decided to confront Thomas.

Instead of telling Thomas everything I'd gathered, I decided to give it to him piecemeal. He was lying down on his bed as I mentioned what the first girl had told me. When he tried to say the girl was lying on him, I started naming the five other girls I'd spoken to. The way his body suddenly jerked on his bed, someone would've thought my words were hitting him like bullets.

Thomas confessed to everything, and showed real contrition. He explained that his motive had been to try to get the same sort of respect he saw people giving me on campus. His hope was that by claiming he'd slept with all of these girls, people would admire him. As he was confiding these things to me, I was thinking, *How could he realistically expect to gain something so quickly that I had to earn? The respect people give me now came from nearly four years of hard work I've put in here at the Mount.*

Once I learned more about how he was thinking about things, it helped me make sense of some of Thomas's behavior earlier in the year, which had puzzled me at the time. He'd once made a statement about being more black-conscious than me, which had confused me. I realized that he'd been comparing himself to me the whole time we were hanging together this school year. It then dawned on my slow-moving brain that of course it must have been Thomas who had invited Leslie to our room while Karen was visiting me. He had caused that whole fiasco in an effort to make me look bad.

Much to his credit, though, Thomas visited every girl he lied on and apologized to them. One of the girls, named Tamika, had a white boyfriend, and Thomas used to make fun of their relationship. When he went to her room to apologize, the boyfriend—who was a military dude—was there, and this white boy wasn't having it. I chuckled to myself when Thomas told me how close he came to getting his butt whipped by the guy, who later married and had a family with Tamika.

Days before graduation, the same self-castigating urge that got the better of me after Loni was killed overtook me again. The thought of attending a ceremony just didn't appeal to me. My initial impulse was to avoid the ceremony and simply have the Mount give me my diploma. Knowing that my mom would be upset, though, I didn't verbalize my feelings to her or anyone else close to me, but when I had a seemingly chance encounter with a Mount professor, I mentioned my indifference to attending graduation. He, though, intimated to me that I was slated to receive an award during the ceremony. This, plus my mom's excitement, helped me overcome my urge not to attend.

Karen came to see me the day before graduation, and we walked around campus. We'd never taken the time before to enjoy the beautiful scenery the Mount's campus offered. She was wearing a form-fitting red dress, and I found myself staring at her. As we were headed back to my apartment, Karen told me, "It seems like being up here for you is like having a retreat in the mountains."

There was no denying that I had blossomed at the Mount, intellectually and, in some ways, personally. When I walked on stage to receive my degree, accompanied by a proudly displayed Malcolm X button pinned to my robe, it was as a magna cum laude graduate. When my name was called a second time, it was to honor me with the John M. Kolon Memorial Award for leadership. That day, for me, was a great culmination of four years of focused effort.

My mom was there with Uncle Wilbert. Karen, friend and fellow DC native Darryl Rose, and Fr. Quickley were there as well. None of my street buddies could make it to the ceremony, though, and this greatly disappointed me. My mother beamed like the bright morning sun as she held onto my degree and award. She valued the importance of education more than I was able to appreciate at the time, and my graduation was due, more than anything else, to the sacrifices she had made for me from the very beginning of my life. Everything I'd accomplished was rooted in the foundation she'd laid down.

Movement

On Marvin Gaye's classic 1971 album, *What's Going On*, there's a song called "Save the Children," which asks, "Who's willing to try to save a world/that's destined to die?" Whenever I listened to those words, I felt as if DC's legendary crooner was speaking to me. That song's message touched me so profoundly that I had some of its lyrics printed underneath my senior photo in the Mount's 1990 yearbook. From my vantage point, nothing else needed to be said.

The cause that Malcolm and so many others had dedicated their lives to was now my raison d'être. Black Nationalism and Pan-Africanism had become, in my view, the best ideologies for black people to adopt, and ADO offered me a practical way to carry out these ideologies in my own life. I was fully committed. After graduation, I began to spend much of my time getting to know the other ADO members and understanding how the organization functioned.

Besides Brother Eric, I became pretty close with Shaka, another founding member. Brother Eric, Shaka, and another founder, Herb, had started out as a singing group when they met as students at UDC. Shaka lived in the basement of his family's home uptown just off Georgia Avenue Northwest, and I would visit there frequently. He had a heavy bag hanging in the basement, so we worked out and talked a lot. Brother Eric was a Southeast cat and still lived there, so he and I communicated more by phone.

Talking to them as much as I did brought me up to speed on what was generally referred to as the "conscious community." ADO and the broader conscious community became like my new nuclear and extended families, so to speak. Getting involved with ADO, I experienced the same feelings of connection and kinship I got after being accepted first on H Place and then in Trinidad.

Aside from the white establishment, and the many centuries of injustice it had inflicted upon African peoples throughout the world, the conscious community viewed the black bourgeoisie as its primary adversary. The term "black bourgeoisie" was popularized in a book of the same name written by sociologist E. Franklin Frazier. Traditionally, the black bourgeoisie functioned as a clique that required members to have the "right" skin color, income, and social status, and we enjoyed criticizing them as turncoats against the black struggle. We felt that it was far more important for black and African peoples to understand and embrace a radical black ideology, identify with African-centered cultural traditions, and stand in opposition to America's corrupt government.

Being a dedicated member of ADO was quite a time commitment. Aside from the weekend study groups, which were generally at Brother Eric's home, we all had to attend weekly group meetings at the Watha T. Daniels Library. My becoming so involved in ADO was cutting into the time Karen and I spent together, and she began to complain about not seeing me enough. I was still very into her, but at this point, my commitment to the black struggle came first, and my increasingly radical views posed a growing concern for her. She viewed me as a man with a bright future, but my unyielding position regarding what I saw as my purpose meant that we were now on opposing sides of what I saw as superficial issues, such as celebrating Christmas, living in a house with a swimming pool, and driving a 7-series BMW. She was determined to experience and obtain those things, and I was resolute about not doing so.

Karen frequently expressed her fear that I was going to give away all the money I was bound to make. She had one particular nightmare that made me laugh, in which she was being interviewed as the wife of a well-known activist, with our future children at her side. All of them were decked out in tattered clothing, wearing shoes pocked with holes. We laughed about it, but we both knew there was a growing divide between us that neither seemed willing to cross.

Though it wasn't clear to me then, I wasn't equipped to handle what Karen was offering me, a complete and far-reaching union. Nothing in my experience to this point had prepared me for this. We went places and conversed about almost anything. Her family, especially her mother, openly accepted me, but the time I spent with her was more like an extracurricular activity. Relationship-wise, I was probably still in grade school!

Another problem was my failure to give Karen's ideas the same regard I gave to the conscious community, especially ADO members. Intellectually, Karen was probably the brightest bulb of my peer group, ADO included. She was on HU's dean's list and always made very clear, cogent points in discussion. She even supported me when I later went to grad school at HU by going to class with, and a few times for, me.

But she wasn't an ADO member or a part of the conscious community. She hadn't read any of the core books, nor did she possess the prerequisite anger toward the white man and his crimes. When she began expressing some concerns about Shaka, one of the ADO founders I was getting pretty close to, I treated it like banter. As clear as I was about the shortcomings of religious belief, I couldn't see that Black Nationalism and Pan-Africanism were, in effect, beliefs that also featured some divisive pitfalls.

Shaka and several other ADO members had African names,

and I began to use one as well. *Simba*, a Kiswahili word that means "lion," was a short-lived community group in DC that I had formed while still in college. After its demise, I started intermittently referring to myself by that name. I first came across the term while reading Dr. Jawanza Kunjufu's multivolume work about educating black youth, *Countering the Conspiracy to Destroy Black Boys*. One chapter discussed an African-centered rite of passage program called simba.

It was commonplace for people in the conscious community to adopt African names, but large sections of the black community still viewed this as a bit strange. To some, the names were difficult to pronounce. Others, incorrectly, saw the name change as a religious conversion. People would ask me, "You Muslim now?" Things got much better for me when *The Lion King* came out several years later. Kids' faces lit up whenever they heard that I had the same name as the main character.

One of the benefits of being in ADO was the opportunity it gave me to do more public speaking. I enjoyed speaking, as I had at the Mount, and folks seemed to like hearing me talk. Brother Eric encouraged me in this area and told Shaka that he was comfortable allowing me to represent ADO on any position. However, the more I spoke publicly, the more concerned I became about authenticity. I knew of at least two other brothers in the conscious community who, though they were great public speakers, weren't living what they preached. And as my involvement in the black consciousness movement increased, I couldn't help but acknowledge that despite our powerful rhetoric, we adherents of Black Nationalism and Pan-Africanism had accomplished very little from a practical standpoint. This affected me to the point where I began to shy away from speaking publicly and became more concerned with manifesting some tangible results of my activist work.

During the summer after graduation, I worked at Institutional Buyer's Mart, a small, local company owned by Keith Johnson that secured contracts with the DC government for office supplies. One day a friend from his high school stopped by the company's office. His name was Hoke Glover, but he went by Yao; Keith told me he was a poet. I had never personally met a dude, or anyone for that matter, who identified himself as such. Yao seemed like a nice fella, though, and the poetry thing had me curious. My intrigue turned into a sort of fascination when I had the opportunity to hear Yao read his poetry one day. I was trying to recruit Keith into ADO, and he invited Yao to come along to one of our study groups at Brother Eric's. Yao read a few of his poems, and I was greatly impressed. There appeared to be an effortless fluidity to every word he read. I had never met anyone who could make written words sound so mysteriously appealing. The way he read gave me the impression that there was some deeper meaning behind his poems that I couldn't quite grasp.

Right then, Yao became the primary focus of my ADO recruitment efforts. I felt that the compelling way he expressed himself was something that had to be of benefit to the organization. Both Keith and Yao soon became ADO members.

While I was getting deeper into ADO, I also embarked on my professional career. I started working at Ernst & Young in September of 1990, along with about 30 other first-year auditors. Our responsibilities included assisting with audit work for various clients and preparing for the Certified Public Accountant (CPA) exam. We were all required to pass within a few years of being hired. The exam, which took place over two and a half days, was administered every May and November.

Despite taking it four times over a two-year period, I never passed all four sections. At the Mount, I had been one of the top accounting students in my class. Accounting came pretty easily for me, but by the time I got to Ernst & Young, my focus had been redirected to the black consciousness movement. My performance at work was mediocre and this mediocrity extended into my exam preparations. The fact that I possessed no passion for accounting became quite evident.

Instead of focusing on the CPA exam, I decided to enroll in HU's African Studies graduate program in January of 1991. I wanted to strengthen my ideological foundation. Since my salary at Ernst & Young was good, I didn't pursue a scholarship that could be better used by someone financially less fortunate. The HU graduate program's approach to learning about Africa was interdisciplinary. We delved into the continent's immense culture by reading African literature and watching cinema. We had to study an African language, and my choice was Kiswahili. (The more popular term "Swahili," as I quickly learned, was the name given to a watered-down or more Arab-influenced form of the language.)

We also examined the effects of economic policies by discussing the political environment of post-colonial African states. Despite the fact that the overwhelming majority of African countries had by now won their independence, the sad reality was that the former colonialist nations of the West dictated Africa's economic policies. These policies, which were often handed down under the auspices of the World Bank and International Monetary Fund (IMF), often had harmful political and social consequences. Though slavery and colonialism were things of the past, oppression at the hands of the West had merely adopted a more palatable form, called "neo-colonialism."

One of my professors, Dr. Luis Serapiao, challenged some of the basic tendencies of Pan-Africanism. He argued that radical thought spent most of its time criticizing governments and groups tied to established governments, but offered up very few solutions to the problems at hand. He also attacked the widespread belief that weak peoples or nations could unify in order to become strong. In response to that belief, he was fond of saying, "Nothing plus nothing plus nothing equals nothing." At the time, I couldn't offer up a strong counterargument, so I simply tucked away his insights for later reflection. It took me years to gain an understanding of the shortcomings that generally come from basing one's life on reacting to injustice.

I was initially disappointed by the program's lack of concentration on ancient African history, but I began to see the importance of examining the contemporary problems Africans faced. We learned, for example, that female circumcision was primarily a way for men, under the guise of tradition, to control women by limiting their sexual enjoyment. It was one of the first times I truly recognized the dangers posed by traditions that I otherwise thought positive.

My burgeoning interest in Africa easily outpaced anything accounting offered me at the time. However, my accounting work helped me learn more about Africa in a very direct and unexpected way. One of the benefits of working at Ernst & Young was the extended vacation time we received. Brother Eric had a relationship with a guy named Prince Kolani, who was sponsoring a three-week trip to Lomé, the capital of Togo. Prince Kolani was a native of DC who received his name, he told us, from the chief of a small village in Togo after promising to build a much-needed health clinic there.

I decided to go, but there were challenges involved. This would be my first time on an airplane, and the airline tickets alone would cost more than $1,000. Growing up the way I had, travelling didn't carry much value to me. Before going to West Africa, my longest trips had been in a car to visit relatives in North Carolina and Philadelphia. The idea of spending more than $1,000 on a trip without having something tangible to show for it—like a leather coat, a Fila sweat suit, or several pairs of New Balance tennis shoes—would not even be a consideration for most of the dudes I knew from the streets of DC.

In late July, Brother Eric, Shaka, Prince Kolani, and I all caught a plane to New York, where we then boarded an Air Afrique plane for the nearly nine-hour flight to Dakar, Senegal. When the plane touched down in Dakar, everyone on board clapped to demonstrate their appreciation to the flight crew for getting us there safely. We stayed on board the plane for about an hour, probably to refuel, before heading to Abidjan, Ivory Coast, for a longer layover. From there, we had a rough final flight coming into Lomé.

Karen and I had broken up not long before, and I was probably showing less excitement than I might have under other circumstances. Shaka, though, had the excitement area covered—he talked the whole way from DC to Lomé. Upon our arrival in Lomé, we were greeted like celebrities by a delegation of people affiliated with Prince Kolani. They carried our luggage, drove us to the residence where we were staying, and gave us a big feast. We stayed in someone's home just off Liberation Avenue, the capital's main street—and one of the few paved roads I saw in the city.

In spite of the poverty, Lomé was teeming and vibrant. People were out in the streets everywhere. There were none of the things around that I associated with cities, such as pay phones, fast-food joints, or storefront churches. Women were walking with big loads balanced on their heads like it was nothing. (I remembered Malcolm calling this ability "mathematics," and saying that it was innate.) The people we encountered seemed to be genuinely happy and at peace.

We visited the consul at the US Embassy, and he warned us about the anti-government sentiment that was rampant throughout the city. We didn't tell him that the people we were staying with were rebel sympathizers. In fact, most of the people we met were against the government of Gnassingbé Eyadéma. Eyadéma was one of Africa's "Big Men," because he had been in power for almost a quarter century. Trained in weaponry and war by the French, he was part of a group that took power from a democratically elected government in a coup d'état in 1963, and then he staged his own takeover in 1967. Most people feared that Eyadéma was so adept at holding onto power in Togo that the anti-government movement would be unable to bring about any political change.

After getting settled, the guy we stayed with served as our tour guide. We walked to nearby parts of the city and rented a truck for longer trips. Riding on the city's rough terrain felt like being on a Kings Dominion roller coaster. The cost of living was amazingly inexpensive compared to living in the States. Six of us ate at a decent restaurant for less than 10,000 CFA francs, or $35. One morning, Brother Eric, Prince Kolani, and I bought fresh coconuts from a woman who skillfully cut them open, so we could drink from them.

Now that I was single again, I didn't hesitate to open myself up to women I met during the trip. I visited one young woman whose mother had recently divorced her 81-year-old husband, a rich government official in Mali who had three other wives. She was the youngest of seventeen siblings. She spoke five languages and was on break from her studies in Belgium. Her dream was to become an international tour guide. She had travelled all over the world, including two visits to the United States, and was very politically astute. We talked about Malcolm and the challenges confronting African development. When I told her about the great hospitality I'd experienced in Lomé, she informed me that part of their kindness was due to my perceived status as an American citizen.

The trip really brought home to me that Americans may be one of the few peoples in the world who feel comfortable speaking only one language. While in West Africa, I felt inadequate meeting all these so-called second- and third-world people who could speak at least two languages, and often more.

During our stay, we also visited nearby Benin and Ghana. In Benin, we spent the day at the once-great castle of King Béhanzin. Long past its better days, the castle served as a museum in honor of the Kingdom of Dahomey, and we learned about its history from the sixteenth to the nineteenth century, when King Béhanzin defeated the invading French. In Ghana, we spent two days in Accra, the capital city, where we visited the national museum and the W. E. B. DuBois Cultural Center. DuBois had been harassed by the US government in his later years, so he accepted Ghanaian citizenship at the invitation of the country's first post-colonial president, Kwame Nkrumah. The cultural center was actually the house where DuBois lived from 1961 until his death on the eve of the March on Washington in August 1963. His tomb was there as well, along with the ashes of his second wife, Shirley Graham DuBois, who died in 1977. I had read several of DuBois's books, including his autobiography and *The Souls of Black Folk*, and I had been influenced by his way of viewing black people as part of the African diaspora.

I fully embraced this unifying black ideology, especially the idea that all black people were linked through a shared African identity, but I could not ignore what confronted me daily while in Togo, where most people I met simply identified me as American. Whenever I told them, "I'm African, too!" they just politely nodded before asking me where I lived in America and what I did there. They all wanted to get my address in the "land of opportunity."

I began to understand something I'd read in Frantz Fanon's book *Black Skin, White Masks*: "The discovery of the existence of a Negro civilization in the fifteenth century confers no patent of humanity on me." What this meant to me was that the psychological lift that I, other ADO members, and other Pan-Africanists derived from studying ancient African culture offered no benefit whatsoever to present-day Africans. Their needs were not being met, and our preoccupation with the past—no matter what importance we attached to that knowledge—could be viewed as an avoidance of the unfortunate conditions facing so many contemporary Africans.

Faced with this dilemma, I struggled to figure out my role in the ongoing fight for black liberation. I reasoned that maybe my work in America could offer economic benefits to Africans on the continent. The challenge was to find ways to make that happen, and I was determined to commit myself, uncompromisingly, to the task.

While I was in Lomé, working out afforded me some solitude to ponder these issues. I started running up and down Liberation Avenue by myself most mornings. I also had the good fortune to stumble upon a local boxing gym, and they were nice enough to let me work out on the heavy bag and hit the punching mitts. Of course, the best fighter there wanted me to help him find a way to America. I promised to give whatever assistance I could.

Spending time alone was good for me, because there were tensions brewing between some of us during the trip. There were times when I was mad at Brother Eric, Shaka, and especially Prince Kolani, who tended to be somewhat controlling. During one tense occasion, Brother Eric confronted me: "Maybe you might wanna hit me, brother?"

My issue at the time wasn't with him, but he'd gotten his point across. I immediately calmed down, realizing that my being so agitated was totally unwarranted. Later on, there were even times when Prince Kolani and I were like buddy-buddy.

What was happening with Shaka was a different matter altogether. It seemed like he had suddenly changed, or perhaps a part of him we had been unaware of began to show itself. He was openly critical of Brother Eric for no apparent reason. On our last night in Lomé, we all had dinner at the home of Dr. Edna Tounou, an American expatriate and educator who had been living in Lomé since marrying her Togolese husband 22 years before. After observing Shaka's behavior, she took me and Brother Eric aside and urged us to "watch out" for him. The week before, we had visited the International Christian School of Lomé, which Dr. Tounou told us she had founded in 1969. Dr. Tounou surprised us by being among the people at the airport the next morning who gave us a warm, almost family-like farewell.

During our nine-hour layover in Abidjan, someone from Air

Afrique informed Prince Kolani that we would not be allowed to board our direct flight to New York. Prince Kolani surmised that some other people had been given our seats—people who probably had powerful connections in Abidjan. When the airline manager told us that it wouldn't be until the following week before we could get another flight, however, my youthful rashness got the better of me. I threatened the manager with bodily harm and gave the duty officer from the US Embassy quite a difficult time when he showed up. Part of my anger was fueled by the fact that I was due back at Ernst & Young in just a few days. That, and we were all pretty much broke.

Fortunately for us, the US government representatives didn't hold any grudges due to either our political philosophy or my impulsive behavior. The duty officer helped us check into a hotel for the night. In the morning, another embassy official gave each of us a $400 loan, courtesy of the US government, so we could stay in a better hotel and make do until further notice. We checked into the Hotel Tiama in a section of the city called the Plateau.

At out most vulnerable moment in a faraway country, my recently acquired penchant for meeting West African women came in handy. When we had our initial layover in Abidjan on our way to Togo, I had met a stewardess who worked for Air Afrique named Fofana Fanta, who I learned made her home in Abidjan. I called her to let her know that we were back in her city.

Fofana came by the hotel to collect me, and then took me away to introduce me to some of her family and friends. Along the way, I noticed how industrialized Abidjan was, and that most of the people were stylishly dressed. We even located an Ernst & Young office, and they allowed me to call the DC office to inform them of my predicament. We spent a fair amount of time together over the next few days. One afternoon, we had a long conversation, and she told me that her goal was to get married within the next two years, before she turned 25. She also told me that if her husband were to take a second wife it would not be to her liking, but she would accept it. After a four-day stay in Abidjan, we got seats on a flight to New York with the help of Fofana and her boss. She even made sure that we had seats alongside one another.

Over the nearly four weeks we spent in Africa, I did plenty of reading and writing. Of all the reading material I consumed during my sojourn there, this passage by the eleventh-century Muslim scholar Abu al-Rayhan Muhamad al-Biruni struck me most profoundly:

> It is our duty to proceed from what is near to what is distant, from what is known to that which is less known, to gather the traditions from those who have reported them, to correct them as much as possible and to leave the rest as it is, in order to make our work help anyone who seeks truth and loves wisdom.

Deep down, I was still reeling from my breakup with Karen, but my adventures in West Africa kept my mind distracted from painful thoughts. She and I got back together soon after I returned, though, but Karen was no longer as into me as she had been before. I felt pangs of regret over putting so much time into ADO at the expense of our relationship. I tried to give her more of my focus, but I could tell that she didn't feel the same way she had before we broke up.

Overall, though, my trip to West Africa reinforced my commitment to bringing about change in the world. I felt less and less tolerance for the injustices life inflicted upon humanity, especially poor black people. Though I accepted that fate was the ultimate controller of what happened in the world, I was headstrong in my belief that my will could have its way, and I could make a difference. In other words, I still felt that life would yield to my will if I was determined and forceful enough.

My old street buddy from Ham AC, Tonyson, appreciated my fortitude and determination. He'd recently come home from a stint at Lorton and was determined to leave the streets behind. He started working at Jiffy Lube and then got a job as head mechanic at a repair shop in Capitol Heights. He also started going to church. We talked frequently, and he admired how seriously I took my education, because he felt education was the major element missing from his own life.

In his view, my only problem was my unwillingness to believe in God. I didn't see that as an issue though. My position on faith really hadn't changed since my grade-school days. Belief just didn't work for me, and the memory of our eviction from Fort Totten was still strong enough to reinforce that conviction whenever I called it to mind. I was essentially agnostic; I wanted to be sure that God existed. After talking to someone like Tonyson, a true person of faith, I would tell myself, very passionately, *If God could somehow come to me, I would happily accept God.* But without that, I saw no reason to change my position.

Hard as it may sound to believe this, the most exciting part about working at Ernst & Young was performing audit work for one of its biggest clients: the United States Postal Service. I'd been working for a year before getting assigned there. This assignment meant I travelled to select post offices all over the country to perform audits, and this gave me the opportunity to visit cities like Chicago, Miami, Los Angeles, Memphis, and New York. Suddenly I was becoming quite the traveller.

In each city, I was given use of a company American Express card to rent a car and a $35 per diem for meals. With no one supervising me, I did my work and then spent most of my time touring whatever city I was visiting. I would jump behind the wheel of whatever rental car they gave me and be in the wind. In Chicago, I visited the DuSable Museum, drove by the Robert Taylor Homes housing projects, spent time in black bookstores, and toured Malcolm X University, where his 1963 Oldsmobile (with 58,411 miles on it) was on display. I even tried to knock on the front door of the Nation of Islam's leader, Louis Farrakhan, only to be denied access by a member of the group's Fruit of Islam security force.

Aside from the opportunity to travel, and a steady salary, Ernst & Young also offered me further lessons in the importance of being organized. "Keeping your work in front of you" was the company gospel. We lived and breathed to-do lists. Whatever assignments were not completed by the end of the day got placed on a to-do list that your supervisor reviewed in order to check on the status of things. Ideally, you wanted items to be completed—and off the to-do list—as soon as possible. Every job had a concrete time frame for completion.

Another unexpected benefit of working at Ernst & Young came in the form of music. At that time, my musical tastes were pretty much limited to R&B and go-go. I never really embraced hip-hop because of my deep attachment to traditional instruments. But when I was young, my mom would listen to gospel music on Sundays, and whenever I heard Tramaine Hawkins's "Goin' Up Yonder," it grabbed me. I'd gotten more exposure to music by white artists at the Mount, and I felt that love songs like Chicago's "If You Leave Me Now" and the Bee Gees's "How Deep Is Your Love" could hold their own in any genre of music. While at the Mount, I worked for a while as a plumber's helper, and when I rode shotgun in the pickup truck, the radio was always set to the local country station. Some of the songs were catchy, and I really dug how similar country music was to the blues in terms of how it told stories.

Jazz, though, had never appealed to me, despite its emphasis on traditional instruments. Most of the jazz I'd heard turned me off with its fast pace and lack of melody. However, when I purchased my first car after working at Ernst & Young for almost two years, a used 1987 BMW 528e, my musical scope began to broaden a bit.

I began listening to a lot of different cassettes while I was driving. Someone turned me on to a Coltrane tune called "Naima." Being a sucker for ballads, I started listening to it every day. Since the song was on a tape between other Coltrane tunes, I had to fast-forward the cassette in order to hear it. Inevitably, I would hear some of the other songs as I got preoccupied with driving, and they began to grow on me.

Before long, I got turned out by Coltrane's rendition of "My Favorite Things." Though I didn't know much about horns, especially the soprano saxophone, Coltrane's talent for riffing impressed me. Steve Davis's big bass sound, supported by McCoy Tyner on the piano and Elvin Jones on the drums, had my head bopping hard as I drove up and down the highway to clients' offices. That song opened me up to appreciating Coltrane's faster-paced tunes. Then, a senior manager at Ernst & Young named Rene LaVigne gave me three tickets to Wolf Trap for a tribute concert to the great Miles Davis, who had just died in September of 1991. Performing was one of Davis's legendary bands: Herbie Hancock on piano, Ron Carter on bass, Wayne Shorter on saxophone, and the thunderous Tony Williams on drums. Young Wallace Roney performed in Miles's spot. Williams played so fast and hard that I thought he was gonna tear a hole in his drums.

There were plenty of benefits to working at Ernst & Young, but they weren't enough to compensate for the unpleasant culture at work. One of my long-term assignments was at the Mobil Corporation headquarters in Virginia. I really disliked the break-time conversations I had to endure with many of my white coworkers. I began eating with the black copy room and mail room workers. On a few assignments, I came close to taking things back to the streets. On two occasions, male coworkers said things I deemed overly disrespectful, and they got offered up. On both occasions, they were pretty surprised, and fortunately, neither took me up on the offer.

I knew it was only a matter of time before my departure from Ernst & Young was requested, either at the company's bidding or mine. One foreboding sign came after I'd been there for nearly two years, when I received a poor review. And I still hadn't earned my CPA. My prospects at the firm were getting dimmer, and for my part, I had no desire to advance further. In truth, I felt lucky I'd been earning a decent wage without having been called out for my apathy about my work.

Looking back, it was obvious that this internal tension, between my working for a classic white-establishment firm and my desire to become a full-fledged Pan-African activist couldn't last for long. The tension showed itself in a rare exchange with my mom. She was from the generation of blacks who struggled during the '50s and '60s to gain access to equal opportunities. Now here I was, 30 years later, complaining about my role in a place where she would not have been welcomed when she was my age. When I brought up the idea of "struggle" as we used the term in the context of Black Nationalism, she was incensed, and snapped, "The 'struggle?' You're going to struggle at your damn job! That's where you're going to struggle."

But by now I was far too independent, and too set in my position, for her words to have any effect on me.

By the end of 1992, I needed a career change but had no idea what direction to pursue. About a year before, an elder in the conscious community had turned me on to a black book distributor in Queens, New York, and I used that connection to order books for a grade-school class Karen was teaching at an independent school in DC. My friend Keith Johnson, who was the Student Government Association president at UDC, ordered *The Autobiography of Malcolm X* in bulk from me. I made a decent profit from these sales, but nothing that made me consider bookselling as a profession.

An opportunity to make more money presented itself when

ADO decided to host an event dedicated to black women, called the African Sistas Conference, at a church in Southeast DC. Yao, the poet I'd heavily recruited to join ADO, had recently acquired a vendor's license and, inspired by the recent birth of his daughter, planned to sell inexpensive jewelry, incense, and various other items at the conference. He offered to display my books after hearing that I was considering ordering some. I took him up on his offer and ordered several boxes of books I thought the attendees might purchase.

Sales from the conference were lackluster. In fact, I didn't even recoup the money I'd put out. This placed me in a slight dilemma, because I had boxes of books but no venue at which to sell them. However, Yao offered to hold onto the books and sell them for me whenever he vended.

Soon, I started helping him with setup and sales. My first time was the Friday after Thanksgiving, 1992; we set up shop on Georgia Avenue in front of HU's Wonder Plaza, and business was booming—in just four hours, we raked in almost $500. I was psyched, and my mind started number crunching. Based on how well we had done that day, I reasoned that if I dedicated myself to vending full time, I could generate enough revenue to match my Ernst & Young salary. Seemingly by coincidence, a week later, Yao told me that he needed a partner. I immediately started making plans for my departure from the white establishment.

On February 19, 1993, I left the offices of Ernst & Young for the final time and stopped at a Best Buy to purchase a folding aluminum table for $98. The next day, I loaded my car with that table, some books, and other items Yao had given me, and I set up shop on the backside of HU on 4th Street, just beyond the school's popular Quad area. Pulling up in my black BMW, dressed in a suit with an overcoat, and ready to duel with the February cold, I made my leap into entrepreneurship.

I quickly learned that full-time vending wouldn't generate the revenue I had anticipated. It had been nearly 20 years since I had celebrated Christmas, so I wasn't aware that Black Friday was one of the year's biggest shopping days—I thought the sales we'd made that day would be just like any other. Now that I wasn't vending during the holiday season, my daily sales ranged anywhere from $50-$100.

Making matters worse, I had assumed, incorrectly, that I was due one more paycheck from Ernst & Young than I actually received. I was anticipating using that last check to pay down my credit card and pay off some significant bills. Now that I wasn't going to get it, my leap into entrepreneurship looked more like a collapse, but I couldn't go back. I was dejected and despairing about the whole thing, and there appeared to be no way out of my predicament.

Then, I stumbled upon a little surprise. The very next time I went to my bank, the black-owned Industrial Bank of Washington (IBW), my checking account balance was $8,000 more than it should have been. Immediately, I started looking at everyone around me in the bank, as if they all knew there was money in my account that didn't belong there. After I left, I thought about that money all day and into the night until sleep overtook me.

When I woke up, guilt was waiting on me. *There has to be some type of mistake,* I thought, so I spoke to an IBW representative later that morning. I explained the situation and she listened patiently, without saying too much. Once I had unburdened myself about that money, I left the bank feeling relieved.

Days passed, though, and despite my having brought it to the bank's attention, the money was still in my account. I waited a few more days before getting up the nerve to take any of the money from the account. With much trepidation, I used my ATM card to take out $300. Doing withdrawals from an ATM became a daily ritual until I felt comfortable enough to write checks from my account. Wherever it came from, and for whatever reason, that money appeared just when I needed it most.

I used some of the money to order more books from distributors in New York. Black literature was popular with the students and professionals we served, so Yao and I decided to dedicate at least 60 percent of our display space to books. During the week, I set up at HU, while Yao went downtown near DuPont Circle. He also recruited a friend who had attended Bowie State University with him to operate a third vending stand. In addition to our three regular vending stands, Yao and I would pay fees to vend at other local and out-of-town venues on the weekends.

The vending license and most of our merchandise belonged to Yao, but I contributed my accounting knowledge and business experience. Yao and I were equal partners, but the business had no name and nothing was formalized. Coming up with the proper name for our venture was a challenge. Our two overriding objectives were to provide superior customer service and to develop a business rooted in African-centered history and culture. Since I was studying Kiswahili at HU, I looked to that language for a name to encapsulate those two qualities. *Karibu*, which means "welcome" or "come in," was simple, catchy, and a representation of our dual aim, in my opinion. Yao agreed, so we set up Karibu Company Inc. as an S corporation in DC. I owned 50 percent of the shares, while Yao and his wife, Karla, owned the other 50 percent.

Since Yao and Karla had started the vending operation, I felt it was proper to put Yao down as president in our articles of incorporation. I was named vice president, and Karla was listed as the secretary. We also opened a company bank account with IBW, my generous benefactor. I began to develop an accounting system for the business. It was rudimentary at first, but over time it became more sophisticated. We both understood that if Karibu was to be taken seriously, it had to be constructed as a real business.

We dreamed about having a store, a place people from the community could frequent. A woman from a neighborhood development association started helping us find a storefront. The association was ready to help us secure a loan, and even found us a location in Anacostia Southeast, but the owner of the building backed away from the deal. A guy we knew who went by DJ Renegade, a former disc jockey who had become a poet, had been working with me at the HU vending stand, and he suggested that majority-black Prince George's (PG) County in Maryland might be a good place for our a store. Yao and I didn't have the money for a stand-alone store, so I looked into Landover Mall and The Mall at Prince George's Plaza, two popular shopping centers in PG County. Both malls offered temporary pushcart and kiosk locations in the common areas. Karibu scraped up just enough resources to open both a pushcart in Landover Mall and a slightly bigger kiosk in PG in mid-October of 1993. Since the malls were open long hours on Mondays through Saturdays, and six hours on Sundays, we needed to shut down our vending stands. We also had to hire more employees to help us maintain the hours.

We were excited about Karibu's expansion, but money was real tight. I took a big hit in income. In 1992, I had earned more than $30,000 working at Ernst & Young. At the end of 1993, my earnings for the year were just $13,000, though that was in part due to our commitment to put most of our earnings back into the business. I was still living with my mother in Section 8 housing, which made it possible for me to withstand such a significant pay decrease. Yao and Karla, who lived with her parents, had to care for their newborn daughter.

Not too long after opening up, I received a surprise visitor at the PG kiosk. Joe Horning had somehow heard about my new venture, and he showed up to visit me. Filled with excitement, he congratulated me and offered to schedule some time to talk to me and meet Yao. Seeking to get some business advice, Yao and I soon met with Mr. Horning in his downtown office.

The day after our meeting with Mr. Horning, he called me and stated bluntly, "You need to do a buy/sell agreement." I understood him as saying that I needed a legally binding document to protect my business interests in Karibu, in the event that Yao and I stopped getting along. I listened patiently and thanked him for his advice. However, I was offended that this white man would suggest I do something that might compromise the trusting relationship between Yao and me. After all, we were both ADO members committed to the black struggle. Though I respected Mr. Horning, especially for his business acumen, I felt the advice he offered crossed over into an area he had no business treading upon. Mr. Horning was one of the few successful business people I knew, and by far the wealthiest, but that was the last time I sought out his advice.

Besides, things really picked up once we opened in the malls, especially at our PG kiosk. In less than six months, the mall manager approached us about moving into a storefront. I leaned heavily on my good personal credit to purchase more books, bookcases, and everything else that was needed. The same company that I used to finance my BMW charged me a high interest rate to use their monies again, but we were able to pay off that debt fairly quickly. In August 1994, Karibu opened an 800-square-foot store. Our Landover Mall operation wasn't as lucrative, but after more than three years of Yao struggling in that pushcart, we opened up a 450-square-foot store there in May 1997. Before long, Karibu was consuming my life.

Before I'd left Ernst & Young, Karen and I had broken up for good. She told me that I was too intense. What had started out two years earlier as my first serious romantic relationship had finally run its course. In effect, Karen had grown distant, doing to me what I had done to her with my commitment to ADO—but the difference was she no longer wanted to be with me. In one desperate attempt to hold onto the relationship, I started bawling in front of her at a downtown McDonald's, and as I peered at her through my tears, I remember her face and eyes looked frigid. When I finally told her

I felt it was over, it was really a case of my putting words to what she had already done. She probably had been hoping I would have said something long before I did. She expressed admiration at how I was choosing to live my life, but made it clear that she wouldn't be living that life with me. When she popped up with a new boyfriend not too long after our breakup, it hurt me pretty bad.

During our final breakup conversation, I remember telling her, "I'm going to be happy." I didn't know at the time where my need to say something like that was coming from, but I remember feeling defiant when I said it. Perhaps I was speaking from a determination to overcome the pain I felt in those moments. By not being with her, I was stepping into uncertainty, but I was resolved that happiness would one day be mine. I had never been as vulnerable with anyone else as I'd been with Karen. The thought of our not being together caused me greater pain than I had ever felt. All of the other things I cared about couldn't cover up this fact.

But my devotion to Karen did not mean that I hadn't been unfaithful. I had slept with a young woman I met through a friend when Karen had been out of the country, travelling to Spain for three months. Maybe it was guilt, or nervousness, but my sexual performance was dismal. It seemed like I climaxed within seconds. A few hours later we were at it again, but the same thing happened. Earlier that night and the only time I'd ever done so, I bragged about myself sexually—I kept calling my penis John. Just before I closed the young woman's passenger side door as she was dropping me at the Metro station early the next morning, she let me in on something.

"We'll have to do this again, but next time, please bring Sam and leave John at home."

I experienced some quick and ugly retribution for my infidelity. During my time on the streets, I had heard many a dude speak of getting burned by a girl. Several days after the indiscretion, when my trips to the bathroom became a little more painful, I gained intimate knowledge of exactly what getting burned meant. It took a trip to a doctor and a few weeks of medication to get rid of whatever I'd contracted. Karen returned from her trip the day I took my last pill.

Despite what cheating might indicate about whether I truly valued my relationship with Karen, it took me a few years to get over losing her. Whenever someone told me they had seen her, my heart rate increased and I became uneasy. I even talked to other women about my feelings for her, but Brother Eric became my main confidant, and he spent many late nights listening to my lamentations. He tried to console me by saying Karen would probably come back to me after she'd been with another guy or two, but the thought of Karen having sex with someone else hurt me even more.

Working in retail gave me plenty of opportunities to meet women, but I couldn't seem to establish any relationships. It felt like I was always on the outside looking in. Other guys were partying on life's fun train while I was struggling just to get on board. There was one woman I dated seriously, who was pretty and very mature, but she moved to Atlanta.

Part of the difficulty was finding someone who embraced a black radical ideology. DC was overflowing with appealing black women, but the overwhelming majority of them were not conscious. I was determined not to experience another disappointment like I had with Karen. Despite my consistent efforts, though, I just couldn't establish a solid relationship with anyone.

Many of the women I took out wouldn't see me beyond one or two dates, because I was very honest about my ideological positions. A lot of women were turned off by my conversation. I terrified one woman when, for our first date, I rode her around Trinidad, Little Vietnam, and a few other rough areas in Northeast. Needless to say, there was no second date. Finding someone with whom I could be myself, and be truly vulnerable, seemed like a never-ending pursuit.

I was not without companionship through this period, but

nearly every woman I had sex with after Karen became a one-night stand. I got the impression that a few of these women thought that once we had sex they would be able to control me, but I refused to lose focus on my work. In other cases, I was the one who lost interest. I turned down sex numerous times, and many of these times, I came to regret it. I compared myself to my friends who'd had numerous sexual conquests. I was frequently lonely, and often by myself at home with nothing but my work and my radical ideology. Feeling desperate and bored, I would reach out to one of my former sexual conquests or a girl who had previously shown interest in me, only to discover that they had moved on.

I always thought my focus and dedication would make me more appealing to women, but it appeared that wasn't the case. I told myself, *I'm young, fit, smart, educated, hardworking, and enterprising. Why can't I find the right girl?* I couldn't escape the frustrating and disheartening pattern of either turning away women I didn't truly like or being rejected by the ones who really interested me.

I couldn't shake the loneliness. ADO, Karibu, and early-morning runs were the fixtures in my life, and the enormous energy they required helped me push the loneliness to the periphery of my thoughts. But by 1994, ADO began to diminish from my life, due to internal issues within the organization. Shaka was never quite the same after our return from Togo, and his behavior caused a rift. What Karen first noticed and Dr. Tounou tried to warn us about concerning Shaka broke open. Without warning, he and the other founder, Herb, advanced the idea that they should take permanent control of ADO's leadership.

Brother Eric and the rest of us saw this demand as unreasonable. We embraced having an organizational structure where it would be possible for new people to come into the group and, through their skills and effort, move into leadership positions. Shaka was undaunted, though, and created even more tension when he took aggressive steps to assume total control. He went to court and had

ADO's bank account frozen. Then he convinced his older brother, who was also a significant member, to side with him in the dispute. Everything came to a head at a big meeting. Brother Eric was always the most highly regarded ADO member, and the organization probably would have gone in whatever direction he favored. Shaka was keenly aware of this, so continued trying to get Brother Eric to join his side. However, Brother Eric remained steadfast in his opposition to Shaka. The rest of us were relieved and looked forward to moving beyond the power struggle and getting things moving again. The timing appeared right for us to really expand our efforts. After several attempts, I had recently secured tax-exempt status for ADO.

But something within the membership had changed. The internal schism had soured too many members, and their commitment was not the same. It was like no one could get over the pain of what happened. After a while, the only ADO program that still drew active participation was the outreach work at Lorton, and most of the people who participated were not ADO members.

The Lorton program, which consisted of biweekly group discussions, had started because of my relationship with Singleton, who was still serving time there. He was initially held in a medium-security facility, but he later enrolled in a treatment program, called Unfoldment, that allowed him to move to the minimum-security facility. Singleton never had a drug problem, but getting into that program offered him the chance to cut down some of his prison time. Through our letters, Singleton was aware of my developing black consciousness, and the next time there was an opportunity for an outsider to visit the Unfoldment program, Singleton wangled an invitation for me to speak to the participants. I was able to address nearly 100 inmates about the importance of black history and culture. They enjoyed the lecture and asked me if I'd come regularly, and that eventually became ADO's prison outreach program.

As ADO members became less active, people associated with

Karibu started accompanying Yao and me on our biweekly visits. I saw the prison outreach as a natural extension of what Karibu was seeking to do with black literature. Our employees and close friends jumped at the chance to offer inspiring words to inmates. Even a few of my street buddies like Tonyson, who had spent a few years locked up in Lorton himself, came with us to visit and see old acquaintances. A friend of Karen's from Chicago was one of the most frequent volunteers. We shared poetry and other literature with inmates, and they, in turn, invited us to their big family-oriented functions. Both parties looked forward to the visits. The hour-plus commute during rush hour didn't bother us at all. I would frequently bring Singleton books with money inserted between select pages. Even after the Unfoldment program was shut down and Singleton was released, the prison outreach work continued. By the end of 1994, ADO was effectively defunct, but the inmates thought that all of the Karibu personnel and others who came to visit were also members of ADO.

The end of ADO came at a meeting in January of 1995. There were only five members present, including Brother Eric, Yao, and myself. At the time, only Yao, me, and one other member named Kofi Adisa were actively working in an ADO program. Brother Eric discussed a plan to revitalize the group, but the rest of us resisted, feeling that ADO had become too theoretical, and Brother Eric conceded the point. For me, Yao, and most former ADO members—including Brother Eric—Karibu was seen as the practical outgrowth of the organization's ideological foundation. I wasn't interested in public speaking anymore. My preference was to work behind the scenes and build an institution dedicated to black consciousness, and Karibu was the manifestation of that desire.

My mom's negative feelings over my commitment to black struggle never changed, but she was supportive of me nonetheless. She never wavered in this regard.

Of more immediate concern was her worsening mental state. When I would come home on breaks from the Mount, her disposition was what it had always been. During the summer after my graduation, however, her mental state began to worry me more. It was as if she began to let herself go shortly after the ceremony. She started turning on the electric oven and leaving its door open, even though all the utilities were working fine. I would come home in the evenings to a scorching living room and kitchen. When I spoke to her about it, she simply complained about being cold. I couldn't reason with her. I needed to get my mom some help but wasn't sure how to do it. Dealing with her in this capacity was something I'd never done before. There were people in our family who were aware of my mom's long-standing issues, however, and I was hopeful that some of them would be willing to help.

I put out a call to family members who I thought could best aid me. Uncle Wilbert, who lived in Greensboro and had come to my graduation, was the family member I knew best and talked to most. He was the first person I called, and he was more than willing to help. I also had a cousin named Wilbert who agreed to help— Cousin Wilbert was actually older than my uncle, and during my years in college, he had given me a lot of encouragement. He lived in DC, so I would see him and his younger brother, Curtis, fairly regularly. With both Wilberts on board, I felt very comfortable moving forward. The fact that they were both older than my mom and had known her for her entire life was a big plus.

We devised and carried out a pretty simple plan. Uncle Wilbert drove up from North Carolina on a weekday in mid-April of 1991 and met Cousin Wilbert. Both of them arrived, unannounced, at our apartment around noon. Cousin Wilbert, whose impromptu visit would not cause too much alarm, knocked on the front door of the apartment, which was located on the top floor of a two-story building, while Uncle Wilbert stood farther back, out of view. My mom answered the door as I sat nearby in the living room.

As soon as she swung the door open to allow Cousin Wilbert to enter, he pulled her into the hallway, where uncle Wilbert jumped in to assist. My mother, already startled by the attack, did a double take when she noticed Uncle Wilbert's face. I kept my distance as they managed to get her inside one of their cars.

We drove to DC General, where we turned her over to the staff on duty. After what seemed like a fairly short wait, a staff member came out and gave us the bad news. He told us that she was definitely psychotic, but, without my mother's consent, they could not administer any treatment or provide her with any services. Thus, there was nothing they could do to help us out. Despite our efforts, my mom had won out. She came stepping out from whatever room they had her in as defiant as ever. She told the people who'd examined her that they were the ones who were crazy. Conceding defeat, we hurriedly rushed my mother to the car and went back home.

Without any other options available to us, my uncle and cousin departed, and I was left alone to listen to my mom's tirade about our betrayal. However, in the days that followed, I remembered one thing the gentleman at DC General told us: they could give my mother treatment if the police brought her to them. Therefore, I would have to find a way to get my mom arrested.

Then it hit me. My mom's penchant for using the oven to heat the house offered me the opening I needed. I made a quick visit to the resident manager at Franklin Commons and informed her about what was going on. She was aware that my mom had some issues, so she sent her a letter of warning about the danger that leaving the oven on posed for everyone living in our building.

As expected, my mom ignored the warning, which gave me an opening to call the police. I made the call a week after our visit to DC General. The police arrived, I showed them the letter, and they arrested my defiant mother. They took her to St. Elizabeths Hospital in Southeast DC, where they gave her Haldol, a drug used to treat psychosis and schizophrenia. For me, it was strange sleeping at home for the first time without my mom being there.

I went to visit her, and was very surprised when she told me that she wasn't angry over what I did. Holding up her index finger, she said, "You've always been my number one!" She had never expressed anything like that kind of emotion toward me before. Her entire disposition had changed. It was as if a part of her that the sickness had covered up for so long was finally revealed again, and that made me feel better about what I'd done. The drugs made her calmer, too.

After a few weeks, my mom was transferred to Washington Hospital Center, which was only a few blocks from where we lived. Even though she was nearby, it was still strange not having my mom right at home. Karen gave me wonderful support during that time, which helped a lot.

By mid-May, my mom was back at home, but now her normal feistiness was replaced by a listless stupor. Her proud homemaker days were a thing of the past. When I came home after work or grad school, she would come sit at the dinner table and just stare at me. However, her disposition was much more pleasant than it had been when I was younger. I felt guilty about being impatient with her.

I was terribly conflicted. On one hand, I had a life filled with work, grad school, ADO, and a girlfriend—or the steady search to find one. On the other hand, I was suddenly thrown into a position of being a caretaker for my mom, who for all of my life had been so independent she'd never even held conversations with me. Now, my mom was demanding my attention. In my earlier years, there were times when I'd felt embarrassed by the behavior that earned my mother the nickname Red Baron. Now, what I felt was a sense of burden.

Part of my frustration came from just not knowing how to handle this new person who needed my attention. My mom, for the first time, just wanted to be in my space. All of a sudden, I could see the love she had for me all over her. It was like her face was now the stamp of her spirit. However, I couldn't engage in a normal conversation with her. I was perplexed. I started telling myself that in time I was going to build a better life for her, and this idea brought me comfort.

I accepted the fact that I was probably the only one in the family who, in the end, could get my mother the help she needed. My family knew that my mom had issues, but when I was younger, they had to consider the very real possibility that getting too involved would have caused her to lose me. Uncle Rudolph had offered to raise me in Greensboro, but my mom categorically refused. They were sort of stuck observing what was going on from the periphery. I could appreciate their predicament. It must have been very difficult for my family to figure out how to deal with the situation. There was a child involved, and my mother, despite her mental issues, was doing a good job in that area. Even Aunt Mary, who certainly had good reasons for not being in my mom's fan club, gave her credit for the job she did in raising me.

Over the next few years, my mom and I made adjustments to our new reality. She became dependent upon me, to some extent, and I had to adjust my schedule to accommodate her. Every weekday, I did drop-offs and pickups at the Barney Senior Center in Adams Morgan Northwest, where she spent the day in activities with other elders. I also took her to medical and dental appointments. In many ways, she was like a new person. She was nice to everyone who stopped by to see us. When ADO members came to the house, she greeted them warmly and generally headed upstairs to give us space to strategize and socialize. Her Red Baron outfit was gone, and the walking stick adorned with nails was now just part of Little Vietnam lore.

I even got my mother to start reading. Even though my mom was a college-educated former teacher, I had never seen her pick up a book. So I was thrilled when she read *Family*, a novel by J. California Cooper that I had gotten for her. Cooper wrote wholesome stories about unpretentious Southern people, and I felt it would be a nice book for my mom to get into. She seemed to like it.

Even more enjoyable for her was a long-overdue trip down South. In April 1992, she rode with three of her cousins, including Wilbert and Curtis, to Goldsboro, North Carolina to spend some time with her sister, Irene. I arrived two days later before stopping in Greensboro to spend some time with Uncle Wilbert and his family.

I wanted to seek out professional advice from someone within the conscious community, so I scheduled an appointment with Dr. Frances Cress Welsing, the local psychiatrist whose book had inspired me in college. During my session with Dr. Welsing, she didn't offer any specific recommendations for dealing with my mother. She listened patiently and surprised me near the very end of our session by encouraging me to write a book. Her suggestion was the first of what eventually became a common response whenever I confided in someone about my situation.

The following spring, I invited Dr. Welsing to speak with the inmates in our outreach program at Lorton. I picked her up, and during the drive she told me about meeting Malcolm X in 1956 when she was a young student. She explained that at that time, she saw all people as being the same, but Malcolm spent hours trying to explain to her that white people were devils. Though his arguments didn't convince her, she commented on how patient and respectful he was in his effort to win her over.

By August 1994, I felt it was time for my mom to see the business that her son had left Ernst & Young to build. The Karibu kiosk in the Mall at Prince George's was a day away from moving into its first storefront. I took her to our Landover pushcart first. It had only been a year and a half since I'd first set up a vending table, after leaving the white establishment in which my mother wanted me to continue to struggle. Now, I wanted her to see and appreciate the progress Yao and I had made within the black struggle.

My mother quietly observed all the people traversing the hallways as she sat in the director's chair that Prince George's provided each kiosk. After a few minutes, a worker and I were startled when my mother unexpectedly slumped over in the chair, before almost falling onto the floor. I quickly got her to my car and took her to Washington Hospital Center's emergency room. After examining her, a doctor gave me the awful news: my mom had cancer, and it was pervasive. The cancer had spread to her kidneys, liver, spleen, and stomach. She would need surgery right away. Since first being treated for schizophrenia, my mother had taken to speaking very little. I could only wonder how long she'd been in pain.

All of my mom's physical turmoil and sickness had been going on during my watch. I felt helpless about the whole situation, and questioned everything about how I'd interacted with her. After two extensive surgeries, my mom was kept in the intensive care unit (ICU). I visited her every day. Uncle Wilbert and Uncle Rudolph came to visit from North Carolina. After they saw her condition, Uncle Rudolph pulled out his checkbook, but I told him to put it away. I still had hope for a victory over the cancer and, to my mind, taking money from him would have been accepting defeat.

Near the middle of September, my mom had to undergo another major surgery. Things looked pretty grim. The next day, I received a call from her chief doctor. It was close to midnight, and he had news for me. I wrote the following in my journal:

> *Here I am in the ICU again. Dr. Frazier said there was nothing more for them to do. I immediately called Uncle Wilbert to inform him of the bad, sad news. I can see my mom taking a few gasps of air every few seconds. Only one eye is open and the rest of her body is covered with the exception of her*

left arm. It's the arm on the side where visitors stand, I guess the nurses left that arm uncovered for me to hold. Oh Mom, how you've suffered. I needed a few more years to really try and make life better for you. I wanted you to see more of your relatives in Philadelphia and North Carolina. I wanted to move you into a really nice place.

I just called Uncle Leroy and told him that you don't have much time left. He said he would see me soon. You might be upset by my calling two of your brothers. I did it because I knew they both cared for you. It would have been selfish for me to come here alone without letting someone know. Perhaps this represents letting them (outsiders) into our life. You've shut so many people out of our life. This was your way of dealing with life and the unfortunate circumstances that came your way. (Heart rate is down to 23.) I've decided to change that, Mom. During your life you shut people out. Now, at the time of your death, I'm inviting them in. It's not a betrayal. It's only an attempt at bonding and sharing within our extended family. Mom, I want to break the tradition. (My mother just died 12:08 a.m.)

I just called Uncle Leroy again to inform them that Mom has just rolled out. They want me to wait for them to arrive here. I haven't cried since she's been in the hospital. I don't think I can cry. I've grieved in my mind for so long now. Just to see my mother not live out a full life has been grief enough.

Someone told me that since my mom had been receiving Social Security, the city would pay for her to be buried locally. I decided against pursuing that, though, because I wanted her laid to rest in North Carolina. She never had any real connection to DC, and there were family members who really cared for her down South. When I informed Uncle Wilbert, he was pleased, and he told me the family had a section of a cemetery in Goldsboro where she could be laid to rest.

The services were held at Antioch Missionary Baptist Church in Goldsboro on September 18, 1994. My mom had isolated herself from everyone, so I didn't see anyone else who was fit to deliver the eulogy besides me. And the thought of some pastor doing it who didn't even know my mom didn't suit me. A minor emergency occurred when my relatives learned that I was not going to wear a necktie to the service. After conferring among themselves, they sent a couple of emissaries from within the family to make a few polite requests. I rejected all of their appeals.

The church service went well, and I was pleased by my effort. When it ended, a family member confronted me as soon as I got past the church pews. He was upset that I mentioned my mom and me being on welfare. I was offended by the audacity of this guy telling me that what I knew and lived wasn't true. At the time, I didn't consider how some family members might have been embarrassed by my exposing certain facts from my mom's past. Growing up apart from family had created an emotional distance within me that couldn't be overcome by simply having my mom's funeral services in North Carolina, and I had work back in DC to escape into. I felt that by having my mom buried in the town of her birth, my duty to my family had been fulfilled. So, I decided to head home right after the funeral. I could see that some family members were disappointed, but everyone was respectful of my preference to be alone.

Besides working, I spent the next few days mostly at home. Though it was early fall, I had the heat pumping in the apartment. When one of my neighbors knocked on the door to check on me, I reassured her that I was fine—but right at that moment, my body collapsed and abruptly hit the floor. I had blacked out. The neighbor helped me to my feet and made sure I was okay.

The very next day, a mailman knocked at the door to deliver a package. Before he could depart, I collapsed again. This time the neighbors weren't taking any chances. They called an ambulance, and I woke up while en route to Washington Hospital Center.

I was held overnight for precautionary measures. I told them that I had been keeping my apartment pretty warm, and may have become dehydrated as a result of not drinking enough water. In the morning, a nurse informed me that they determined nothing serious caused my two tumbles, and a doctor would be in soon to give me an update and order my release.

As the morning dragged on, I became impatient about getting released. The doctor was taking a long time, and I just couldn't take the waiting. When it seemed like the doctor would never come, I decided to take matters into my own hands. I pulled the IV out of my arm and slipped out of the room. Shortly after arriving home, hospital security called my house and asked if I was coming back. At this point in my life, my attachment to my work was so important to me that I couldn't stand being away from it for even a day, unless it was on my terms. I made sure to keep the heat down and got back to work without any more problems. I didn't care about what was happening to my health—I just wanted to get back to work.

Beyond work, trying to solve the long-standing mystery surrounding my father became my next focus. Due to my mom's refusal to admit to his existence, I always believed that she was still angry about whatever had happened between them, and while she was alive I had been reluctant to put much effort into finding him. I had obtained my birth certificate a few years earlier, though, and according to that document, my father was Herman Sutton, and he was a mathematician. He and my mother had both been 36 when I was born.

It was taking my mom to be buried down South that opened an unexpected door in my search for my father. While I was there, Aunt Mary told me that Herman Sutton's sister, Loreen Jones, lived in Goldsboro and had even come to my mother's funeral. She gave me this woman's phone number. She, in turn, connected me to Herman Sutton, my mother's ex-husband, who was living in Detroit.

We had a long, pleasurable, and informative phone conversation. He immediately addressed my concerns about whether he was my father. He told me that the last time he'd had sex with my mother was the same year they separated long before I was born in 1968. I wasn't disturbed by his bluntness; on the contrary, I appreciated his directness and willingness to deal with my deepest concerns. I had followed the trail as far as it could take me, and my father's identity remained a mystery.

The city's Medicaid plan paid for my mother's $50,000-plus hospital bill. However, the bill I incurred for my short visit to the same hospital was a different matter, as I had no medical insurance at the time. I also owed American Express for my mom's funeral expenses. I had charged the costs (more than $6,000) with the expectation that all of my uncles (with the exception of Atward) would help pay. When only Wilbert and Rudolph contributed their share, I couldn't make the full card payment. Fortunately, Amex gave me an extension, but the bill needed to be paid soon. I was in the lurch, and Karibu was still too fragile to alleviate any of my personal financial burdens. I looked into doing accounting at night, but the time required was prohibitive.

The only other skill I possessed that could bring in money was the sweet science, so I turned there. The thought of boxing professionally had crossed my mind as a teenager, but school was always a greater priority, and I was turned off by the thought that being a fighter would limit me. But now I felt desperate, so when a guy named Antwon, who had recently opened a boxing gym in Riggs Park Northeast, stopped by the PG store and invited me to start working out there, I jumped at the chance. The gym was actually on my way home from work, so that made it very convenient. Getting used to taking blows to the head again was the real challenge.

Just as I was getting back into the rhythm of training, some financial relief arrived in the mail. I received a letter from Washington Hospital Center indicating that it was forgiving my debt. Someone had told me that the hospital sometimes wrote off bills, so I had sent them a request for debt forgiveness. It was such a relief to have this financial burden off my shoulders; without the hospital debt, I was able to shoulder my responsibility to Amex. I immediately dropped the idea of boxing professionally and put all of my focus back on building Karibu.

While boxing at Antwon's, though, I established a good rapport with Beethavean "Bee" Scottland, a young and extremely talented fighter who had just turned professional in February of 1995. Antwon was his father figure and had nurtured Bee through the amateur ranks, and a lot of people in DC had high hopes for his boxing career. Unfortunately, by the end of 1997, Bee fell out with Antwon and his manager and gave up boxing. His record was a disappointing eleven wins, four losses, and two draws. That wasn't a terrible record, but it wasn't indicative of the talent Bee possessed.

Even though I had stopped going to the gym by the end of 1995, I continued running every other day and I did my best to keep up with the fight game. I watched all the major bouts on television and pay-per-view and I tried to attend as many local fights as possible. I frequently ran into Curtbone, who shared my passion for boxing and was now managing a fighter.

Curtbone had somehow managed to avoid a long prison sentence for his involvement with Rayful Edmond. Rayful caught a "kingpin charge," meaning he would spend the rest of his life in prison without the possibility of parole. Others close to Rayful received long sentences as well. In the end, though, Curtbone was only convicted of money laundering, for which he spent four years in prison, and he never snitched on any of his old squad members.

At one fight I attended while I was still working at Ernst & Young, I ran into Curtbone while I was dressed in business attire. After he introduced me to a friend he was with, he pointed at me and said to the guy, "You wouldn't believe that he used to be one of us." I had left the streets, but I still ran into many of the people I had known out there. I had seen Little Gary Terrell at a boxing match about a month before he was allegedly tortured and killed.

Going to the fights offered an occasion for people from all walks of life to intermingle. DC was an underappreciated fight town with a history of talented fighters, but in the mid-1990s, it saw a kind of golden age in boxing. A number of homegrown fighters were winning titles or making noise on a global scale, such as William Joppy, Mark "Too Sharp" Johnson, Derrell "Too Sweet" Coley, Keith Holmes, Sharmba "Little Big Man" Mitchell, Israh Girgrah, Andrew Council, and Demarcus "Chop Chop" Corley. At one point, there were five simultaneous world champions who all came from the DC area.

But the fighter who really captivated me at the time was a Philadelphia guy named Bernard Hopkins, whose nickname was "The Executioner." How he survived the streets of Philly, spent nearly five years in prison, lost his first match, and still managed to achieve world prominence fascinated me. When he won the International Boxing Federation (IBF) middleweight championship in a 1995 rematch against Segundo Mercado at the Capital Centre in Prince George's County, I was on hand.

Yao was keenly aware of my interest in boxing. After he and Karla purchased their first house, he hung a heavy bag in the basement so we could work out together while talking about the business. I was so focused on staying fit that the possibility of Karla and their children's being disturbed by the noise we made punching that bag never crossed my mind. Yao never talked to me about how Karla felt about it, perhaps because he viewed the bonding as good for building Karibu.

In mid-1998, when Yao learned about my interest in Bee, he suggested that I consider managing him. After doing some investigative work and speaking to Antwon, I concluded that Bee had been mismanaged. Besides his first loss, an exciting fight against a talented local fighter named Allen "Boogaloo" Watts, his other defeats had been out-of-town matches in or near his opponents' hometowns. I didn't think Bee's handlers had built him up properly, and as a result Bee had been required to rely too much on his innate talent.

Before embarking on this new venture, I wanted to get the best available advice. I had gone to school with the daughter of Mike Trainer, the man who masterminded the career of the great Sugar Ray Leonard, and she kindly set up a meeting with her father for me. We agreed to meet at his office, and I came there with a bunch of questions typed out. When I arrived at his office in Maryland, he greeted me wearing a polo shirt and shorts. We had a mostly one-sided discussion filled with cautionary advice. He told me, "If this guy you're looking to manage doesn't have the potential to become a world champion, then don't waste your time with him." And, "If you were supposed to meet Ray Leonard at 7:00 a.m. to run and you arrived at 7:05, he'd be gone. When I was dealing with Ray Leonard, I didn't have to tell him to train." And, "There are very few decent people in boxing, and everyone has their hand out."

At the end of the discussion, he looked me over, asked what I did for a living, and issued his final piece of advice: "You should probably stick with what you're doing and leave boxing alone."

Bee's talent was undeniable. Throughout the summer, stories floated around local gyms about the time he busted open the eye of William Joppy during a sparring session. Joppy was the current two-time WBA middleweight champion, and he openly acknowledged that Bee was a good fighter.

Before summer's end, Bee and I made a handshake agreement that I would manage him. My first act as manager was to help him and Antwon reconcile. I knew Antwon had a game plan for getting Bee to a championship, and I wanted to implement it. First, we would keep Bee fighting locally against mediocre opposition until he regained his confidence. We would review tapes of the potential opponent before agreeing to take a fight, and we would never take any last-minute fights, especially if they were in out-of-town venues. Unless we had a chance at a fight with significant implications, we would keep Bee away from tall southpaws because, as a lefty himself, he had trouble with that type of fighter. Three of his earlier losses had come against such opponents.

Despite the occasional hiccups, Karibu was operating pretty smoothly, and this gave me some time to focus on building Bee's career. I began going to the gym every day to watch him train. His trainer was Adrian Davis, a former fighter who had Joppy and several other world-class fighters in his camp. Bee had a day job as an exterminator, and if for whatever reason his work prevented him from getting to the gym, Antwon and I would spar with him in Antwon's home gym. The head shots Bee delivered didn't affect me too much, but the body shots would stay with me for days. I also began driving to Bee's place in Maryland to run with him in the mornings.

I reached out to a promoter who held fights at a venue in Glen Burnie, Maryland, called Michael's Eighth Avenue. This guy had staged nearly half of Bee's fights and treated him very well. He was excited to put Bee back on his cards again. Bee's return bout was a six-round decision victory in September of 1998 at Michael's Eighth Avenue. Two of his next three fights were in Glen Burnie, and he won them all. Antwon and I understood that a good-looking record was important in boxing. Our goal was to get Bee to 20 victories and hope that an opportunity for a bigger fight would open up for him.

As a newcomer to the boxing business with no deep connections, I had to work extra hard to get Bee fights. I developed an extensive contact list of promoters and matchmakers throughout the country. When harassing these promoters failed to deliver fights frequently enough, I began paying for Bee to fight at a local promoter's venue in Virginia. The promoter would put Bee on his card as long as I paid the purse for both Bee and his opponent. These opponents were known as "duckpins"—guys the promoter would set up for you so that your fighter could literally knock them down. Duckpins were generally beatable, provided your fighter was in shape. Bee won all these fights easily and gained more confidence.

When reigning super-flyweight world champion Mark Johnson called us about a fight, Bee was a year into his comeback, had won all six of his fights, and had just received a national ranking with the United States Boxing Association (USBA). Johnson was defending his own title in DC on ESPN2 and was also promoting the card. He wanted to do a rematch between Bee and Boogaloo Watts, the guy who gave Bee his first loss. Their first fight had been a barn burner, and a rematch in DC was a no-brainer. At the time of the first fight, Bee was a bit inexperienced, and some people questioned his handler's decision to take the fight in the first place. Now, Bee was riding high on his winning streak, and Boogaloo was coming off a knockout loss. The rematch made sense from our perspective, so we agreed to take the fight.

The bout was originally scheduled for eight rounds, but was later cut down to six to accommodate the main event and some other preliminary bouts that were all being televised on ESPN2. After the main event, all the ESPN people started breaking down the camera equipment and packing up to leave. These people were out-of-towners and didn't realize how important this fight was locally. I looked around frantically and spotted Teddy Atlas, the highly respected analyst for ESPN and a world-renowned trainer who once helped train Mike Tyson under the tutelage of Cus D'Amato. I scrambled over to him and asked, "Can you stay and watch my guy fight, Mr. Atlas?"

Atlas, who had just stood up and placed his suit jacket over his left forearm, gave me a solemn look then answered, "Okay." He stood right there during the entire fight, never sitting back down, and watched the action very attentively.

As the rounds went by, Bee was throwing the harder shots while Boogaloo was landing with more frequency. Boogaloo was open for a right hook, and Bee was inching closer and closer to landing it. But the fight's being reduced to six rounds played in Boogaloo's favor. Bee threw too few punches and lost by a unanimous decision. Antwon, Adrian, and I were terribly disappointed, and Bee cried like a baby. Later, Boogaloo came strutting out from his locker room, spotted all of us huddled up around Bee, and yelled out, "I love you, Bee!" There was just something about Bee that brought out the best in Boogaloo.

Bee rebounded with an easy victory over another duckpin fighter. Then he was offered a hometown fight as the headliner against the number-two ranked IBF contender, Thomas "Ice Tea" Tate. A three-time world title challenger, Tate had only been knocked out once, by the all-time great Roy Jones when he was in his prime. Bee put up a good scrap but took a ten-round decision loss.

It was getting much easier to get Bee fights, and this allowed me some time to focus on him as a fighter. One of the things Bee struggled with was transferring what he showed during his impressive sparring sessions to his fight nights. He wasn't as confident as he always tried to make us believe. He was also unwilling to fully exert himself during training and had a few technical flaws. Bee was aware of his talent, and that sometimes worked against him. Adrian was the only one who could get Bee to give more in training, but he was oftentimes busy with his title-holding fighters. I couldn't get through to Bee, though, and Antwon never backed me up on it. Their attitude was that since I'd never fought professionally, they didn't have to heed my advice. My job was to simply get Bee fights.

As I was seeking to make better headway with these issues, on the night of August 1, 2000, Bee delivered a devastating performance en route to a seventh-round TKO. After nearly two years of effort, the fighter I was accustomed to seeing in the gym every week showed up on fight night. I was thrilled! He had secured his 20th victory, won nine of his eleven fights under my management, and was back in the USBA rankings.

I really enjoyed being Bee's manager. For one, it gave me a close-up view of the fights. To see two highly trained fighters test their skills against each other was always amazing. Being at or near ringside, where the action was, and feeling the energy from the crowd, was exhilarating. And I liked making a difference in Bee's career. I could chart its development, through the dips and the climbs. In effect, I was a chronicler who was also part and parcel of a genuinely uplifting story.

On the financial side of things, I was just starting to receive payment for my work. During my first two years managing Bee, I collected no fee for my services because the purses were so small. Now that Bee was earning bigger purses, I could start recouping the $5,000 that I'd laid out, paying for duckpins, purchasing equipment, and covering Bee's annual licensing and medical expenses.

Bee didn't see it that way though. He had grown too accustomed to my not getting paid. After one victory, he asked if I would forgo collecting my management fee so he could use the money to pay for a repair to his truck. I wouldn't agree—I had put forth a lot of effort to help get him a national ranking, and he knew it. He had even confided to me that his wife told him that I was doing more for him than most managers would.

In November 2000, Bee and I rode to Baltimore for his annual neurological exam. The trip ended up being my final act as his manager. Early the next month, I received a call from a match-maker who informed me that someone else had called him claiming to represent Bee, so he was calling to let me know.

I called Bee's cell phone but didn't reach him. Next, I called Antwon and told him what happened. His response told me what I feared most: "Man, you know how that niggah Bee is."

Naw, I don't know.

From Antwon's attitude, I knew he'd either cosigned on whatever Bee had done, or hadn't done enough to stop him. Thinking that Antwon was somehow involved in Bee's departure stung me, because I thought he and I had developed a really good rapport. He also fought professionally, and I served as his primary sparring partner. We had gone nearly 50 rounds in prepping him for an upcoming fight. I had even gotten the *Washington City Paper* to do a front-page story on the fight, which Antwon won with a first-round knockout.

All the work I'd put in with Bee and Antwon and *bam!* Just like that, I was no longer Bee's manager. It was like all my work meant nothing. Bee avoided me and I didn't go out of my way to find him, either.

Several months later, I heard Bee was scheduled to fight George Khalid Jones on ESPN2. I later learned it was a short-notice bout that came through Adrian. Promoters frequently called Adrian for fights, and every time he had approached me about Bee taking one of those bouts, I politely turned down the offer. These fights were always against a tough opponent backed by the promoter offering the fight. In essence, Adrian's guy was generally being brought in to lose, and the Jones fight was no different. He was an undefeated light heavyweight with fifteen victories, eleven by knockout. He was a tall southpaw who had started his career as a cruiserweight. He was now fighting 20 pounds below his former weight, in part due to a recent stint in prison that had led to a serious lifestyle change after a conversion to Islam.

The fight was being held on the *USS Intrepid*, a World War II naval ship harbored in New York City, and Jones was from nearby Paterson, New Jersey. His promoter and manager was the legendary Lou Duva, the man largely responsible for the careers of great boxers like Evander Holyfield, Pernell "Sweet Pea" Whitaker, and Meldrick Taylor.

At the weigh-in, Jones came in at 174.75 pounds while Bee was only 170.75 pounds. Bee had never fought above the super-middleweight limit of 168 pounds. Making matters even worse, I later discovered that Bee hadn't worked out for days leading up to the fight because he had twisted an ankle during a run.

After the first few rounds in the fight, Jones began landing some serious blows. Several times, Max Kellerman, the ESPN2 analyst, mentioned that the referee should consider stopping the bout. But Bee hung tough and eked out a few of the later rounds on the scorecards. In the tenth and final round, Bee fell to the canvas with less than a minute remaining, and the referee waved the fight off. As Bee lay on the canvas, dejected, I felt vindicated. I had been wronged and part of me wanted him to pay for what he did to me. I sent a few emails to friends who knew what had transpired between Bee and me.

The next day, I was working at one of the Karibu stores when Henry "Discombobulating" Jones, a local ring announcer and one of the few decent people I had befriended in boxing, called me.

"You see the fight last night?" he asked.

"Yeah, I saw Bee get knocked out. That's what he gets for leaving me the way he did."

"Did you know that Bee was in the hospital? Look on the front page of Fightnews.com."

I hung up the phone and logged on to Fightnews.com. Bee was in a coma after undergoing two surgeries to relieve swelling on the brain and was in critical condition at New York's Bellevue Hospital. The sense of satisfaction I had felt from seeing Bee on the canvas the night before turned to astonishment. Six days later, on Tuesday, July 2, 2001, Bee died—the official cause was listed as "blunt impacts to the head with subdural hemorrhage."

Bee's death received national attention. *GQ* magazine did a story. National and local news programs ran coverage. Reporters from the *Washington Post, USA Today,* and other papers wrote stories. Senator McCain, a champion of boxing reform, called for "a thorough and complete investigation" into Bee's death. His wife even filed a lawsuit through Johnnie Cochran's law firm. Poor management was never mentioned as playing a role in Bee's death.

Bee's funeral was held at Metropolitan Baptist Church, and his wife asked me to serve as a pallbearer. George Khalid Jones and Lou Duva were in attendance, as well as many other people from the local boxing community. Antwon spoke during the services. I never met the guy who had taken over managing Bee.

Bee and I never spoke again after the day I took him to get that neurological exam in Baltimore. Antwon told me that Bee had admitted to him that at least I kept him busy fighting. As the person who had nurtured Bee, guided him through the amateurs, and was there every step of the way, Antwon took the loss very hard. The harsh truth was that Antwon and Bee's new manager didn't make Bee stick to Antwon's game plan, and the resulting tragedy weighed heavily on Antwon.

Real fighters fight, and Bee was a real fighter. There was no quit in him once he stepped into that ring. The energy that brought Bee to boxing is the same thing that brought me and many others to the sport. I've always known that true fighters place themselves in very vulnerable positions. They're risk-takers, and they need caring people on their team who can protect them from themselves. I truly believed I had done that for Bee as his manager, and that put my heart at rest when I pondered his tragic end.

When I thought back on my meeting with Mr. Trainer, I had

to admit that his advice was very prescient. There were only a few good people that I'd met in the boxing world. I'd certainly been used, in terms of my time and financial resources. But I still appreciated the experience I gained being involved with the sweet science, Bee's death notwithstanding.

Before my foray into boxing began in the fall of 1998, that year had been quite challenging for me. First, I had finally obtained my master's degree in African studies from HU after nearly seven years of juggling ADO, Karibu, and my various personal issues. I was fortunate that my professors gave me a lot of flexibility in taking African thought and applying it to what I was trying to do with Karibu. My thesis paper used the philosophy of Amílcar Cabral as a foundation for examining black bookstores as sites of cultural resistance in the United States.

DJ Renegade, who was Cape Verdean, had first turned me onto Cabral. Cabral was a Cape Verdean born in nearby Guinea-Bissau who became an agronomist after studying in Portugal. After gaining immense knowledge of the various languages and cultures of the peoples living in the Guinea-Bissau countryside, he used this knowledge to become the leader of the independence struggle against the Portuguese colonial masters. Though he was less well known, many considered Cabral's revolutionary ideas as highly as those of Che Guevara and Frantz Fanon. He was murdered in 1973, but the political group he helped form, the African Party for the Independence of Guinea and Cape Verde (PAIGC), won independence for both countries eight months after his death. Amazingly, his ideas even inspired the Portuguese soldiers he was fighting against to stage a successful military takeover of the authoritarian regime in Lisbon upon returning from the war in Guinea-Bissau.

As much as I enjoyed studying and learning, I didn't have any interest in pursuing a PhD. Teaching at a university didn't appeal to me. I didn't see it as being practical enough. From my viewpoint, building a financially viable cultural institution offered me an opportunity to take things beyond the theoretical. Accomplishing this with Karibu, I now believed, would be the greatest contribution I could make toward the struggle of African peoples.

The second challenge I faced concerned Karibu itself. The four-year lease we had signed for our PG store was nearly up, and negotiations for a renewal were at a stalemate. When the leasing agent I was negotiating with surprised me with a letter giving us 30 days to vacate the premises, it was like getting hit by a vicious left hook. I was staggered so badly that I slept in the store after reading the letter that night, and I informed Yao the next day that I feared my time with Karibu was done.

Fortunately, the general manager of the mall, Henry Watford, helped me navigate through the situation. In a matter of months, I had climbed off the canvas and negotiated Karibu's expansion into a store twice the size of its previous space. We also miraculously obtained new financing for the store and reopened in early August. In a relatively short time, our PG location generated a million dollars in revenue annually. Before 1998 came to a close, we also opened a kiosk at an enclosed mall in Forestville, Maryland, which gave Karibu three locations. As the company approached its sixth year, I had a sense that we weren't pushing uphill anymore. We had momentum on our side.

I was proud that our commitment to accounting played a critical factor in all of this. A few years after forming Karibu, we retained Carter & Associates, a local accounting firm owned by a friend named Patrick Carter, to compile our year-end financial statements. The cost wasn't cheap, especially considering our struggles at the time, but we were able to use those documents to secure Small Business Administration (SBA) loans to cover the costs of the business's expansion. Yao and I understood that having timely and accurate financial statements gave banks and potential investors a clear picture of our business. We refused to allow anything that was under our control to limit our potential growth.

My primary role was to oversee Karibu's expansion. I scoped out prospective locations, negotiated leases, created budgets for store build-outs, and obtained the financing needed for all of it. I also was responsible for supervising the receiving department, located in the basement of our PG store.

Meanwhile, Yao focused more on operations. He hired and diligently trained a new buyer, named Ayem, who was responsible for submitting weekly orders to publishers and wholesalers to restock the company's shelves and fill customer special orders. Yao also wanted to take on the challenge of handling the company's bookkeeping, and he became proficient in a high-end accounting software program to maintain the books and produce internal financial statements.

We ended up putting a lot of money into the build-out of each Karibu location in order to establish and uphold a high standard for our customers. Each store had hardwood floors, custom-built bookshelves, and good-looking storefront and in-store signage. We always tried to implement the latest inventory control and point-of-sale technology in our stores. Yao and I read *Publishers Weekly* religiously in order to stay up on the trends in the bookselling and publishing industries.

Though Yao and I were responsible for Karibu on a macro level, we didn't feel that either of us could afford to step away from the day-to-day store operations. Each of us managed a store, with the idea that this would help us lead our growing number of employees by example. We attempted to demonstrate that the revenue Karibu generated was a by-product of the great service we provided our customers.

As a team, I felt Yao and I balanced each other out pretty well. I was the risk-taker, the one who was always willing to make big moves and chase down opportunities for the business. Yao was more deliberate and thorough when implementing a new idea.

If you're going to run a bookstore, it really helps to love everything about books. Both of us loved literature and were always willing to engage people in conversation about it. Yao was generally more into poetry, fiction, and religious books, while my interests ran more to history, biography, and business titles. We genuinely enjoyed discussing books, and the people in the community who came out to our stores responded well to us.

The hard work and long hours we put in really began to pay off. By the end of the 2001 holiday season, we had added two more stores to the fold. In October 2000, we opened a store in Iverson Mall, and exactly one year later we opened our largest location yet at a brand-new outdoor mall called Bowie Town Center. The company now had four stores and one kiosk, all in PG County. DJ Renegade's advice back when we were vending at HU had served Karibu quite well.

Everything was going so well with Karibu that it seemed like even unexpected misfortune couldn't slow us down. After Lerner Enterprises, which owned Landover Mall, shut the entire place down in 2002, we rebounded a few months later by opening a unique location in the common area of the Pentagon City Mall in Arlington, Virginia. We then expanded our Forestville kiosk into a store in November 2003.

By the time Karibu opened its sixth store on Black Friday in 2005, at Security Square Mall in Baltimore County, we were recognized as the largest black-owned bookselling business in the country. Our sales were closing in on $4 million annually. We had nearly 50 full- and part-time employees. The company had established credit terms with hundreds of book publishers and distributors. We had even published a few books ourselves, and produced DJ Renegade's poetry CD. I began to envision Karibu existing in every mall frequented by people of African descent. In fact, several people talked to Yao and me about having a regional and even a national presence.

The company became the darling of the country's black book-selling community. Other owners, people who wanted to become booksellers themselves, and even some people from the major publishing companies, were calling us seeking advice. I started serving on the advisory board of the American Booksellers Association (ABA), the nation's lead organization for independent booksellers. Yao accepted an invitation to join the board of trustees for the Hurston/Wright Foundation, an advocacy group for black writers.

Karibu hired a full-time marketing executive named Lee McDonald, and she elevated that aspect of the business to the point where our stores became go-to destinations for established and new authors who wanted to promote their books with readings and signings. We hosted numerous author events featuring both heavyweight literary and pop authors, such as Toni Morrison, Patti LaBelle, E. Lynn Harris, Cornel West, Spike Lee, Terry McMillan, Maya Angelou, and Johnnie Cochran.

As well as things seemed to be going, as with so many partnerships, there were issues between me and Yao. These really broke into the open about five years into our partnership, or roughly around 1998. Unlike me, Yao was raising a family at the same time we were building Karibu. I didn't have those same burdens.

Though Yao worked diligently on Karibu's growth, every year, and with every expansion, he would remind me about all of the new challenges Karibu would have to confront. When we succeeded in overcoming them, there were always more. Our conversations about these were constant.

Yao had a passion for poetry, and he often talked about how his responsibilities to family and Karibu kept him away from writing. He was one of the most sensitive men I'd ever known. For my part, I tended to operate with a focused tunnel vision that sometimes caused me to disregard the feelings of the people around me. At times, I thought of myself as being only as good as what I was going after. If I had a goal, I would run as fast as I could to reach it. The end result was what mattered most, and I often failed to see the emotional damage that resulted from the effort to get there.

My relationship with Yao was almost completely focused on Karibu. We never developed the type of closeness he had with other guys, or that I shared with Singleton. Yao was more of a family man, while I was generally on the go. Due to the issues in my own family, I looked at Singleton and a few of my other closest street buddies from childhood as being like my family. Outside of our time in ADO together, Yao and I didn't share that kind of history. Even though we were both college educated, Yao was from suburban Maryland, while I was rooted in the inner city of DC. When I wanted to attend a boxing event, or go see Frankie Beverly and Maze in concert, or engage in conversations about beautiful women, Singleton was my guy. Even though I had only known Brother Eric through ADO, I felt more comfortable speaking with him about personal issues, due in part to the fact that he, too, had grown up in Southeast DC. My connection with Yao was all about Karibu. Eventually, the work environment, at times, became an uncomfortable place to be.

In spite of these internal issues, Karibu was booming. Yao and I began getting advice from a DC law firm about expanding Karibu nationally. We strategized with two lawyers at the firm on the best way to seek investors for new store openings in select communities throughout the country. The lawyers were also helping us work out an investment arrangement with an NBA player who wanted to get involved with Karibu. I became aware, though, that the attorneys could see the conflicts affecting our partnership. I think some of the Karibu managers were also becoming aware of these conflicts.

Selling books for a living put me in front of people every day, and conversing with them was part of doing good business. I enjoyed engaging in what was often pleasant and meaningful dialogue. Invariably, this also gave me opportunities to meet women. Nearly all of the women I dated, or attempted to date, after leaving Ernst & Young came into my life through Karibu.

Most of these women I met on my own. But in the spring of 1993, the year Karibu started, Yao introduced me to one who ended up playing an enormous role in my life. I was vending at an event in HU's Blackburn Center. Yao stopped by to check on things, and a student he knew from his own time there walked up and started talking to him. She was cute, with big eyes, locks, and an earthy, African-centered style.

After they finished talking, I asked Yao about her and discovered that she was a local jazz singer named Monica Jones. He introduced us before she left. Noticing that I was interested in her, Yao called me a few days later and told me that she was scheduled to sing at a downtown club later that week.

The Ascot Restaurant & Lounge was a modest, dimly-lit room with tables spread throughout. Monica was the featured guest singer for a trumpeter giving his final local performance before moving out west. The event was well attended, but I didn't know anyone there. I was hoping Monica would remember me if I got the opportunity to speak with her after the show. She was good, and blessed with a wonderful stage presence. But I was disappointed when she dedicated a tune to her fiancé, who happened to be in attendance.

In the course of running into Monica on HU's campus and around DC over the ensuing months, we developed a friendship. Sometimes, when I was dropping my mother off at the Barney Senior Center, I would see Monica waiting for the bus in Adams Morgan, so I'd pick her up on my way to vend at HU. I could always make her laugh and she was very easy to talk to, a good and patient listener. Later that year, I went with her to see trumpeter Roy Hargrove perform at Blues Alley. He was one of my favorite jazz artists, and I was thrilled when Monica told me she knew him from her time living in New York. She introduced me to him after his band's stellar performance.

Monica eventually told me that she wanted to set me up with her best friend. She arranged for the three of us to meet at a movie theater in Mazza Gallerie to see *Sankofa*. It was clear there was no mutual interest, but Monica handed me her friend's phone number from the passenger seat of the car just before they pulled off. Her friend and I had barely said a word to each other after the film. Sometime later, Monica came up to my vending stand at HU's campus and asked, "Why haven't you called my friend?" I did my best to dodge the question and not tell her how I really felt. A few days later, though, on the telephone, I mustered up the courage to tell her, "I want to meet one of your friends who looks more like you."

I never called Monica's friend, and Monica never introduced me to any more of her girlfriends. Instead, she came with me to an ADO program at Lorton, on an occasion when I was the main speaker. After that, she started going to Lorton with me on a regular basis. I remember looking at her one day during a discussion with a group of inmates at Lorton in April of 1995, and in that moment, I made up my mind to go for it. That evening, I called her and said, "I would like to put in an application."

She replied simply, "I accept."

Our first date was a dinner Monica prepared for me at her apartment in Adams Morgan. The fact that she was four years older than I was didn't bother me, but she asked me to promise not to divulge her age to anyone else. That night she talked a lot about the Peruvian spiritualist writer Carlos Castaneda, who at that time I had not yet read.

Not long after, Monica told me she was in the midst of a kind of sabbatical from sex, a temporary celibacy period. It was a commitment she had made to herself after breaking up with her previous boyfriend. I considered myself a soldier for the long haul, so I told her that I was willing to hold out until "whenever."

On several occasions, Monica was adamant that she wanted to know, immediately, if I ever developed feelings for another woman. She didn't have the type of positive relationships I had with my former love interests. Aside from the guy who chose to marry his girlfriend, the other guys she'd been with had either been abusive or unfaithful, and she wanted nothing to do with them. Her real displeasure and pain, though, was focused on her father. Their relationship was distant; he'd had very limited involvement in her upbringing. He was married and still living in the area, but even though I expressed an interest in meeting him, Monica refused to call him.

The relationship Monica and I had wasn't plagued with such issues. I wasn't abusive. I didn't have any interest in being with someone else. I never saw myself as not being involved with any future children we might have. Things were going pretty smoothly. One day, while hanging out at her place, she surprised me by announcing that her temporary celibacy period was over. After six months, we finally had our first night together. In the morning, after we were awake but still lying in bed, Monica had a smile on her face that just wouldn't quit. As I looked at her, wrapped up in her own thoughts, I couldn't help myself, and blurted out, "You just happy to have a man!"

Monica couldn't deny it. It was all over her face.

By early 1996, though, Monica started complaining that I wasn't spending enough time with her. I told her that Karibu and grad school took up all of my time—but she then pointed out my habit of slipping off to the movies alone, something I'd done for years. She also didn't understand why I visited her place so infrequently.

I made excuses, but the real truth was that I couldn't explain why I didn't spend more time with her—in part because I didn't understand it myself. She was everything I told myself I wanted in a woman. I'd pined for Monica Jones and I felt lucky to be dating her. Yet I felt uneasy whenever the words "I love you" rolled off my tongue. My behavior was a mystery to me, and I didn't know how to articulate any of this, so I simply made a promise to her: "Once I finish grad school and Karibu gets stable, we'll spend more time together. You'll see; next year will be *our* year."

On the night I received that vicious letter from the leasing agent representing the Mall at Prince George's in the winter of 1998, I also received a voicemail from Monica. She was breaking up with me. My promise to spend more time with her had gone unfulfilled, and she was fed up. I was distraught.

Within a few days, I convinced Monica to take me back. I didn't like the idea of being alone. A few months later, we were talking on the phone when she made an announcement: "I would like to get married, and I would like for the person I marry to be you. If you're not trying to, then I'm gonna have to move on."

We had been together for three years, but the idea of marrying her was not in my plans. I wasn't going to be forced into something like that, so we broke up again. My thoughts turned again to a woman named Cynthia, who I had known since the first grade at St. Anthony's. After Karen and I broke up, I had dated Cynthia off and on, but her lack of black consciousness dampened my passion. Monica and Cynthia were familiar with each other and were friendly, but while I was with Monica, she had frequently accused me of having feelings for Cynthia. Eventually, my feelings for Cynthia were overtaken by my guilt and fear concerning Monica.

I daydreamed about being with Cynthia, but I felt guilty over breaking up with Monica. Why was I reluctant to marry her? What was wrong with me? Would I ever be able to find another woman who was as good for me as Monica? I struggled with all of these questions, but Monica represented everything I believed I wanted in a woman. Soon, Monica and I were engaged; we made plans to be married in the fall of 1998. She moved into the apartment in Southeast where I was living after my mother died.

As the wedding date drew closer, though, doubt kept rearing its head. The sort of feelings I'd always imagined having for my future wife just weren't there. I discussed this with a friend who told me that if Monica had at least 85 percent of what I was looking for in a woman, then I would do well to marry her. I felt confident placing a check in that box, but I still had general feelings of doubt. One main question obsessed me: *What if there's someone else out there I'm supposed to be with?*

Around this time I began a process of reflecting on and considering all the other women I'd most cared about or been attracted to in my life, past and present, to somehow gauge whether my feelings for Monica would transcend how I'd felt about all the others. I even reached out to a few of these women in the effort to better understand how my feelings for them compared to what I felt for Monica.

Though I didn't disclose any of the details to her, Monica knew I was going through this elimination process, and she seemed okay with it—especially once I realized I didn't care for anyone else I'd ever met as much as I cared for her. She was also okay with the fact that I'd recently filed papers to legally change my name to Simba Sana, which was Kiswahili. *Sana* means "to make or forge," and I wanted to choose a name that represented movement and action. My journey to find my father had left me feeling unfulfilled, with no attachment to my given name. Simba Sana just felt right to me.

On October 10, 1998, Monica and I were married in DC in a simple, nontraditional ceremony. Yao served as my best man, and the same girlfriend Monica had tried to set me up with served as her maid of honor. Some of my family members from North Carolina were there, and the day was quite lovely.

We didn't do the honeymoon thing, because I wanted to stay focused on work. A year later, we purchased a house in Bloomingdale Northwest. Our plan was to enjoy our marriage for three years, then have a child. Our daughter Zendaya was born on the night of March 20, 2001.

Now that we had a child, I saw it as my duty to work even harder to provide, so we saw each other even less. I remained married to my work. The issues Monica had with our not spending time together never got better.

Love

THERE WAS ONE PARTICULAR LINE IN THE HIT 1995 movie *Heat* that really hit home with me—when Al Pacino told his estranged wife that he was only as good as what he was going after. It was as if something in the darkened theater slipped down from the screen, ascended from the floor, and poked me in the chest. That movie was so good that I saw it twice in the same week, and though it was years before Karibu's takeoff, my marriage, or my deep involvement in boxing, Pacino's onscreen admission echoed in my mind from time to time.

By this stage of my life, I was starting to struggle to understand myself better. The Pacino character's admission was relevant to me because I understood that I was almost completely task-driven in how I approached things. I began to wonder about my lack of emotion. I often used to wonder what it felt like to be a machine; I mean, if it were possible for a machine to feel, what would that be like? Like most guys, I got excited when a pretty woman walked by and would occasionally get upset about certain things. I could get teary-eyed watching a movie, and I would swear that Donnie Hathaway, my favorite male singer, possessed the gift of osmosis with his ability to convey feelings. But by this point in my life,

I began to wonder whether some of the emotional components existing in a typical human being were missing in me. I was becoming more aware that I didn't seem to have the same emotional experiences as others around me.

But the life I'd created for myself by this time was such a maelstrom of daily activity that it didn't allow for very much introspection. I was a workhorse and I thrived on getting things done. "I can see you drawing a line through one of your to-do-list items as we speak," a young woman once said to me over the phone when we were discussing a business matter. And that's exactly what I was doing. I had achieved a lot in my life up to this point, and along the way I'd built up a level of self-confidence that told me there was almost nothing I couldn't accomplish. The success I was finding with Karibu fed my ego more than anything. My narrow-minded focus on building Karibu opened the door to my fostering some unhealthy relationships: the most critical being the one with myself.

By this time, my preoccupation with the sweet science was second only to my involvement with Karibu. Watching major fights on the weekends, serving as a sparring partner, and sometimes even forgoing my normal running route to drive up Route 50 so I could personally do early-morning roadwork with my fighter gobbled up much of my off-work time.

Monica had never tried to discourage my involvement with Bee's career and even attended a few of his fights. But on the day of his funeral, we got into an argument and she stayed home. To me this was telling; though I couldn't be sure, I thought that resentment over all the time I had spent with Bee must have been at the root of her refusal to attend.

By the time Zendaya was born in March 2001, Bee and I had parted ways, and he died just over three months later, so boxing pretty much became a non-issue. When I occasionally went to a fight or sought some other respite from my daily routine, Singleton was still my main hangin' buddy.

Monica and I were rarely together unless we were visiting someone or attending an event. On the days I picked Zendaya up from the Howard University Early Learning Program (HUELP), Monica would be working or visiting friends. When she was with Zendaya, I was at one of the stores. By the time Zendaya was about three, she would sometimes ask why we didn't spend time together as a family. That innocent question spoke directly to the disconnect in our five-year-old marriage.

Karibu had grown to the point where the company could afford to hire managers for every store. I was still the receiving manager at PG, so I was very familiar with that location's staff. The manager there told me about a personal problem one of his part-time staff was having. Daphne, who was a very solid evening worker, had been dating a guy for six years, despite the fact that he had a live-in girlfriend. According to her, the guy was very controlling; she'd recently broken off their arrangement, and now she feared for her safety.

Daphne was someone I'd barely noticed to this point. Every time I saw her, she was wearing loose-fitting jeans and tennis shoes, and I viewed her as a bit timid and weak-minded. The situation she'd created for herself only furthered that impression. However, I had a genuine concern for her well-being, and her predicament, which was resolved without incident, led to our getting to know each other. She eventually felt comfortable enough to intimate that her previous demeanor toward me had been shaped in part by her sense that I was rigorous and stern.

Daphne, who was the same age as me, was from the South and had come to DC to attend HU. As was typical with most blacks from out of town, she knew very little about inner-city DC. She wanted to hear live go-go music, so I offered to take her to hear Lissen Band, which at the time was the hottest group on the scene. I had taken a female employee and her sister out to hear go-go music one time before, and it hadn't caused any uneasiness with

Monica. In my mind, this outing appeared to be just as innocent, and, besides, Singleton was coming along too.

On a Friday in early summer, I picked Daphne up from her brother's apartment in Northwest DC. She jumped in the car wearing a tight-fitting beige outfit with some heeled boots, and her hair was styled in a cute, medium-sized Afro. She looked completely different from how I'd ever seen her before. My man Singleton, who we picked up en route to the club, was all over Daphne for much of the night. When he finally left her alone on the crowded dance floor, she came running over to me and said, in a little-girl voice, "Some guy smacked me on the butt as I was making my way through the crowd." She had a fish-out-of-water quality that, combined with the ex-boyfriend situation I'd helped her with, made me feel that I needed to protect her. At least, that's what I told myself. And she definitely gave off the impression of being available, or at least easily approachable. My earlier judgment of her had morphed into a kind of interested concern.

Before long, Daphne became one of our go-to people for selling books at off-site events (where the store would bring books to sell at an author event or festival). She agreed to cover one event in July 2003, and asked if it was okay to bring a friend who was in town for the weekend. Monica was out of town and Zendaya was away visiting family, so I decided to stop by the event and then take them to hear Lissen Band afterward. I told myself this was another innocent outing—but the timing of it, the fact that Singleton wasn't going to be there, and the slight ripples of excitement in my toes were telling signs.

Upon my arrival, I was surprised to learn that Daphne's friend, Kamiya, and I already knew each other. She had been in my auditing class during my internship at HU—and she looked almost exactly the same as she had nearly fifteen years before. In other words, she was still the same girl I hadn't had the nerve to approach at the bus stop on Georgia Avenue. My delight at realizing who she was came to me at the same instant as a quick stab of regret.

After the off-site event, I drove the three of us to hear Lissen perform at a club on U Street Northwest. Curtbone and a few of his boys were there, and the band was crankin'. Toward the end of the concert, Kamiya, who was standing beside me, looked up at me affectionately, and said, "The band sounds really good. I'm really enjoying myself." The look she put on me made a dude feel real good.

Later that night, I was lying in bed, my mind all wrapped up in thoughts of Kamiya. I still couldn't get over how good she looked, and how lucky I felt to have run into her again. The fact that she lived in Miami, and I knew I needed to travel there in several months, only made me fantasize more about her and what could have been. Even after Monica came back from her trip, I'd be lying in bed next to her but I'd be thinking about Kamiya. I'd never thought this much about another woman since I'd gotten married. Usually my energies were focused entirely on work. It was as if some dormant part of me was suddenly awakened. I didn't understand how this woman, someone I hadn't seen in so many years, and had never really known well, could evoke so much emotion in me that my wife couldn't.

Of course, I felt guilty about this. I still thought of Monica as the perfect partner for me. Even though I knew she didn't elicit certain feelings from me, I thought this meant that I was simply not an emotional dude. Or that perhaps something else was wrong with me.

Kamiya was causing all of these feelings to tumble out of me that I hadn't known existed. What this was like is not easy to explain. As it is for a lot of people, Friday is my favorite day of the week. For me, this is especially true of Friday afternoon, when I can really start to taste the coming weekend's succulent possibilities. Even a disappointing weekend can't dull the allure of next

Friday, especially if you're knowingly or unknowingly seeking something. Every moment I thought about Kamiya placed me in this Friday-like mindset. The idea of being with Kamiya became a pleasant mental escape.

It was one thing to lose myself in my work and not spend much time with my wife. It was another thing altogether to have these kinds of powerful feelings for another woman. Though I sometimes vacillated, privately, about my romantic feelings for Monica, I knew that our relationship was solid. But Kamiya had awakened a fervor in me that I couldn't contain. This, more than anything, helped me come to a huge realization: I didn't have those kinds of feelings for my wife.

During a summer weekend trip we took together to New York City, I made a difficult announcement to Monica. I admitted to her, as I had admitted to myself, that I didn't love her. Then I readied myself for her angry reaction. But to my surprise, there was none—and I did my best to keep the discussion about our relationship short. I also didn't want to open any doors for her to ask what might have spurred my confession.

Whether due to guilt over admitting that I didn't love Monica, or for some other psychological reason, I didn't pursue ending our marriage. Maybe if I had been a bit stronger at that point in my life, or more self-aware, I would have insisted that we take steps to end it immediately. My decision to confide in Monica about how I felt was my way of attempting to respect our relationship. Perhaps I hoped that *she* would suggest we part ways. Whatever the case, my fantasies about Kamiya continued unabated.

Later that month, Monica, Zendaya, and I went on a vacation to South Carolina, the first real getaway in our five-year marriage. After all this time, we had finally taken a vacation, but the irony was that I wanted to be elsewhere, and with someone besides my wife. While Monica and Zendaya were preoccupied in our room, I stepped out to call Daphne. As insensitive and desperate as this act may have been, my recent confession had freed me from some of my psychological burden. I felt compelled to act on my thoughts about Kamiya by telling someone else about them besides Singleton—someone who could possibly help me to fulfill my desires.

Her mood was somber as I confided in her about my feelings for Kamiya. When I finished, she said, "I'm happy for you two." But she refused to give me Kamiya's number when I asked. And I could tell, despite what she'd said, that she wasn't really happy for me or for Kamiya. Acknowledging the truth of my feelings for Monica, coupled with my irrational fixation, led me to make a desperate move. I got the main office number at the company where Kamiya worked, and the operator connected me to her. She politely listened to me explain how I felt about her. I told her that my marriage was an unhappy one—and I took the extra step of telling Kamiya that it would be ending soon. Then I told her about my upcoming trip to Miami in December and asked if we could see each other there. She seemed very flattered by all the effort I'd expended to get in touch with her, including my brief conversation with Daphne. In a very pleasant tone, however, she rejected my request to see her.

Strangely enough, I wasn't too upset or disappointed by this result. All of the buildup, all of my fantasizing about Kamiya, faded away just as quickly as it had come upon me. Again, at the time I had no explanation for why this was happening—I still didn't really understand how and why I was experiencing all these different feelings. But now I had a less exciting thing to deal with: marriage to a woman I now understood I did not love.

I couldn't avoid the reality of how I'd failed Monica. As a husband, I may have been a good provider, but my inability to make an emotional connection with my wife was bottom-basement low.

In this sense, my foolhardy pursuit of Kamiya wasn't a total disaster. It helped me to another powerful realization: I wasn't completely lacking in human emotion after all. I had just gotten myself into a relationship where I was unable to realize or express those emotions. But getting to know Daphne and running into Kamiya had opened me up to a part of myself that had been in hiding. Now that the vault was open, I was in the mindset of a Friday afternoon.

My hope, given how easily our talk in New York had gone, was that Monica and I could make a smooth transition from husband and wife to being just friends. After we returned from our trip, I waited about a week before saying anything. We were both getting dressed early one morning when I told her, as casually as I could, that I wanted to buy a small, multi-unit building somewhere in Northeast or Southeast and live in one of the apartments, so we could separate. Monica's reaction, however, was not casual, and what I took from it was that any effort on my part to end our marriage would result in difficulty. Based on how well our conversation had gone in New York, my initial reaction to this was surprise—and still more overwhelming guilt.

The following months moved along with no issues, at least on the surface. In October of 2003, we celebrated our fifth wedding anniversary with an overnight stay in a hotel in Georgetown. Monica seemed content with how things were going, but now there was something else brewing in me.

As crazy as it seemed, it had to do with Daphne. I couldn't believe it, even though it was happening inside of me. Whatever *it* was I didn't have a name for at the time. But *urge*, I later learned, was the best word to describe the force driving my actions. I was told this happened to busy people, especially men, when they reached a certain age. The company's stability had allowed my life to slow up enough for my newly released roving eye to begin having its time. That this was happening at Karibu, the place where I spent most of my time, was not surprising, in retrospect. Whenever I saw Daphne at the PG store, I started getting goose bumps. She dressed no differently than she had before, but her appearance suddenly began to have an effect on me. It became harder and harder to concentrate on my work. I even began taking notice of and responding to a fragrance she wore.

She invited me eat with her at the Outback Steakhouse in the mall one afternoon. She was nicely dressed in blue slacks and a lighter-colored blouse. It was quite a pleasant change to see her walking toward me in heels rather than in her usual tennis shoes. As we sat down and conversed over a nice little meal, she told me that Kamiya had bragged to her about my impromptu phone call to her job. At the time, I didn't understand the depth or history of their relationship. My mind was far removed from all that—because now, increasingly, all I could think about was *Daphne*. I wanted to tell her how I was feeling, but knowing that she was aware of how I'd felt about Kamiya so recently held me back. I resigned myself to taking pleasure in just being with her.

I struggled every day with the urge to act on my feelings for Daphne. But I still couldn't come up with a comfortable way to broach the subject with her—until I got some help from the last place I would've ever expected it.

Monica was headed off for a trip to New York, and we had a difficult conversation before she left. Clearly, she hadn't forgotten about my admission, or my statement about moving out. During her weekend away, I made plans to invite a few friends, including Daphne, to our house Saturday night to watch the Roy Jones vs. Antonio Tarver fight. Daphne was the second person to arrive. While my buddies were in the basement watching one of the preliminary bouts, Daphne and I sat at the dining room table and talked.

"The feelings I thought I had for Kamiya were mistaken. It was really you all along who I was developing feelings for. I just didn't understand it at the time," I revealed to her.

"I feel the same way for you," she admitted. I was excited; my urge to be with someone else had found another resting place. She didn't flinch when I told her that I was going to let Monica know about my feelings for her, and that I wanted to be with her. Just as with Kamiya, I easily convinced myself that it was love fueling my desire to be with Daphne.

I didn't understand that Monica's permission wasn't required in order for me to end our marriage, but psychologically, that was how I felt. When she returned, I told her I wanted to be with Daphne, and now she responded in a way that made it clear to me that my admissions were causing her pain.

I related this later to Daphne in a phone call, and she reacted with dismay. She explained that she wasn't looking for a serious relationship. Now I was in a quandary. I had just been rejected—or at least, set back—by the woman I had told my wife I wanted to leave her for. Thinking about being with Daphne had been so pleasurable that I had convinced myself we would be together. Clearly, whatever I was feeling didn't match up with the reality of the situation. At bottom, I was disappointed that the feeling I had viewed as love was terribly misplaced.

But I still wanted her. The lofty dream of being with Daphne degenerated into an intense urge to simply be with her sexually. Now, I was cornered by my sexual desire on one side and the powerful guilt I felt about leaving Monica on the other. In secret, I made arrangements to meet Daphne on an early Friday afternoon at a parking lot near the University of Maryland, College Park. From there, I drove us to a hotel. The excitement building inside of me was far beyond anything I had ever experienced with Monica.

After I quickly undressed, Daphne took control: she put me on my back and commenced giving me the best blowjob I'd ever experienced. In these moments, there was no business to run. There was nothing requiring me to exert all my energy and focus to accomplish a myriad of tasks. There was no need to be in control. I was thoroughly enjoying being submissive and vulnerable to the situation at hand.

Though I'd never been able to describe it, I understood at that moment that this is what I'd always wanted sexually. When Daphne finally brought me to the point of climax, I completely let go of myself. There was no pressure, no pain, and no struggle as I experienced an indescribable sense of joy. Everything that I'd built up around myself, from years of effort, momentarily ceased to exist.

After these moments passed, Daphne's whole disposition changed. She suddenly became a completely different person, sullen and distant. She wasn't down for any cuddling or even conversation. The excitement I'd felt on our way to the hotel was replaced by a cheap and unsatisfied sensation as we gathered our things and departed.

As soon as I walked through the foyer at home, I learned that my modest attempt to keep my rendezvous secret had failed.

As a result of the entire fiasco, Daphne, who had just been offered the job to become Karibu's new and much-needed buyer, left the company. Now, we had an important position to fill but no one to place in it. Yao was the only one at Karibu who could do the job, but as the COO, his time was very limited. My reaction was to leave the decision up to Yao. I felt bad about the possibility of him being burdened with extra work because my dealings with Daphne ultimately led to her departure. To my chagrin, Yao decided to hire Monica, who had been expressing an interest in working at the company. I began to feel more and more trapped in the work environment that had always been my refuge.

I now fully understood that I had deep personal issues that I had to address. An older friend had told me that a person's deeper personal issues generally showed themselves when that person reached his thirties. He suggested that I seek a therapist. I was 35, and I realized I had behaved so erratically with the whole Daphne debacle that this wasn't such a bad idea. This friend turned me onto his therapist, Mr. Harvin. We started having weekly one-on-one sessions at his downtown office. As I recounted what happened with

Kamiya and then Daphne, he interrupted me, asking, "I bet it felt good, didn't it?" He explained that what I'd felt for them was not love but merely lust and infatuation. "Love is something deeper," he assured me, without offering any further explanation.

Mr. Harvin's assessment was that the way I'd dealt with my harsh upbringing had caused me to develop workaholic tendencies, which had hardened me to the subtler things of life.

"You're always in motion. You need to be still sometimes and learn how to enjoy those moments," he advised.

He also told me that I'd made a mistake by telling Monica that I didn't love her. It was "the things you did for her that made her feel loved," he insisted. In his view, my admission had blown up the marriage, and it would have to be rebuilt if we were going to stay together.

"Very few marriages maintain the initial high that's there at the beginning," Mr. Harvin told me as reassurance. But the whole time he was talking, I was thinking, *But I want one of those special marriages.* I was still on empty about my marriage, but I continued going to the sessions. Mr. Harvin suggested we begin including my wife. After a few months of joint sessions, Mr. Harvin complimented me on the strides I'd made to rebuild our marriage.

My desire to leave the marriage had waned, but I still wasn't excited about it. I was like a boy who desperately wanted to leave home, so he joined the travelling circus, only to return after being duped out of all of his possessions. Therapy couldn't resolve what was always missing from my feelings. It did, however, help me delve further into myself, and further my understanding of what love was not.

From December until the middle of May of the following year, I didn't engage in sexual activity of any kind. Although Daphne periodically crossed my mind, I had no urge to call her. I even stopped masturbating. Sex, however, wasn't the main thing on my mind. It was what sex results in that preoccupied my thoughts.

Having two children had always been one of my primary aims for getting married. I'd spent so much lonely time by myself as an only child that I didn't want the same thing to happen to Zendaya.

A month after my final therapy session with Mr. Harvin, Monica and I began discussing a second child, and by the end of 2004, she was pregnant with a boy. Things between us became pretty settled again, but as before, we still weren't spending much time together. Monica and I developed a routine where we more or less split Zendaya's pick-up days during the workweek. On my non-pick-up days, I'd be off doing my thing. On the weekends, we did occasionally make time to do things as a family.

Besides working at Karibu and spending time with Zendaya, I was drawn back into boxing. In the spring of 2004, I started going to Midtown Youth Academy, an old gym located near 14th and Belmont Street Northwest. Three days a week there, Zendaya played games and learned how to jump rope from me while I labored under the tutelage of Eugene "Thunder" Hughes, an old-time former fighter who owned the gym.

Though Midtown was past its heyday, there were still some decent fighters who frequented the place. I sparred damn near every amateur and professional fighter there. Before long, I was serving as the primary sparring partner for Oliver Musampa, a Congolese raised in France who had come to the United States with a dream of becoming super-middleweight world champion. By this stage of my life, Karibu had become less of a challenge, and I realized how much I still enjoyed the whole experience of putting on gloves and headgear, spreading Vaseline over my face, climbing through the ropes, and practicing the art of hitting without getting hit. Boxing has been called "the theater of the unexpected," and that phrase perfectly describes what kept me feeling so alive in the ring. Unfortunately, I was still so focused on my own issues, and using boxing to bring some excitement to my life, that I never seriously considered finding an activity focused primarily on Zendaya. Despite my enjoyment of the sweet science, I vowed to stop boxing once my son Talib was born on August 14, 2005. Having an infant at home wouldn't allow time for being in the gym. Neither Monica nor I planned it, but four-year-old Zendaya was there to watch her little brother come into the world. Before the birthing, I figured that one of the nurses would make me take her out of the room, but everyone carried on as if she wasn't there. I thought it was wonderful that Zendaya got to see the whole thing. She was very attentive and calm throughout.

In honor of Talib's birth, Oliver and I did one last session of intense sparring, and thus ended my latest boxing stint. When Oliver then moved to New York to embark upon a professional career, I became his manager. That was something else I hadn't planned, but his good-naturedness and focus impressed me.

Having a second child failed to improve my frustrations with my marriage. Even before Talib's birth, the increasingly desperate urge for carnal pleasure had been one of my primary motives for planning a trip to Las Vegas that July. The other reason was to watch Bernard Hopkins fight. It had been ten years since I'd seen Hopkins win the middleweight title, and he had never relinquished it. He racked up a record-breaking 20 middleweight title defenses and became the undisputed champion of the division. This fight would be a defense against a young and strong former Olympian, Jermain "Bad Intentions" Taylor.

I had become such a fan of Hopkins that I had already travelled out of town on a few occasions to see him fight. I was on hand when he broke Carlos Monzón's record for middleweight title defenses in Reading, Pennsylvania in February of 2002, and I sat ringside two fights later with mixed emotions as he beat my friend and former two-time WBA middleweight champion, William Joppy, in Atlantic City in December of 2003. Those trips had been all about boxing.

This latest outing to watch Hopkins fight, though, seemed to be the perfect way to fulfill my sexual needs. I'd never been to Las Vegas, which was the undisputed capital of big boxing venues. Over the years I'd heard a lot about how prostitution was partly legal in Nevada, which I associated with an atmosphere of greater sexual license. One friend jokingly told me that a guy could hire a Jennifer Lopez look-alike for $150. Another told me that a brothel called the Chicken Ranch, located about 60 miles from Vegas in Nye County, was the place to go.

The thought of sleeping with a prostitute had never interested me before, but I was pretty desperate at this point. The sexual urge that drove me into the whole situation with Daphne had been quieted for a time afterward, but never left me. Now I wanted that thrill again—but this time, unlike two years earlier, I no longer had any thought or hope of leaving my marriage. Not only had my desire to leave the marriage subsided, but we'd even moved forward with having a second child.

Regardless of how it had helped me learn about myself, the situation with Daphne had ultimately been a fiasco. Now, paying for sex, and the emotional distance that entailed, had a greater appeal to me. I'd already travelled to many Hopkins fights; this time, I would have an added layer of secrecy and remove in my effort to find a sexual outlet.

My suite at the MGM Grand, the hotel/casino where the fight was being waged, was marvelous. I wasn't into gambling, but I enjoyed seeing the crowds and experiencing the casino atmosphere. The full experience of sitting ringside for a big fight in Vegas was, for me, almost better than the action itself. Watching all the boxing luminaries and celebrities in attendance styling and profiling was quite a sight.

The fight itself was kind of disappointing; Hopkins showed too much respect to Taylor and gave away the early rounds. He came on late and hurt Taylor with a right that caused him to fall back against the ropes. The crowd jumped to its feet, but Hopkins failed to get the knockout and lost a split decision. I had the pleasure of meeting Taylor after the fight. The humbleness he showed after I congratulated him on the victory made me feel better about Hopkins losing.

The crowd that spread out around the casino after the fight looked promising for what I had in mind—even *I* could tell, by the way they sort of hung around the casino floor, which women were prostitutes. While they seemed easily approachable, the problem was that none of them were attractive to me. If I was gonna give myself over to a prostitute, I wanted it to be someone who appealed to me physically.

The next morning, I saw Hopkins himself walking through a lower-level corridor of the MGM. He was moving briskly with several family members in tow, wearing a baseball cap tight over his head, and shades—probably in an effort to keep a low profile or hide any puffiness around the eyes (Hopkins was remarkable for never sustaining cuts during his fights). Quite naturally, he wasn't in a jovial mood, but a woman I approached from his group told me it was okay to greet him. As I walked up, he stopped briefly, turned in my direction, and shook my hand. After I expressed how good it was to meet him, he gave me a stern yet polite thank-you before continuing down the walkway.

I had woken up with the much-heralded Chicken Ranch on my mind. I called and spoke to a woman who I assumed was the madam. I inquired about the number of available black women there, and she told me two were currently in residence. (While I had been seriously attracted to Shelley during my time at the Mount, my radicalization into Black Nationalism and Pan-Africanism kept me from looking at white girls in any kind of sexual/romantic way.)

The openness of the road and surrounding hills along my route to the Chicken Ranch provided a peaceful respite. When I arrived in the early afternoon, the parking area surrounding the old-fashioned house was largely empty. The madam I had spoken to over the phone promptly guided me to an empty saloon filled with thick, dark-brown tables. Shortly thereafter, two scantily dressed black women sat down at my table to begin our little encounter.

We engaged in some tense, uneasy banter; right away, I felt like a fraud for trying to act interested in two women who were totally unappealing to me physically. They reminded me of the prostitutes I had seen after the fight. It was hard for me to concentrate on anything they were saying. All I was thinking about was the time, effort, and money it had cost me to come out there. I couldn't take it, so I got up and spoke to the madam.

In response to my request to see more women, regardless of color, the madam leaned over and pressed a buzzer. All the women on the Ranch came scrambling into the main room, where the madam and I were, and lined up across the back wall. I noticed the two black women in the line and I felt embarrassed. They knew I wasn't going to pick one of them.

I hurriedly scanned the line for an attractive woman, but no one stood out from the group. *I came all this way for this? I've got to blend with somebody!* But I couldn't find one who caught my eye, and as the seconds passed, the pressure to pick someone came down on me hard. I started glancing from left to right as several of the women shifted back and forth and began muttering unpleasant words about me. A few more seconds passed before I finally caved to the pressure and selected a generously shaped white woman.

By this point, everything felt wrong. Once we reached her room, she began running down some prices for various services. And they weren't cheap. That did it; I mumbled something and bolted from the room in embarrassment, zooming past the madam at the front desk on my way to the rental car. Whatever the Ranch had to offer other men, it just wasn't for me. When my flight touched down at National Airport, I felt even more sexually frustrated than when I had departed.

After Talib was born, my wife and I would still have sex occasionally, but I still didn't feel any real connection with her. For whatever reason, I could not surrender to her sexually. After each time we were together, I would get up early in the morning to put in four miles of roadwork, then be off to Karibu.

When Hopkins secured a rematch with Taylor back in Vegas, at the Mandalay Bay, that December, I made plans to return despite the frustration I'd experienced the first time. This time, however, I was determined not to come away from the trip unsatisfied. A few months before the fight, I began courting Rachel, a younger woman I met through a former Karibu employee, and eventually I invited her to stay with me in Vegas. She knew about my wife, but she readily agreed to go. I planned to fly out early to catch the weigh-in and take in the prefight atmosphere, while she would arrive on the morning of the fight.

The main highlights of the fight, for me, were seeing Mike Tyson up close and talking to the legendary trainer Emanuel Steward, one of my favorite personalities in boxing. The rematch was almost identical to the first fight: a slow and cautious start, a second-half surge, and a controversial Hopkins loss by decision.

My room was in the swankiest part of the Mandalay Bay, an all-suite tower that was only accessible by taking some spiffy express elevators. Rachel absolutely adored the suite, but now that she was here, I didn't feel the same about her. Another fiasco! My determination to figure out a way to have sex with another woman in Vegas had blinded me to the fact that there was no chemistry between us.

I tried to make the best of the situation. We ate in a nice restaurant and walked around the resort. As we engaged in some pleasant conversation, I did my best not to beat up on myself for all the planning and expense I'd devoted to get Rachel out here, only to realize that she was doing nothing for me sexually. After we got back to the suite, neither of us made an attempt at being intimate. We slept on opposite ends of the bed.

Sunday morning, I couldn't wait to drop Rachel off at the airport. I was wild to somehow seek out another opportunity. On the night of the weigh-in, I had spotted a pretty young white woman in a long white dress getting off an elevator. I greeted her as I approached from the opposite direction, but she had walked past without acknowledging me or even saying a word. Then, on Sunday evening, I spotted her again standing by a fake palm tree near a bar across from the casino area. She was alone, dressed down this time in a pair of tight blue jeans, looking at the people dancing. In my desperation, I saw possibility in front of me. I quickly gathered up some nerve and asked her how she was doing.

"What do you want?" she snapped, as she turned and glared at me.

"I just wanted to say hello to you. I didn't mean to offend you."

The young woman's face softened, and she told me her name was Rebecca. Though I hadn't been sure when I saw her on Friday, I now realized with certainty that she was working as a prostitute. Before long, I learned her price was $500, and she knew where the closest ATM could be found. When I placed those crisp $100 bills in her hand, I would've sworn to anyone that I was the one who was profiting from the exchange, not her. She could've demanded much more, and I would've gladly paid it.

I told Rebecca what she'd probably heard hundreds of times before from other men: Unhappily married. Internally miserable. Desperately in need of affection. We sat in the suite and talked for a while before things got physical. When I confessed that this was my first time with a prostitute, she was far from shocked. She made things comfortable for me. She complimented me on my tenderness and helped me put on a condom. Everything went smoothly. But just as I got into a nice rhythm with my stroke, she started repeating a phrase like a chant, a mantra.

"Fuck this white pussy. Fuck this white pussy."

The irony of her words slowed me up a bit. My political and

229

cultural beliefs had kept me away from pursuing white women ever since college, yet my sexual needs had finally broken through all that. Here I was gettin' down with a college-aged snow bunny, and even though she was a prostitute I felt more at ease with her sexually than I ever had with my wife. Getting with Rebecca was the first time I'd had intercourse with someone else since Monica and I first started dating. Those few minutes with Rebecca allowed me to climb out of the dungeon of sexual frustration in which I'd trapped myself. Despite the explicitly financial nature of our encounter, I experienced a measure of emotional liberty with her along with the pleasure.

Afterward, I tipped her another $100 to show my appreciation for the experience.

Amid these trips to Vegas, I knew I wanted and needed more. Not knowing where else to turn, I went back to Daphne. Our reconnecting required us to work through her initial anger at how things had gone down before. I told her I wasn't looking for a relationship, but I hoped she would be my mistress. She refused. She did get something out of the sexual chemistry that existed between us, but for the time being, she wanted to keep things nonphysical.

"You're going to have to get comfortable with the discomfort in our relationship," she told me.

I was so dissatisfied sexually that I readily accepted the terms she laid down. She lived with her boyfriend and I, of course, was still married, so we established a routine of talking on the phone during work hours and regularly meeting for lunch downtown.

Before long, Daphne had turned me out emotionally. She would ask me if I wanted her to wear certain outfits for lunch: skirts with no stockings, tight slacks with high-heeled shoes, hair pulled back or hair styled some other type of way. Every so often, she would tease me with a plan for us to get together after work. I'd get all excited and clear out my schedule, but the outing would never materialize. I was captivated by the sexual energy that existed between us.

When I told her that she was a master of seduction, she explained that, for her, it very often wasn't a conscious thing. From a young age, sex had always been a component of her relationships, and much of what she did or became involved in wasn't planned. "I would find myself in situations, and things would just happen," she confided. She was in therapy over issues stemming from her childhood, but she said that she didn't see any real hope of establishing a healthy long-term relationship; after all, despite the live-in boyfriend, she was now involved with me. My willingness to respect the boundaries she was setting made her feel comfortable enough to open up to me. This helped us develop a new, deeper, more open friendship. Daphne became like a female version of Singleton: things that I felt forced to keep to myself, when at home and at work, I could later discuss with her.

Despite everything that had happened previously, the closeness we developed caused me once again to wonder whether there was a deeper connection between us beyond just friendship. I was confused, and still trying to sort out the meaning of my deeper feelings. I had done the therapy thing, and wasn't sure it had more to offer me. My work with my therapist ended up focusing on patching up my marriage. But I had a friend, Ayem, Karibu's former buyer, who practiced Yoruba, a religion popular in certain parts of West Africa, the Caribbean, and South America. He was aware of my confusion, and he suggested I visit his spiritual guide for help. Mama Ime Kuti, an elderly woman always dressed in African lapa skirts, lived in a rented house in Beltsville, Maryland. With an air of authority, she listened patiently as I opened up to her about Daphne, my marriage, and the sexual urges bearing down on me. After consulting with the Ifa, Yoruba's oracle system, she told me that the relationship Daphne and I had established was close, but it would eventually lead me into darkness. The possibility of coming to love did exist with Monica, she said, but if I did not accomplish it—but continued to stay in the marriage anyway—then our children would resent me.

Some of the principles of the Yoruba religion intrigued me, and, as I knew I needed help to resolve the struggles over my search for love, these principles ultimately led me to place a lot of trust in Mama Kuti. I started making regular visits to see her. Every week, she talked about the various orishas, or minor gods, imbued with particular characteristics. When she explained that my energy was aligned with the Shango orisha, known for living a full life and having numerous women, I was pulled further in. I found it easy to open up to Mama Kuti about my intimate desires; the relief I found in talking to her was like stretching out on the beach on a cool summer evening.

I'd already made a lot of bad or inexplicable decisions. But my confused quest for love (or sexual satisfaction, at the very least) was making me as gullible as a third-grader. Before long Mama Kuti was also giving me guidance regarding the business, in particular my relationship with my partner. Over the months, I began engaging in additional Yoruba practices, and Mama Kuti became my spiritual guide. For her part, she started confiding in me about problems with her landlord, who lived upstairs. A take-care-of-your-mother sort of instinct kicked in, and when I discovered that the owner was open to selling, I took out a loan for the Beltsville house and put Mama Kuti's name on the title.

Emboldened by my newfound spiritual practice, I continued trying to satisfy my carnal urges. Whatever Daphne was giving me, it wasn't enough. I started yearning for a longer-term arrangement with a willing partner—a true mistress, not the friendship/flirtation I had with Daphne. I saw no way to leave my marriage. Having a wife, two children, and an ever-expanding business made the idea of leaving the marriage seem impossible. I even told my wife on one occasion that she needn't worry about my ever leaving her. This was not a promise without some cost, however. The only respite I could find in this situation was the excitement of being in the arms of another woman.

By the end of 2006, the basement of our house served as my sanctuary within the marriage. There was a lounge area consisting of a dark purple foldout couch and a 40-inch television. A water-filled, black leather Ringside heavy bag and a red double-end bag hung from exposed wooden joists in another area. My desktop computer and metal file cabinet were next to the basement window, facing the street. Everything I needed to keep myself preoccupied when away from Karibu, or not engaged with the kids, was here.

Night after night as one day transitioned to the next, I'd tell myself to go upstairs and get in bed next to Monica, like a good husband. But after getting some work done—and looking at pictures of attractive women online—the couch would call to me. Fantasies of being with other women, some I'd known and others I could only imagine meeting, dominated my thoughts. My penchant for sleeping in the basement, something I'd developed over the course of our marriage, had become my full-time modus operandi by the end of that year. We never applied the word "separation" to our living situation, but by January 2007, I gave up the pretense that we were sharing a bed together. After the children went to sleep and before they woke up, the basement was my home within the home.

I started breaking out of my normal routines. I'd always been very thrifty, spending virtually no money on myself, even as Karibu grew. In late January 2007, though, as I was walking by a watch store in Pentagon City Mall, a nice chronometer caught my eye. I walked in and tried it on. When the clerk told me it was an Omega Seamaster, with a price tag of $3,000, I uncharacteristically pulled out my platinum American Express card and paid for it after receiving a small unsolicited discount. I'd only purchased one other watch in my life, which had cost about $100.

I then went upstairs and bought a Dell computer and a snazzy flat-screen monitor. Then I walked into Nordstrom and picked up a few $100 Façonnable shirts. That was big for me—if a shirt was more than $50, I considered it to be too expensive. A few months later, I had a closet full of colorful Façonnable.

These were merely material items, but my behavior symbolized something of greater significance. The drudgery of my life had worn me down. The neglected me began to take over, and some of his actions were more honest but not so wholesome. January was also the month my search for a mistress began in earnest. I tried to keep my wife from knowing about my attempt to engage in extracurricular activities. My plan was to stay in the marriage and find another woman to fill the emotional and sexual gaps existing at home.

I didn't have much to hide. I pursued two attractive women who initially seemed open to being involved with a married man. We had the type of discussions that only a man as unfulfilled and wanting as me could hang his hat on. But after so much buildup, the prospect of any liaisons was snatched away when they both rejected my proposals. Desperation won out when I settled for sex with a prostitute at the Crystal City Virginia Marriott, and then later with a part-time stripper in Southeast DC.

Then I met a woman named Darcy during halftime of a Wizards basketball game at the Verizon Center. Darcy was a light-complexioned, voluptuous, and sharp-tongued real estate agent who had moved to DC from down South after getting separated from her husband. A few days after the Wizards game, we had lunch at Union Station. She was the only woman I'd ever met who openly bragged about her breast size. I didn't find Darcy to be as refined as the two other women I'd pursued, but she made up for that with her willingness to become involved with a married man. Since Darcy was a real estate agent, she offered the perfect cover for our mixing business and pleasure. One of the houses I'd purchased for investment purposes in Baltimore was undergoing renovations, and I planned on having Darcy sell it. In April 2007, I drove her to Baltimore on a Friday afternoon to see the house. Afterward, we had the rest of the day to ourselves. I decided to make a quick stop at the neighborhood mall, which was just up the street.

Mondawmin Mall was located in a tough area of Baltimore City and, like the old Landover Mall just outside of DC, was frequented primarily by lower- and working-class blacks. Since the curtain hadn't quite closed on the workweek, the mall was sparsely populated, but Darcy, dressed in tight jeans and a form-fitting blouse, was jolting most of the guys who happened to be walking around. Seeing so many other guys taken by her looks, combined with the fact that we still hadn't done anything of a sexual nature, should have heightened my desire for her, or so I thought. I had been courting her; on one occasion I even purchased a $50 bottle of pink Moët she'd requested I bring her as a prerequisite for an early-night rendezvous. When I had arrived panting heavily at her doorstep later than she had instructed, the bottle of Moët was permitted entrance, but I was left standing outside.

Now, the coveted day was upon me, but I felt no quickened heartbeat. Instead, I was possessed with a calm detachment from what was happening, which was bizarre for me while in the presence of a romantic interest. When we arrived back at Darcy's place, the strange sense of detachment stayed with me. She pulled out that turncoat bottle of pink Moët, but I wasn't into drinking wine, so she poured herself some. The chilled glass of Moët stared at us from a glass coffee table as we nestled on her brown leather sofa.

As we sat looking at some photos in one of her albums, I couldn't help but notice that she was topless in several of them. Periodically, she got up from the sofa, always making sure that her right breast brushed generously against my shoulder. Darcy was setting the stage, yet I still hadn't made a move, so she got a bit more direct.

"You need to stay with me this evening."

What I'd been diligently working toward for several months was finally within grasp. But once again, I faltered in the moment. The thing that overwhelmed me was how lurid it all suddenly seemed. And I wanted no part of it. So I left.

On my way out, I pulled out my cell phone and called Singleton, my most trusted confidante. "I just left Darcy's house. I can't do it, Joe!"

"What, you scared man?"

What was going on with me had nothing to do with fear. The next morning I sat on the living room couch with water-filled eyes as the springtime daylight shone outside our window. Monica was looking at me as I kept saying, "I have to do this! I have to do this!" And though I couldn't articulate what *this* was, I was able to state resolutely, "Whatever it is I'm looking for, it's not sex."

My mind had gone to a place I still couldn't understand. I had reached some type of impasse. I'd recently finished reading a spiritual novel called *Eleven Minutes*, by celebrated Brazilian writer Paulo Coelho, and the central point of the story was that to engage in sex without being in a loving relationship was to be in darkness.

In the days that followed, I began to notice that my urge to have sex, which had been unbearable for so long, was dissipating. At the same time, I no longer felt like I was alternating between an acute loneliness and a desperate yearning for intimacy. Those days were unexplainably pleasant. I was somehow more attuned to everyday life, and everything around me appeared more vivid. I remember that I kept grinning to myself like I was tipsy.

Not long after, I saw one of the two women I'd pursued the fall before for the first time since she'd rejected my proposal. I called out to her, and her body appeared to tense up when she recognized my voice, as if she were bracing herself, but she politely turned around to speak with me.

"I want to apologize for how disrespectful I was to you before," I said.

Her shoulders relaxed, and a smile of relief spread across her face. I was pleased that my apology could so visibly remove the tension my presence had obviously caused her. I felt a bit lighter myself. In fact, I wanted to unburden myself some more.

I contacted the other woman, and she agreed to meet me for lunch. After I apologized to her in similar fashion, she opened up and told me about her ex-husband and their failed marriage. For me, it was enjoyable to engage in a pleasant conversation with an attractive woman without feeling burdened by the base motive to have sex.

When I told Daphne about these encounters during our next lunch date, I was surprised to see her react angrily. Daphne, it was clear, enjoyed hearing about my mistress-seeking adventures; she didn't see why I felt the need to do what I'd done. For my part, I couldn't really give her a reason for my actions, or for why my feelings were changing. I didn't know how to explain that I was starting to understand that what I had been seeking was not bringing me the satisfaction I needed.

By this point in our relationship, Daphne and I had come quite a way in establishing what I felt was an unlikely but good friendship. She trusted me with things she felt uncomfortable sharing with her boyfriend. I'd held to my promise not to make any sexual advances toward her. I even offered her advice on getting back with her boyfriend when they'd briefly broken up. She let me know, on several occasions, that I was an important person in her life. For my part, Daphne was the woman I could open up to without being judged for my behavior. What I hadn't yet realized, however, and what Daphne's angry reaction was alerting me to, was that the path I was embarking upon would eventually leave me with nothing to confide in her about.

One woman I didn't apologize to was Darcy. Rightly or wrongly, her willingness to become my mistress didn't inspire me to extend her the same overture of contrition. After leaving her house that

Friday in April, I wanted no further dealings with her, business or pleasure. That meant I needed to find a new agent to sell the house in Baltimore.

I'd met a real estate agent named Trian on February 15, 2007, at the Black CEO Conference held at the Baltimore Convention Center. She was yet another woman I'd seen at the Verizon Center. She and her boyfriend, a guy named Dave I'd met through a mutual friend years before, would always enter during the second quarter of Wizards games, looking elegant as they walked to their front-row seats.

The Black CEO Conference was hosted by my old friend Finney, from the Mount. He contracted Karibu to sell books for Chris Gardner, author of the bestselling memoir *The Pursuit of Happyness*, which was later made into a movie produced by and starring Will Smith. Gardner had struggled to care for his young son during a time of homelessness, then overcame those circumstances to open his own successful stock brokerage company. Tavis Smiley would also be speaking. My plan had been to attend the luncheon to hear Smiley and then let two employees work Gardner's evening event, but Finney asked if I would come back for the dinner portion of the program.

That evening, I was walking with Finney's friend Anthony when I saw Trian standing alone at the back of the room, looking a bit sullen. She was dressed professionally in a red sweater, black slacks, and black patent leather shoes. I'd already seen her so many times at Verizon that I felt as if I already knew her, but we'd never met, so I decided to speak to her and introduce myself. The three of us exchanged business cards and made small talk. When Trian told us she'd originally planned to only attend the luncheon and hear Tavis Smiley speak, Anthony started going in on him.

I thought Anthony's criticism of Smiley was unfair. I was actually familiar with Tavis from doing numerous offsite events for him. He'd also come to Karibu plenty of times, and I knew the folks around him were pretty solid people, so I defended him. I told Trian and Anthony about the extent of my dealings with Tavis, and I cited the names of his publicist and road manager as evidence.

Trian looked at Anthony, then at me. "I agree with him," she said, nodding her head toward Anthony. I was pissed. At the next pause in our conversation, I politely excused myself and walked over to the signing table to check on my staff working the event. Despite that, though, I thought Trian was attractive and had a pleasant disposition, and she was clearly very professional. When Gardner started signing his books, I gave Trian a copy. However, I had no intention of doing business with her, and I threw her card in the trash as I departed the convention center.

A few weeks later, I was surprised to find an email in my inbox from Trian, thanking me for the copy of the book and reminding me that she was the woman I'd seen with Dave at the Wizards games. I sent an email back to her, noting that I hadn't seen her at the Verizon Center recently, and she replied that it was because she and Dave were no longer together. She gave me her contact information and offered to take on any needs I might have regarding real estate.

It was Thursday, May 3, 2007, when I met Trian just outside the parking garage in the Harborplace Mall and then drove us to the house for a tour. She liked the place and agreed to list it once the rehab work was completed. After we got back to Harborplace, she accepted my offer to treat her to lunch at the Cheesecake Factory.

Almost immediately after we began talking, I realized how intelligent she was. We talked about business, about Anthony and Dave, and about our families. She started talking about her deceased younger brother, Patrick. According to Trian, he'd lived a fascinating life, and she regretted how little they'd seen of each other as adults. Right in the midst of reminiscing about him, she stopped and said out loud, seemingly, to herself, "I never talk to anyone about my brother."

When I told her about Paulo Coelho's *Eleven Minutes* and the impact it had made on me, she suggested I read his most popular book, *The Alchemist*. By the time we finished talking, more than two hours had elapsed, and we parted ways with a promise to meet again the following week. I picked up *The Alchemist* that weekend and tried to email Trian about it on Sunday, but twice my email was bounced back, before the third one finally went through.

The following Wednesday I met Trian again, and as promised, I brought her a copy of *Eleven Minutes* and gave her my early opinion of *The Alchemist*, which I'd just started. I opened up to her about my unhappiness in my marriage, and I immediately felt a sense of relief. I had once again reached a point where the idea of staying in my marriage seemed unbearable. After listening to me for a few minutes, Trian expressed her belief that whenever things aren't working out between couples and they decide to part ways, then they should do so amicably. She was critical of men who tried to be financially unfair to their spouses during a divorce.

More and more I sensed there might be something special about Trian, though I couldn't put my finger on it. Instead of going straight home after, I took a little ride through the city. I just didn't want to go home. Earlier that day, Monica and I had gotten into a series of exchanges about the future of our relationship, in person and over email, and I knew we were going to get into it again when I returned to the house. When I finally pulled into the driveway, it was almost midnight, and the lights in the house were on. By the time I came through the back door, however, everything was dark. I headed straight to the basement with a sense of relief at having delayed our talk, at least for one more night. But just as I was settling in on the basement couch, I heard Monica coming down the stairs, and we started in again on the subject of our relationship and its future.

I felt that my recent arrival at an understanding that the desire for sex outside of one's marriage was unwholesome, coupled with my unwillingness to be committed to Monica, meant that our marriage was no longer tenable. I knew I wanted a committed relationship; I just didn't want it to be with her. I told her what I felt. Divorce had to be our next step, I believed; we began talking about that prospect. It had now been four years since I'd first realized I didn't love Monica. Finally, I thought, our marriage would be coming to an end.

The next morning was Friday, May 11. I was sitting on the living room couch reading *The Alchemist*. The story's protagonist, Santiago, had just met a girl named Fatima while travelling through the desert, and knew instantly that he loved her. When he looked in her eyes, it seemed to him as if the entire universe stood still. Upon seeing her for the second time, he professed his love to her.

At that moment, something came over me, too. It seemed like my mind froze, and, in that instant, I felt this immensity beyond description. In that instant, I also had a vision of Trian as an old woman. Somehow, I realized, it was as if Trian belonged to me, and I to her. I felt more certain about it than anything I'd ever felt in my entire life.

The words I'd spoken to Monica in the basement the previous night must have freed me, because sight and action became one. I jumped up from the couch, grabbed my cell phone, and ran out the back door to the middle of the alley. Instinctively, I knew that it was best for no one—especially my soon-to-be ex-wife—to hear what I was about to say. I dialed Trian's number and as soon as she answered, I swung for the fences.

"I don't care if you never speak to me again, but I must tell you this. I *know* that you're the one for me!"

My entire body was trembling. I recounted to her everything I'd learned and thought about her from the moment of our initial conversation. I told her that I would be happy to continue talking to her and meeting chastely until she knew me better, but that as far as I was concerned, my own feelings for her were clear. Before we finished talking, I asked if we could see each other later that night, but she was noncommittal.

Later that day, Trian sent me an email, in which she stressed that as much as she appreciated what I'd said, she would never consider having a relationship with a married man. I followed up with her several times, begging her to meet me that night, and she eventually agreed. Excitedly, I called Singleton and asked him to drive me there, because I wanted him to meet her. When I jumped in his ride a few hours later to head uptown, I told him, "This woman's going to be my next wife."

The next day, Trian mentioned that the latest issue of the *Washington Afro-American* newspaper contained a picture of her from a recent event. Since Karibu sold the *Afro*, it gave me the perfect opportunity to personally deliver several copies of the paper to her parents' house, where she was visiting that day.

They lived in a gated community in PG County, Maryland. The house was large, serene, and nicely decorated, and just beyond the back deck was a pleasant-looking lake. Trian's mother was very friendly. After I left, Trian told me that her mother had voiced some suspicions about my motives for being there. Since Trian hadn't told her about my profession of love, she tried to throw her off by telling her that I was married. Her mother didn't buy it.

Everything felt different now. For the first time in years, I felt unburdened of the emotional weight of maintaining my dreary marriage. I moved quickly to alter my life. Dealing with Monica was the first thing. I wanted to unburden myself in all respects. I was so excited about what was going on between Trian and me that I told Monica about my new relationship just three days after we discussed divorce.

I was taken aback, though, later, when Mama Kuti seemed displeased by the news. When I announced to her over the phone that I'd met someone, she got real quiet. Before we finished talking, she gave me an exceedingly long list of spiritual tasks to carry out in preparation for my next visit.

When that visit arrived, Mama Kuti was brooding as I entered the basement of the house. We sat on the couch, and I listened as she offered up an unfavorable spiritual assessment of my relationship. Undeterred, I requested that we consult the orishas. Typically, Mama Kuti used cowrie shells to communicate with them, but this time she cut up a coconut into four pieces and used them instead.

We posed question after question to the orishas. Mama Kuti would ask the questions as I tossed the coconut pieces. None of the readings she was giving me based on the various combinations were positive. According to her, Trian's supposed financial and emotional problems didn't bode well for a loving relationship. Even after the orishas indicated that Trian would be faithful to me, Mama Kuti added her own interpretation, as her index finger veered off at a 45-degree angle along the beige carpet: "She'll be faithful for a time but eventually will stray."

I was despondent. Here was the person to whom I'd entrusted my spiritual development, and spent almost a year confiding in about my search for love—and now she was telling me that the woman I knew I loved was not good for me. I believed Mama Kuti, with the help of the orishas, had the gift of foresight, but what she was telling me now went too far. If she'd advised me to take things slow with Trian based on us not knowing each other, I could have better accepted her advice. Her words, however, went beyond caution. She was, in essence, telling me that Trian was a damaged person and unworthy of marrying. In my heart, I knew that wasn't true. After I left Mama Kuti's house, I drove around for hours in a sad state with my cell phone turned off.

I met Trian at her office later that night. She'd been worrying; since that momentous Friday-morning phone call, we'd seen each other every day and spoken on the phone constantly. She'd been calling me, wondering what happened at Mama Kuti's. One look at my sullen face, and she knew something was wrong.

After I recounted what had occurred at Mama Kuti's, Trian was unfazed. She readily acknowledged that she wasn't perfect—she even showed me her earnings—but she took issue with her supposed unfaithfulness. She assured me that she'd never cheated on anyone she'd dated. She said she'd be happy to meet Mama Kuti to address her reading directly. Trian's response, and in particular her willingness to face Mama Kuti, impressed me. I also thought that her suspicion of Mama Kuti had some merit—how could someone claiming to be a spiritual guide make a false accusation about a stranger's character? The sight of Mama Kuti's finger veering off after she saw me smiling in reaction to the orishas' indication that Trian would be faithful was burned into my memory. The negative behavior she'd displayed since I first told her about Trian started me wondering. Had I been a mark all along?

Trian calmly brought up the house in Beltsville I'd purchased for Mama Kuti. Mama Kuti had promised to secure a tenant to help cut down the mortgage payments I was making, but she hadn't found anyone, and she'd made it clear she was unwilling to contribute anything toward the payments. Trian suggested that I get Mama Kuti to sign a quitclaim deed to surrender her ownership in the property—she said that if Mama Kuti was truly my friend, then she'd willingly take her name off the house's title.

When I spoke to Mama Kuti the next day, she got downright nasty. She tried to make it seem as if I was in the wrong for asking her to take her name off the title. When she finished making her point, the phone went *click*. I looked at my cell in shock, then immediately started driving toward Beltsville.

As I made my way up Route 1, I dialed Mama Kuti again. I was in a different state of mind when she answered. I was seething, and my tone of voice made that clear. She'd never heard me talk like this before. I informed her that I'd be at the house very soon.

I called Brother Ayem from the car and told him what happened. He confessed that she routinely hung up on him, too, which only infuriated me more. He tried to calm me down, but I was too far gone. I was angry with myself as much as with her. I felt foolish and helpless over putting myself in such a situation. When I arrived at the house, Mama Kuti either refused to answer the door or else had departed before I got there. I didn't have a key and decided against trying to break in, so I drove home after calming down.

When I told Trian about the incident, she offered to handle the situation. I left Mama Kuti a message letting her know that Trian would contact her. After several attempts to avoid her, Mama Kuti finally agreed to allow Trian to see the house. Amazingly, by the time their meeting concluded, Mama Kuti had offered Trian an apology, verbally committed to signing the quitclaim deed, and promised to move out.

Mama Kuti's sudden about-face confirmed what I feared about her. The opportunity to take advantage of me had probably been too good for her to pass up. When I first visited her, back when I'd been seeking answers about Daphne, she may have seen it as akin to stumbling upon a mark poking his way around in the dark. I told her what I was looking for, and she promised to serve as my guide in finding it. Her true intentions, it turned out, were not so positive.

Less than a week later, I pulled up in front of the house in Beltsville and saw two big moving crates sitting in the front yard. I didn't need Mama Kuti to tell me she was sorry for whatever she'd done. By signing the quitclaim deed and moving out, she did all the apologizing I could ask for.

Brother Ayem also stopped going to see Mama Kuti shortly thereafter. We had both been marks, and I had been the most foolish. But I didn't have any hard feelings. Despite her manipulations, I appreciated the things Mama Kuti told me that had been helpful in my struggles, and a few years later, I even reached out to her again to see how she was doing.

Getting to know Trian in the typical way of becoming familiar with someone wasn't a priority for me. Whatever had occurred to me on Friday, May 11, had told me all I needed to know about her. On the surface, however, we shared very few things in common. She was the product of a stable upbringing with two parents, and she'd had little to no exposure to the streets. Like me, she'd gone to private schools, but had spent a lot of time hanging with her white classmates. As a result, she wasn't too much into R&B or funk, and especially not go-go or jazz. She also didn't follow sports, despite having a father who was a radio sportscaster and a son, Jimmie, whose father was a former player for the Washington Redskins.

Trian also wasn't into black consciousness. Due to my involvement with the movement, she assumed that I was going to encourage her to grow locks or twisties and demand that she wear Birkenstock sandals. To her relief, I liked women in high heels as much as she enjoyed wearing them. Trian was elegant and favored business attire. I, on the other hand, didn't adhere to any sort of professional dress code. Jeans and athletic shoes were part of my daily uniform.

She loved holidays, especially Christmas, while I had no relationship to such family traditions. I hadn't celebrated Christmas since the age of five or six. While black consciousness and its general disdain for European holidays gave me a further reason to not celebrate Christmas, the truth was that I didn't celebrate holidays whether they were European or African. My childhood circumstances hadn't allowed me to develop any fond memories of holidays.

What we did share was a joy of reading books and watching romantic comedies. Both of us also had a tendency to go full tilt after becoming involved in a group or activity.

Most significantly, though, we had each refused to give up on finding love, despite spending years in unfulfilling relationships. Just a few months before my sudden Friday-morning profession of love, Trian, for the first time in her life, had made a conscious decision to be single. Before then, ever since she was a teenager, she had always had a boyfriend, fiancé, or husband. She even told a friend that she was going to stop dating because the next guy in her life would not only become her next husband, but he would also *know* that she was the one for him. In the first moments after my crazy Friday phone call, she remembered this promise to herself.

I struggled to find the best way to explain that alarming call and my subsequent behavior. My sense of *knowing* what I'd suddenly become aware of on that fateful morning wasn't a matter of choice, or making a decision. "I didn't choose you!" I stated emphatically to Trian on several occasions. I was simply doing, in effect, what I had been shown to do. How else could I have known she was *the* one despite being practically a stranger?

Sex, which until recently had occupied such a prominent place in my life, wasn't the focus of our relationship. I was certainly very much attracted to Trian, but I wasn't in any rush to have sex with her. We spent time discussing our previous relationships. During those conversations, I told her everything about my sexual experiences before and during my marriage. None of what I told Trian put her off. What mattered to her was seeing my words backed up by my behavior.

The twists and turns that brought Trian and me together caused me to see, quite intimately, how a series of little coincidences could culminate in one intense moment of clarity. I find it hilarious, looking back, to consider how my giving Trian a book entitled *The Pursuit of Happyness* brought us together.

The more Trian and I talked about our lives, the more we were amazed to find out that we'd been in separate orbits around each other for years. Trian had frequently attended events at my grade and high schools, but I never met her because I wasn't involved in any after-school activities. Both of us were 1986 high school graduates who had wanted to go to Georgetown University, but didn't apply. Instead, both of us applied to Syracuse University, where neither of us was accepted. When I told her about my having dated Karen, I discovered that she'd dated Karen's brother.

I continued taking steps to spend the rest of my life with Trian, one of which was telling her to pick out an engagement ring. After a few days, she emailed me a picture of one. On Friday, May 25, Singleton and I went to a fight card at the DC Armory to see the brothers Lamont and Anthony Peterson score TKO victories. I was fascinated by the Petersons because, like me, they were once homeless as little boys growing up in DC. My mother and I, at least, had had the benefit of staying in a shelter, but they were out in the streets shuffling between the Greyhound bus station and any other place they could find. After the fights ended, I went to Trian's condo in Southwest. I gave her a crumpled-up paper bag—but in it was a nicely packaged engagement ring purchased from the Tiny Jewel Box, a renowned antique jewelry store in downtown DC. After going to see her mom and dad, she accepted. My proposal came only two weeks after my crazy Friday-morning phone call; none of my actions had been instigated, or even in any way urged on, by Trian herself. I felt calm and certain.

From my freshman year at the Mount, when I'd started seriously reading books again, till the spring of 2007, when I read *Eleven Minutes*, I had largely avoided religious and spiritual books. The extent of my exposure to such literature was the New Testament Gospels, *The Negro Church in America* by E. Franklin Frazier, and *Message to the Blackman in America* by Elijah Muhammad.

That stuff just wasn't for me—or at least, that's how I felt during those years. The essential tools I used to make my way through life were reason, logic, planning, and determination. Coupled with enormous effort, these things made me feel unstoppable. For a long time, I had never looked for anything in life beyond my own thoughts, the knowledge I acquired, and the feeling of security I gained from my accomplishments. I had no real relationship to failure, because I'd managed to achieve nearly every goal I set for myself.

Love had been the one thing I just couldn't figure out, though, and the way it had now come into my life filled me with awe. The experience of coming to love forced me to begin searching, again, for a deeper understanding of life—this time, without the help of a spiritual guide. I was greatly aided in this quest when Trian introduced me to a man named Emmanuel, a dark-skinned Nigerian immigrant married to a nurse named Sue, who was white and from a conservative family. After Trian helped them purchase a home in Maryland, they'd become friends.

When Trian told them about her whirlwind engagement to this strange man, they asked to meet me. Emmanuel and I quickly slipped into a conversation about Africa. Seated in his comfortable lounge chair, drinking dark beer and talking good-naturedly about his country, he kept mentioning his spiritual guru back home. When I mentioned I was having some struggles in my life at the time, he offered to ask his guru a few questions on my behalf. But after my experience with Mama Kuti, I no longer saw the need for a spiritual guide or guru.

Before we left for the evening, though, he gave me a copy of a book called *The Awakening of Intelligence* by Jiddu Krishnamurti. The book was a collection of group discussions and interviews conducted by Krishnamurti over several decades during his travels through the United States, Europe, and India. Initially, the book frustrated me because of Krishnamurti's tendency to answer the questions posed to him by audience members and interviewers with another question. However, I quickly caught on and started to really enjoy it. Krishnamurti spoke about love in a way that seemed to me very unique and sensible. Until I read his book, I had no way of explaining what had led me to fall in love with Trian the way I had. It was easy for me to embrace what he was saying, because it was what I'd just experienced.

Krishnamurti had a profound way of looking at aspects of human existence outside of prevailing assumptions. One of his primary assertions had to do with the limitation of human thought. He pointed out that thinking was merely a response of memory, and thus always limited. This is similar to how a computer is always limited by its programming. As he saw it, memory was like programming in that it was limited to using past life experiences and acquired knowledge as the basis for human conditioning.

Thinking about Krishnamurti's ideas brought back to me the words of Marie Gadsden, an elderly woman I'd met through a professor right after graduating from the Mount. She had spent her career working for the United Nations, and lived for many years all over Africa. The professor had told me that she was very wise, so I made an effort to get to know her. At that time she was caring for her dying husband, and they were both very much in the twilight of their lives. During one of our visits, Mrs. Gadsden told me, "The more that you know, the more you know there is to know that you can never know."

I never forgot those words, but it took me nearly two decades to really appreciate and understand the meaning behind them. She was essentially saying the same thing as Krishnamurti; that is, there was a fundamental limitation to the acquired knowledge that I was using to guide myself through life. As long as I operated solely from this knowledge and conditioning, no matter how successful I became, my life would be defined by limitations and repetitiveness.

Now, I felt I was starting to be able to see that true reality, or the beyond, was unlimited in how it encompassed all possibilities, not just the knowledge I'd acquired in the past. The only way to experience this limitless reality was for the mind to accept its limitations. And by accepting its limitations, the mind could then move beyond itself.

Krishnamurti argued that this type of understanding was beyond one's mental or intellectual grasp, and could only occur when the mind was brought to stillness without effort; any effort applied to the mind to bring it to stillness was still within the realm of thought. Krishnamurti referred to this unforced stillness as a "timeless moment"—an instant without thought.

This was all new to me, but I connected with the phrase "a timeless moment" when Krishnamurti wrote about love. He kept reiterating that the way for someone to come to love was to first discover what love is not. This was as far as the mind could reach; by accepting this limitation, the mind could be brought to a timeless moment. After reading this, I thought back to my strange experience on that Friday morning. *Is that what I experienced that day?*

When Krishnamurti later described a timeless moment as sight and action being one, it seemed like he was actually describing what occurred to me. I thought about my mad dash from the living room couch to the alley to make that early-morning phone call to Trian. The moment before had been sudden, unexpected, and unforced. My natural intelligence, as Krishnamurti called it, had stepped in, moved my thoughts to a secondary place, and forced me into action. Krishnamurti's idea of the timeless moment seemed to characterize my own experience.

At first glance, what Krishnamurti was saying seemed counterintuitive, but when I put aside all of my preconceptions, it made sense. If love was sourced from the beyond, then it was undoubtedly unlimited, could not be fully understood by something as small as the mind, and would only come when thoughts were stilled. I discovered that this explained why I *knew* that I loved Trian in that instant, but didn't know why or how I knew.

Having been married to Monica, going through my degrading search for a mistress, and all of the rest of my dysfunctional behavior were all essential to the process of my coming to love. Those experiences brought my mind to its limitation; they taught me what love was not. When things didn't feel right in my personal life, the pursuit I embarked upon became an important part of this process.

At different periods in my relationship with Monica, it had seemed logical, or reasonable, or safe; but it had always been unfulfilling. Our relationship followed the pattern or formula I learned from the people around me. We had dated; we had shared information about ourselves; we had made a conscious commitment to each other. Our union was steeped in acquired knowledge, but also—at least on my part—fear and guilt. I was fearful of not being able to find someone better for me, and guilt-ridden over not loving someone who appeared to be giving me what I wanted. To me, the relationship never felt right, but I figured that, with effort and a determined will, I could grow to love her. Effort and will had everything to do with my success in life; why couldn't it help me find love?

But instead of my determined will assisting me, it only prolonged my misery. No matter how much effort I put into telling myself to spend time with Monica, there were always other things, such as building Karibu, managing Bee, keeping up with my reading, and caring for Zendaya and Talib, that were more of a priority. I could never bring myself to put the same level of energy and focus on my marriage that I put on these other responsibilities and commitments.

Work was my addiction of choice, and the social acceptance of that addiction helped me to get away with what I was doing—for a while. Work had helped me to escape poverty and the other painful circumstances of my childhood and young life. As money began to roll in and I accomplished goal after goal, it's true, I felt better and better about myself. The work, in and of itself, wasn't bad, but my attachment to it led me further and further away from my true self. I had fooled myself into believing that work was necessary for me to become the person I thought I had to become, instead of engaging in the all-important task of simply seeing who I already was.

My will kept moving me from one activity or project to another, but it never brought me comfort, and it never helped me strengthen my marriage. It was simply too difficult for me to give myself over to something that didn't capture my passion. When I finally slowed down from all the effort and exertion of will, the strong emotions that came out of me toward Kamiya and Daphne represented a respite from the dreariness and monotony of my emotional life. My mind was seeking an escape from the cage I'd been locked into by my determined will.

I looked back on my marriage with disappointment, but I came to accept that what happened had already happened, and there was nothing I could do about that. I needed an empty mind, free of all the clutter it had acquired, in order for my heart and soul to see, clearly, what I was doing.

In this regard, Tayari Casel, a highly respected martial artist who ran a school where Zendaya took classes, helped me realize how important my search for a mistress had been in discovering love. He and I conversed for hours one day at his school. I was telling him about having conquered Darcy on the day I drove her to Mondawmin Mall in Baltimore that Friday afternoon in April. He replied, "Naw brother—you conquered *yourself*."

Tayari was right. It was me, not someone else, who had been defeated on that day and, by doing so, I had unknowingly brought about the final discovery I needed of what love was not. Looking back, I saw what happened with Kamiya, Daphne, and all the rest as a blessing. My sexual urge, so long suppressed, had become exposed. Only after that could I deal with it head-on. To avoid doing so would only have made my inner conflicts, or demons as some might call them, that much stronger.

I could see clearly how the main point of Coelho's story about Maria's descent into prostitution in *Eleven Minutes* had played out in my own life. Like Maria in her own journey to love, I had to discover, in my own way and time, that sex without love was darkness. This type of awareness couldn't be forced by following a dictum or by chasing some ideal. Doing so would only lead me into further conflict with my inner urge to have sex. I had to work through my own disorder in order to come to a better place.

Having to confront my inner urges helped me to realize that cheating was much more than just a physical act. The act was only what could be seen, a mere symptom of something else. It was the inner urge that led to the act. Only the elimination of the inner urge could prevent the manifestation of the inappropriate act.

St. Augustine, the fourth-century African who was later considered the father of Western Catholicism, appreciated the difficulty of dealing with sexual urges. Upon learning that he'd have to forgo sex for two years after converting to Christianity, which meant dismissing his long-time mistress, he uttered his now famous prayer to God, "Grant me chastity and continence, but not yet."

Then, he promptly took a second mistress.

By seeing the ugliness of what my sexual impulses were doing to me and my life, and by then accepting my mind's limitations, I was finally allowed to stumble upon Trian. My upbringing and experiences had conditioned me away from using my innate natural intelligence as a guide.

Love, I came to understand, isn't a conscious thing, or some entity that can be constructed by the mind. Coming to love with Trian wasn't like my marriage or any other previous relationship I'd experienced, and it's nothing like what I'd heard love could be. And though I recognized and acknowledged Trian's beauty, I never had any urge to pursue her. Instead, I experienced, for the first time, love as recognition, a sense of knowing. There was no choice or decision involved. The desire for love had always been in my heart, but it was my journey toward self-discovery that unknowingly helped me experience it. In my case, once I recognized who Trian was, there was no desire to be with anyone else.

Honesty was essential in my quest for love. I wholly disagreed with my former therapist when he told me I shouldn't have admitted to Monica that I didn't love her. It was the truth; the real problem was my own failure to truly see it. Once I became aware of it, I realized that my pre-wedding ceremony behavior, such as not buying an engagement ring and visiting all those various women to compare them to Monica, were clear indications that I didn't love her. By openly acknowledging what was false about my feelings for her, I opened the door to discovering love.

With Trian, I was able to see myself more clearly. From the very beginning, I was honest with her about where I was. She knew about the general state of my marriage, and I made my intentions known to her every step of the way. When I got the inkling that my feelings with her were about more than just business, I told her. Honesty and vulnerability, from the beginning, were of greatest importance in dealing with Trian. Effort, will, and determination, which had always been the keys to how I approached life, played no role here.

Perhaps the greatest thing about coming to love this way was that I discovered it on my own. Reading what Krishnamurti and others had written about love certainly made it easier for me to talk about it, but my own experiences were the basis for this discovery, and nothing and no one could take that from me. I knew I'd done many foolish things over the course of my journey, but finding love made it well worth it.

I wasn't the same person as before. It felt good to move through life no longer alternating between emptiness and yearning to be with someone. I didn't need a rule or a commandment to follow in order to make myself believe that I was moral. Love itself was goodness, and coming to love with Trian allowed that goodness to permeate my being.

I began to contemplate the subject of love and came to recognize that it's been such a great mystery for humanity because we've always tried to understand it using thought. However, I no longer embrace the idea that any particular method or system of thought can grasp love, or bring it about. To really find love, you have to be willing to travel the often harsh and arduous road of self discovery, if necessary, in order to see yourself as you are at any given moment. Krishnamurti called this the clarity of self-knowing.

After reading Krishnamurti and contemplating his work, and my own experiences, I became disappointed by the paucity of good information on the subject of love. One day, while travelling through the city, I was hit by an urge to write down my own description of love. After about a month of poring over my thoughts and tweaking what I'd penned, I finally had something I considered a good description of that which really exists beyond description.

> **Love:** *a deep, never-ending connection, beyond words, that is discovered with no prescribed path, causing a life-altering commitment, not based on thought, knowledge, time, choice, or sex, and without motive, condition, or explanation.*

This description really says more about what love is *not* than what love *is*, but my hope in offering it is to point people in love's general direction, and more importantly, help them see how essential it is to engage in the work of self-discovery. At bottom, defining what love is isn't as important as experiencing it, because to experience it is to know it.

In fact, the human effort to explain and define what love is has led to our collective confusion. In my view, the notion, for example, that we can fall in and out of love with someone, which of course is widely accepted, is actually sadly mistaken. If God is love, as we so often quote from the New Testament, then loving someone else can't be temporary. God certainly isn't temporary. God simply is. Thus, love between two people doesn't fade over time, or due to circumstance, and only ends with physical demise.

I'm a movie buff, and I felt very fortunate to discover that romantic comedies are really onto something about love. The novelists and screenwriters responsible for these movies have figured out what nearly all of the philosophers have failed to uncover: that true love happens in an instant. The plot in romance movies is generally the same: the lead character begins to follow his or her desire for love, and so embarks on the simple-yet-difficult task of seeing him- or herself. And, like magic, the other person appears in his or her life. The consummation of the love relationship is oftentimes inconvenient, convoluted, and seemingly inappropriate, but in the end love always makes the finite world yield to its will.

Time and time again, the really good romantic comedies demonstrate that love is a noncausal occurrence: a case of meaningful coincidence, which brings with it a sense of knowing without the why or the how. Our problem as human beings is that we're afraid of thought being suspended long enough to allow this type of knowledge, which is the only true knowing, to inform us. This is why most marriages are not based on love.

I made many trips to the movie theater during my marriage to watch romantic films; these outings were really prayers and meditations on love. When I went to these movies, I would be alone, and it would be the middle of the day. During those two hours, I ate popcorn and fantasized about what didn't exist in my life. I was yearning for love.

Aside from my own happiness, there was another compelling reason for me to never stop seeking love. I was a human being who had fathered two children, and now I was on the verge of becoming a parent to a teenage boy. The words of James Baldwin were always hovering in and around my thoughts: "Children have never been very good at listening to their elders, but they have never failed to imitate them. They must, they have no other models."

For the children in my life, to see me in a loving relationship would mean more than anything I could say about love. Of course, this couldn't offer them any guarantee that they would find love, but, at the very least, my own journey could serve as an example of what is possible.

Wisdom

MY EXPERIENCE OF COMING TO LOVE WAS SUCH A MI-
raculous blessing that I was convinced life would get a little easier
for me. All of the wondering about finding the right one was over,
and I was no longer conflicted or torn between my desire to be
with another woman and my commitment to my marriage. In fact,
I was stripped of any desire to be with someone other than Trian,
and that commitment felt effortless, as it was not a thing of the
mind. Now, I was looking forward to continuing my life's work
and moving in the direction I'd chosen for myself.

However, the timeless moment I'd experienced represented a
demarcation point, a turn toward an even more intense journey of
self-discovery. There were many more things about myself that I
needed to learn in order to find out who I really was. I soon discovered that I knew nothing about my real purpose or destiny in life,
and my discovery of love opened the door to what I didn't know
about these things, and about the people around me.

My life began to shift in ways that were as startling as they were
painful, and I had to face the fact that my eagerness and haste were
contributing factors in this shift. I was blessed and cursed with a
tunnel-like focus that often created a lack of sensitivity to what was

happening around me. Clearly, this had been a huge problem in my marriage, but it affected many of my relationships. I was like Florentino, the lovelorn protagonist of Gabriel García Márquez's *Love in the Time of Cholera*. The film adaptation of this book is one of my favorites.

Toward the end of the film, Florentino is an old man and has just learned that the husband of Fermina, the woman he's loved since his youth but was not permitted to marry, has just died. No one tells him this, but he's so connected to Fermina that when he hears the ringing of the town's church bells, he senses that her husband has just died. He gets out of bed and promptly sends away his young and gorgeous American girlfriend, who had just been lying in his arms.

Unable to contain himself, he pays Fermina a visit just as she's coming back home from her husband's funeral. As she enters the foyer of her house, Florentino professes that he's loved her ever since he first laid eyes on her 51 years, 9 months and 4 days ago. Fermina, shocked, shouts at him about his grotesque insensitivity and throws him out.

Like Florentino, my quest for love overrode my life's other concerns. As more of my friends discovered that I was getting a divorce, some of them began conveying their feelings to me about my marriage. "Man, I never felt no connection between you two," Curtbone told me one day. Tonyson had expressed a similar sentiment after meeting Monica for the first time. Curtbone and Tonyson were guys who'd spent years surviving on the streets and in prison, in large part by developing their instincts about people. They were far more in touch with those kinds of things than I had ever been. The more I recognized this, the more I began to understand how naive and credulous I was in my dealings with other people. I'd certainly seen this play out with Mama Kuti, but that was only the beginning.

Several women around me also weighed in. During a conversation with a friend's wife named Elanna Gilmore, she asked me, rhetorically, "You have a low EQ, don't you?" At the time, I hadn't even heard of EQ, which stands for "emotional quotient"—I had to look it up on Wikipedia. During a phone conversation with my cousin Teresa, who lived in North Carolina, she offered me this personal insight: "From afar, I always had the feeling from watching you running around in groups that you were really looking for love. But one problem I see is that you don't understand boundaries."

Her comment caused me to think about Cliff Warren, one of my classmates at the Mount. During our first two years there, I disliked him; I thought he was selfish. Once we became roommates during our junior year, though, my viewpoint changed. Cliff was the basketball team's starting point guard and had a true passion for the sport. He also had the benefit of being raised by two loving parents, so he didn't have any overwhelming urge to look outside of his home for attention and affection. After we graduated, Cliff developed a successful career as a basketball coach, met the woman who became his wife, and together they eventually had two children.

Cliff was an adult with healthy relationships, and I was eventually able to see how he represented an important lesson for me. My long-ago dislike of him showed itself in a new light. Now I could see clearly, and for the very first time, that what I formerly didn't like about Cliff had to do with what I spent many years failing to understand about myself.

I gained even more insight into my habit of forming poor relationships from Trian. After dealing with Mama Kuti, meeting with a former mentor of mine who was working as the contractor for the Baltimore house, and then having a brief, unfriendly encounter with a third person close to me, she told me, "You don't realize that most of these people don't like you because they really don't like themselves."

Of course, by now Trian also knew all about my mother and the circumstances surrounding her death. One evening, she had an epiphany and sent me an email. In it, she outlined a theory that the tremendous guilt I felt over not spending more time with my mother once I'd become an adult had helped drive me into unhealthy relationships. Trian pointed out that from a very early age I'd shouldered the responsibility of being my mother's financial provider, and that even if she couldn't articulate her appreciation or her love, my mother surely must have felt those things, just as I struggled to express my love for her as well. My mom had shown me her love by fighting so hard to get me the best education possible. As Trian saw it, many of the choices I'd made about people after my mom's death were driven in part by a buried desire to punish myself, and that I'd felt undeserving of real happiness.

I wasn't certain whether I'd been beating up on myself and shying away from happiness, but I did recognize that I had a tendency to draw needy people into my life. Even I knew, on a conscious level, that you can't "save" anyone; yet, instead of just being a listening ear or trusted advisor, I spent years trying to solve the problems of some of the people around me. Later, at least two of the people I'd interacted with in this way expressed feelings of resentment toward me. Did all this stem from an inner need to make up for my unrealistic and unfulfilled hope of building a life for my mom?

When I realized how much my unconscious feelings about my mother were controlling my life, it was a breakthrough. I could now see how these feelings had shaped all the major relationships in my life. This realization was one thing—but getting myself untangled from these relationships was something else altogether.

Toward this effort, whatever may have been done to me by the people in my life during that time is of no relevance now. After all the emotions and angst over what occurred had subsided, my chief concern in telling this story was to focus on *my* behavior, *my* actions: the things that were within my realm of control. This, I feel, is the only way that looking at these experiences can provide some benefit to me and, I hope, others.

Ending my marriage to Monica was by no means an easy affair. I hired an attorney and we proposed terms for separation. Less than a month after proposing to Trian, I moved out of the basement of Monica's and my house on S Street. My attorney advised against such a move, but I felt that my continuing to sleep in the same house was no longer practical. For a week or so after moving out, I slept in my office at Karibu, in a sleeping bag. In the mornings, I picked the children up from the house and took them to school and day care. Within the next several weeks, I had moved in with Trian, who was renting a condo in Southwest.

Back in 2006, Monica and I had bought a second house in the Hillcrest neighborhood in Southeast, but we'd never moved from our old house on S Street. My hope was that Monica would move into the Hillcrest house and I would return to S Street.

It wouldn't be so simple. I asked my lawyer to file for divorce, but before he could get the paperwork ready, Monica had me served with divorce papers at Karibu's office.

Meanwhile, the company was at a critical juncture. On the positive side, we had an opportunity to expand the business. We had developed a new bookstore concept featuring a unique seating arrangement with a bistro, and I'd negotiated with the Mall at Prince George's to replace our flagship location with this prototype. Their leasing department was giving us $200,000 toward the store's build-out. A broker I'd been working with found us a venture capitalist who was planning to invest $1.4 million in the company. This infusion of capital would be enough to complete the build-out of the new store, pay off some debt, and open two additional stores in new markets. This would be our first step toward greater expansion, with the ultimate goal of opening stores in black-frequented malls throughout the country.

At the same time, however, the differences between me and Yao,

combined with a sudden downturn in sales, served to buckle Karibu's financial legs. Though we'd been discussing a buyout, we still
hadn't been able to work out a price. I'd made an initial offer based
on an earlier business valuation of $1.8 million. The operation that
made that valuation may have been overly generous in its assessment, but Karibu had been at its zenith when they conducted their
study of our business.

2006 brought a shift in the opposite direction. The differences
between Yao and me, which in earlier years had been so beneficial
to the business, now became points of overt contention. We now
had nearly 50 full-time and part-time employees, and I saw it was
becoming harder for them to miss the conflicts between the owners.
Employees began taking sides; morale began to slide. So did our
business. When the DC attorney I'd hired to help negotiate the
buyout used another operation to value our company, almost two
years after the first valuation, they placed Karibu's overall value at
less than $300,000.

With so much of my attention going to the company's internal
affairs, as well my own personal matters, I was overlooking what was
happening all around us. The world outside of Karibu's doors was
undergoing its own turmoil, at least economically. Our company's
growth had coincided with the dot-com and, later, real estate market
booms. The boom in the housing market had padded the pockets of
less-affluent people, and they converted much of their home-value
increases into spending capital. Karibu greatly benefitted from this.
But when the real estate market began its descent in 2006, it had
a direct and immediate negative impact on retail sales. Bookstores,
like most other retailers, experienced a downturn in sales. Karibu's
rise was over, yet I hadn't taken sufficient notice.

Yao and Karla scheduled our first-ever board meeting in early
August of 2007. With their two-thirds vote, I could simply be removed from my position as head of the company. I interpreted
this as a clever power play to take control of Karibu. But what they

didn't know was that over the past year, I had loaned Karibu more than $400,000 of my own money to keep the company afloat.

When they sat down at the conference table for the board meeting, which they'd convened at a community center in Largo, Maryland, a binder-clipped stack of financials was staring up at them—including the documents showing my loans to the company. I'd sent the same materials to Yao's attorney two days earlier via FedEx. Before the meeting commenced, I slid back from the big conference table, got up to depart, and told them, "Just let me know when you want the keys to the office." A few days later, Yao sent me an email informing me that I was in charge and that they'd be willing to accept $200,000 for their share of Karibu.

After nearly two years of conflict, I finally felt free to push through my vision for expanding the company. But since I was essentially going through two divorces simultaneously, my personal affairs became the big monster in the room. I was refusing to give up joint legal custody of our children, which led my wife and her legal team to reject my proposed terms of separation. My divorce case was now threatening Karibu's future—no investor would want to put money into a company embroiled in such a complex and potentially costly dispute.

I was facing another stalemate, but now a sense of financial desperation had set in. In addition to the personal funds I had put into Karibu, a friend loaned me $200,000 to aid Karibu until the investor funds could be injected. This loan, which was fully executed and secured with two homes I owned, was to be used to help Karibu's expansion into the new prototype store. Instead, in a desperate move, I used the funds to pay outstanding invoices from book suppliers. By the following month, invoices were due again, but there wasn't any more money to pay them.

When I told my friend how I had misused the loan money he'd supplied, he was livid. My intent had been to do what was necessary to keep Karibu afloat until things were sorted out, but I had to admit to my friend and to myself that my behavior had been dishonorable. My ambitions for Karibu had caused me to become fiscally irresponsible.

Just when one area of my life had finally come together, another was in a state of utter collapse. Several months after experiencing the wonderful timeless moment that led me to Trian, everything I'd worked so hard to build was falling apart. From nearly every angle, financial misfortune was striking out at me: from the fiasco with Mama Kuti, to the ownership conflict, to what now looked like it would be a protracted divorce case. Even a guy I trusted—a former mentor who had supervised me during my time working at Horning Brothers, and later worked with me on my personal and business properties—absconded with a significant amount of money when he realized financial trouble had come to my doorstep.

There didn't appear to be a practical or reasonable way for me to tackle the myriad issues facing me, yet all through this time I still had a sense that things would somehow get better for me financially. Every entrepreneur becomes used to overcoming what at first look like insoluble problems. And just as my timeless moment had shifted the focus of my reading, it also affected my outlook on getting things done.

How I came to love was such a confounding experience that it opened me up to notions I'd categorically rejected after the painful experiences of being displaced as a child. What I took from those childhood situations was that what happens in life is what you make happen, and generally through enormous effort. Coming to love, however, gave me the impression that I was simply acting out a part in a movie being directed by something outside of my control. If life could make love happen so quickly, so unexplainably, then maybe whatever else I needed would also be provided in similar fashion.

I became less concerned with the day-to-day, even somewhat detached. Being a bit worn out from shouldering so much responsibility for so long, and harboring an inner desire to be taken care of, allowed me to toy with fanciful thoughts such as winning the lottery or stumbling upon some other type of windfall. Thinking like this prevented me from overreacting to so much of the upheaval in my life at the time; however, it also rendered me more passive than I'd ever been. I was like a fighter who'd given away so many rounds due to inactivity that he needed a late-round knockout to pull out the victory. The self-belief I needed to get that knockout was still intact, though. The things that I'd managed to overcome during my life gave me that assurance. Whenever I placed my full effort into something, things almost always worked out for me.

However, that self-assurance worked against me in my custody situation. I made a bad misjudgment, in an incident where I picked my daughter up from school after she'd been called to the vice-principal's office for a disciplinary issue. When Zendaya took the opportunity to tell me what I thought was troubling information about her living situation, I decided to take matters into my own hands and take her home with me.

It felt good to come to my daughter's rescue and give her some much-needed attention. Zendaya finally met Trian, and they got along well. We stayed in Southwest that Friday, then slept at Trian's parents' house the following night. Zendaya told us she didn't like going to Brent Elementary, so I decided to give her a break from school for a few days. I made sure she spoke to Monica over the weekend and called the school on Monday morning to let them know of her absence. Later that day, I took Zendaya to HUELP to see her former teachers and schoolmates. The next day, we visited another school uptown to see how she liked it.

When I returned Zendaya to Brent Elementary on Wednesday, the police had alerted the school that I had taken her. The school counselor, who knew some of what was going on, advised me to depart quickly. I wasn't afraid of the police. My intention at the time was to be there for my daughter. But I never considered how my actions would appear in the eyes of the court. I hadn't yet been to court for any of my divorce proceedings, or discussed detailed strategy with my attorney regarding custody. But Monica and her attorney saw a judge that Monday morning, and this judge awarded her temporary full custody of our children. Legally, my not taking Zendaya to school for those two days was a grave mistake. It got worse. My attorney never told me that I could've challenged that temporary court order. When I finally convinced Monica to move from S Street by telling her that Trian and I were going to move elsewhere, I still wasn't able to spend time with Zendaya and Talib. It wasn't until a December 2007 court appearance that I was able to secure more time with them.

What was turning into a lengthy and difficult divorce case wasn't good for Karibu. As could have been predicted, no lottery win or other financial windfall appeared, so most of the publishers and distributors we ordered books from put a hold on our credit accounts with them. The downward spiral continued as inventory in the stores dwindled, and sales were steadily decreasing. I had run into my old boss Joe Horning at a Whole Foods on P Street Northwest some months previously, in late spring, and told him that I should've heeded his long-ago advice about doing a buy/sell agreement with Yao. I kept him updated about my troubles, and his acute business sense enabled him to offer me some timely advice. He called me in early January 2008 to tell me what I'd been avoiding for months: "You know it's time to shut things down." This time, I didn't toss his words in the trash bin.

On January 24, 2008, the *Washington Post* ran an article on its front page about Karibu's impending closure. The tensions between Yao and me were mentioned, and I was quoted as saying the company's demise was caused by the ownership's "failure to resolve conflict in a peaceful way and also a failure to end relationships amicably."

I did several radio interviews. Michael Baisden, who always did his DC-area book events at Karibu, invited me on his WHUR radio show, and I was also invited onto NPR programs *The Kojo Nnamdi Show* and *Tell Me More*, which was hosted by Michel Martin. My interview with Mrs. Martin went beyond discussing Karibu and its impact on the community. I also spoke about the importance of love, and I admitted that my search to become a whole person had much to do with Karibu's demise.

We initiated a company-wide going-out-of-business sale that brought customers in droves. When Karibu shut its doors on February 8, most of its inventory was gone and the company bank account had more than $125,000 in it. My plan was to use that money to reopen a few of our most profitable stores.

However, two incidents crushed any hope of keeping Karibu alive. First, Karibu still had several outstanding SBA loans, totaling close to $300,000, with Bank of America, and I discovered that the bank had simply taken whatever funds were available a day or two after we closed down. After the tirade I unleashed over the lost money had subsided, it was clear to me that I hadn't fully accepted the reality of Karibu's demise. Later, I learned that if you have funds in a bank you owe money to, that institution can "set-off" those funds by taking whatever is in your account.

Second, Yao had gone to court and convinced a judge to approve placing Karibu in receivership. A few weeks after Karibu closed, I came to the office only to discover that the locks had been changed. The computers and all the information contained therein were now under the control of an attorney appointed by the court. When I met with the attorney at his office uptown on Wisconsin Avenue, he asked me, "What would you say if I told you that I was coming after you?"

"I'd tell you to get in a very long line."

He simply smiled, and I never heard from him again.

As all this was going on, tensions between Monica and me escalated to an unhealthy level. The fact that our children, and Trian, got swept up in this conflict was a source of great and continuing pain to me, not least because I understood how deeply unfair this was to them. After realizing Trian was the one for me, I never considered not being with her. The timeless moment I'd experienced was the most meaningful experience of my life; I wasn't going to surrender the relationship that came about as a result. Whatever difficulties arose would somehow be overcome.

I was struggling, though. I felt boxed in by the situation at hand and I was angry about it. It seemed that the proper thing to do, under the circumstances, was to spare the children a custody fight with Monica. I wrote a letter to the court in April 2008 detailing some of the conflict we'd experienced and explaining why I was giving up custody. During a July court appearance, the judge said nothing about my letter as she awarded Monica full custody, with my consent. I only asked for, and was granted, the right to give Zendaya and Talib gifts on their respective birthdays.

I felt as though I had learned more about Monica during our divorce than I had the entire time we were married—or maybe, for the first time, I was simply paying attention to what she had always been showing me about herself. Before our divorce was finalized in the fall of 2008, I stumbled upon something she had misrepresented to me throughout our relationship. Perhaps she believed that being honest with me about it while we were dating would have damaged my view of her, or even caused me to back away from marrying her. When I questioned her, she refused to give me an answer. She finally admitted to lying to me about it in a letter she wrote me in the spring of 2009, after she learned that Trian and I had gotten married.

I wasn't upset that she had waited until after our divorce to make such an admission. To be clear, I was disappointed more by what I saw as her having been dishonest at the outset of our relationship, rather than whatever it was she was being dishonest about. In a way, I was also relieved. Her confession alleviated much of the guilt I harbored over not being able to connect with her during our marriage. I also saw it as further proof that we were never right for each other. More than anything, I was fascinated by the fact that something in me had always held a question in my mind about our relationship, going all the way back to when we were dating. What I didn't know then, and had just started to learn, was the importance of listening to my inner voice. If I had been more aware of it a decade earlier, I would have realized that the answer to the question that had come into my mind back then was in the question itself. Thus, I didn't need to look outside of myself for any answer.

My eyes had never been more open to the need to engage in self-inquiry. Getting out of the marriage taught me some costly lessons, as had my relationship with my business partner. My spirit had always been trying to speak to me, but I was too ignorant about myself to hear it. From those experiences, I learned that the beginning is really the end, and the end is really the beginning. How a relationship truly starts off is how it ends. There were early signs in both situations that I overlooked, and now those relationships were ending in pain, anger, and loss. This forced me to look at myself, because I was the common ingredient in each relationship.

These were not the only unhealthy relationships in my life, either. Over the years, I'd helped many people, and now I was in need of assistance, but people were either unable or unwilling to come to my aid. I didn't put out a press release or anything, but even the people who were aware of what was going on avoided me.

My relationship with Daphne ended for a different reason. As with everyone in my life, my sudden engagement to Trian had caught Daphne off guard. But instead of being surprised and then happy for me after her shock subsided, she became competitive. Before I arranged for Trian to meet Daphne over lunch at Lauriol Plaza in DuPont Circle NW, I told her every significant detail of our dealings. Daphne showed up wearing a suggestively short, tight skirt. Over the next two weeks, Daphne bombarded me with flirtatious phone calls. I felt there was no choice but for me to confront her.

"I noticed you been calling me a lot since you met Trian. What's this all about?"

"I feel like your relationship with her is going to change our friendship."

She apologized and slowed up on the calls, but her messages were just as suggestive as ever, if not more so. Before much longer I called to let her know that I felt our relationship had run its course. I knew she wasn't going to make it an easy parting. She cried, called me selfish, and tried to lay a serious guilt trip on me, but I held to my position. In hindsight, it was naive of me to expect Daphne to respect my new relationship, after she had seen me demonstrate such disregard for my marriage.

The end of my marriage served as the catalyst for the loss of most of what I'd worked for to this point in my life. It went quickly. By 2009, my business and all of my money were gone. My career as an entrepreneur, which I had worked so hard for so many years to establish, had imploded. My stellar credit rating had plummeted. All the real estate I owned, including the S Street residence, was facing foreclosure. Worst of all, I wasn't seeing Zendaya and Talib.

Throughout all this turmoil, my relationship with Trian remained strong. I had initially told her that things between Monica and me were friendly. When it was obvious that my divorce wasn't going to be amicable, I began travelling down that long and winding road to discovering whom I had married. It was a costly yet valuable journey, and Trian was supportive throughout.

The summer after Trian and I got together was quite enjoyable, but by the following spring my dire circumstances placed some unpleasant restraints on our relationship. Financially, I was handcuffed. Anything aside from going to see a movie was beyond my means at the time. For most of my life, I had been a provider above all; now true love had entered my existence, but money was disappearing from my life. Still, we kept a positive outlook on our future together. The worse my circumstances became, the more we clung to each other.

After Karibu closed in February 2008, I found it difficult to earn money. For months and months afterward, I was in a daze from severing my attachment to being the leader of Karibu. Most of my energy was spent gearing up for a custody fight and being in anguish over the kids. I began tapping into a stock portfolio valued at less than $50,000, since I had no other money coming in.

Trian's clear-mindedness helped me during the time I was still discombobulated from my financial fallout. When both of the cars I had were repossessed on the same night in late May, she offered some advice that helped me gain access to another vehicle to get around in.

Since my days hustling bags at Giant Food, I had always earned enough money to take care of myself. Working gave me a sense of value and allowed me to forge through many unpleasant circumstances. I took pride in being a breadwinner; now, I didn't know what to do. I'd lost my primary means of earning money at a point when I personally and professionally needed money the most. That all this was happening, in part, because of my effort to make an internal change for the better weighed on my mind as well.

I underwent a sort of mental shutdown, and my sense of practicality evaded me. This demonstrated itself in my refusal to file for bankruptcy. Trian brought up the subject on several occasions, but I wouldn't even discuss it. In my heart, I wanted to pay off my personal and business debts. I remember sitting at home watching Deepak Chopra, in a video entitled *The Seven Spiritual Laws of Success*, speak about never walking away from your debts, which further cemented my position.

I made things worse during a court appearance to which I was summoned regarding child support. The judge asked me what my income was, but I didn't have an answer; at the time, I had virtually none, so she tried a different approach, asking me, "Do you estimate you'll be able to earn $50,000 a year?"

"Oh yeah, definitely," I replied

If only I'd known better. Because of the success I'd experienced with Karibu, I was overconfident about making money. But having been immersed in Karibu for fifteen years also meant I'd been in a sort of bubble in which I didn't have to worry about things like updating my resume, going to interviews, or developing skills that would make me more appealing to potential employers.

Entrepreneurship was in my blood, but bookselling was not a profession that offered much transferability, at least in my case. In fact, shortly after Karibu's closing, retail bookselling underwent a serious downfall, in part due to increasing online and e-book sales. Bookstores were shutting down, not opening up. Even if my expansion plans for Karibu had taken off, the industry shift might have been too much to overcome.

Though it was devastating to me at the time, Karibu's collapse may have saved me from a bigger catastrophe down the road. In trying to save the company, I was willing to take on some challenging financial obligations, in what became a terrible recession, all while the retail book industry was dwindling. First, there would have been the buyout money that was going to come from the proposed investor's funds; second, the money my friend loaned me; and finally, the investor, like any reasonable business person, would've been seeking a healthy return.

Even beyond meeting those commitments, I don't know if Karibu could have made it through the period of stagnation and loss that affected the book industry after 2006. The DC/Maryland/Virginia area boasts one of the most educated and well-read populaces in the country, yet bookstores were shutting down throughout the region. In DC, for example, I think it's fair to say that Politics and Prose and Kramerbooks & Afterwords were the only two viable bookstores remaining after the economic downturn ended. Even the two retail book giants, Borders (which shut down in 2011) and Barnes & Noble, left the city. I had my concerns about whether I would've been able to steer the company through the challenges so many other stores failed to meet, but I remained eager, till the end, to take up the task. Running Karibu was the life I'd chosen.

The company's demise left me adrift. I'd gained a lot of confidence from being in business for fifteen years, but none of the projects I attempted in order to generate immediate income were working out. Bomani Armah, a local hip-hop poet and former Karibu employee, released a single in 2007 entitled "Read A Book" that received some national recognition. We worked out an agency contract, but I was unable to get him a book deal. I also helped my boxer friend William Joppy, who was on a recent win streak, sign with a promoter who got him a title shot. Unfortunately, he was near the end of his career. He lost the fight in Canada, and the management contract I presented him went unsigned. He was several fights away from retiring and was simply trying to cash out.

I was forced to look for a job, something I hadn't done since my senior year at the Mount. Back then, it was pretty easy, but now? I learned quickly that 40-year-old former owners of failed businesses weren't necessarily desirable to most employers.

Networking had always been a shortcoming of mine, and this affected me significantly during these difficult years. Joining the local Chamber of Commerce and things of that nature hadn't interested me in the least, especially as a committed Pan-Africanist. During the Karibu years, my professional dealings had mostly been with people in the book industry.

But with the loss of Karibu, all those connections, with the exception of a few, faded away. I'd established some pretty good relationships with several sales representatives at major publishing companies over the years. Karibu was a major account for these guys, but I quickly learned that our relationship was based largely on my company's helping them meet their sales numbers. I didn't get much response to my calls seeking help.

Unexpectedly, the head of an imprint at a major publishing company approached me with an idea for using Karibu's brand to establish an online presence. At that time, books about street life and sex were exploding in popularity among black readers, and I harbored some concerns about the types of titles this publisher was seeking to promote on the website. I was open to the proposal, but after a few preliminary conversations, the imprint dropped the idea without any explanation.

My financial situation became dire. I couldn't find decent-paying work, so I took on a few low-wage jobs and short-term assignments such as tutoring, working on a project for Black Classic Press, and even selling insurance. I quickly fell behind in child support. Since my support payments were based on the assurance about my income I'd made in court, I filed to have them reduced to reflect my actual wages. The judge refused to honor my request. My education and my previous ownership of Karibu worked against me. In effect, the judge accused me of purposely limiting my ability to pay child support.

The financial upheaval I was experiencing at this time made me hesitant about marrying Trian. We were still living on S Street, in my primary residence, which I was fighting to hold onto. I didn't want to bring her into my financial mess, but she told me, "I'm going to marry you anyway, so why not now?" We were married by a civil celebrant in Leesburg, Virginia on March 12, 2009.

Aside from Trian, who was always by my side, Brother Eric and another former ADO member, Gilbert Davidson, came to my aid with some much-needed short-term financial assistance. However, it wasn't enough to save me from the worst repercussions of my situation. I was locked up in DC jail twice, for a total of

40 days and 40 nights. Both times, I was jailed because the court thought I was hiding money that I should have been paying in child support.

My first stint, which occurred in the spring of 2009, was for eight days. The judge had warned me this would happen if I didn't pay up on all of the child support arrears. When I appeared in court with only a partial payment, the judge called for my personal escort to usher me away. Trian and some friends, including the one who loaned me the money for Karibu, took care of the unpaid arrears to get me out.

The following year, I had a court appearance scheduled for March 12, 2010, which happened to be my one-year wedding anniversary. I literally skipped downtown from S Street, exuberant because this was the first hearing set to discuss the possibility of my spending time with Zendaya and Talib since I'd given up custody in 2008. When my ex-wife told this new judge that I was behind in child support payments, the judge called for a personal escort once again. At the time, I was working as a boxing trainer, but the main way I was earning money was by dressing up as a Powerball/Mega Millions lottery mascot at area events. I came to court with pictures of myself dressed in a fuzzy, oversized lottery-ball costume, but that didn't make a difference to this judge.

Outside of the mediocre food and the metal bed with an insufficient mattress, my incarceration was not unpleasant. Both times I was housed in the Northeast 2 dorm, and both times I was fortunate to have a decent cellmate. I read and wrote every day, despite not having access to the law library. In my cell, I found a copy of *The Art of Christian Listening* by Thomas Hart, which treats Jesus's lay ministry as a guide for spiritual growth. I also got ahold of a King James Bible. With so many days and nights available to read, I was able to delve deeply into both books before being released. Trian was waiting for me when I walked out. She had also come to see me on my visiting days.

During my stays, I engaged in some good conversations with many of the guys there and played some mean games of Spades. I also nearly got into several fights. When the guards, or COs as they were called, let us have outdoor recreation, I worked out on the heavy and speed bags. Once other inmates realized I had some boxing skills, it garnered me more respect.

During my second stint, there was a guy from Uptown named Fats whose influence in the DC jail was like that of a made-man mafioso. He was in jail awaiting transfer to a federal institution, and his cell was directly across from mine on the top tier. He had such a rapport with the officers that his cell door was rarely locked. The four pay phones in Northeast 2 were always occupied whenever we were allowed out of our cells, but one of those phones unofficially belonged to him. Only the dudes who were cool with Fats seemed able to use that phone.

As I was being shown to my cell on my first night there, Fats said something to me half-jokingly that I couldn't quite make out. It seemed as if he was trying to test me, but I ignored him. Things between us were strained for the first two weeks. After we were finally allowed outside for recreation and I worked out on the heavy bag, Fats generally avoided making eye contact with me.

But one day, I committed a cardinal sin by using his unofficial pay phone. It wasn't purposeful. We had just finished outside rec, and I was one of the first ones back in. I saw the phone closest to me was empty and I took advantage of not having to wait in a long line. It wasn't until Fats walked up and stood next to one of his boys, who was sitting at a nearby cafeteria-style table, that I realized which phone I was using. By then, I was already into my conversation with Trian and didn't intend to jump off. Fats said nothing to me, but I heard him mumble to his buddy in a low, irritated tone, "Man, I gettin' tired of this niggah."

When I finished, Fats was sitting atop the table by himself. I walked over, stood in front of him, and stated firmly as we locked

gazes, "The phone was available, so I used it. There was no disrespect to you."

In those moments, we reached a tacit agreement, a settlement:
he sensed that I'd probably hurt him badly in a one-on-one fight,
but I was aware that he had probably half of Northeast 2 behind
him. Fats didn't say anything before I walked off. Later, he acknowledged me back on our tier, and from then on, we always
spoke to each other. After he got transferred, several of the young
guys who were under his influence approached me to talk boxing,
and I started training them on the basics of the sweet science.

The most significant incident at DC jail occurred during my
eight-day stay, and the pay phones were once again involved. After
almost coming to blows with another inmate over the use of the
phones, I came back to my cell huffing and puffing. My cellie, an
old-timer from Southeast, could see the displeasure all over my face.

He was aware that I used to box. He also knew about an incident I'd told him about that happened in 2000, when I punched
a Kennedy Center employee. This happened a year after this employee grabbed Monica while she was working at an event there.
Monica had called the police immediately after the initial incident,
but the officers couldn't find him and never followed through on
the arrest warrant that was later issued. A year later, Monica was
still upset about it, so I proposed going up to the Kennedy Center to speak with the guy after a performance. That didn't go well,
and I ended up popping him on the left side of his face with two
straight right hands. I was arrested, found guilty of misdemeanor
assault, and given six months' probation.

My cellie didn't say anything when I first told him about the
Kennedy Center incident. At the time, it was probably easy for a
perceptive guy like him to see how proud I was of defending my
wife's honor that way. Now, looking at me all tensed up in our cell,
he decided it was time to poke a needle in my balloon,

"I know you used to box, but that don't mean nuthin' in here, especially when you could end up with a pair of scissors stickin' out the side of your neck. And by the way, I know you think punching that guy at the Kennedy Center made you more of a man. It actually made you less of one. If you would've walked away from that guy when he refused to speak with your wife, then you would've been more of a man."

I just listened to him as he talked about having to be around killers without being a killer. It was the first time someone who knew about that Kennedy Center incident had openly challenged my actions. After contemplating his words, I couldn't disagree with them. I understood him to be saying that, basically, unless I was protecting my own life or someone else's, getting physical with someone else was a sign of weakness.

Unbeknownst to me, the judge overseeing my case had set a status hearing for April 12, 32 days after my second jailing, and was surprised to see me led into the courtroom in shackles instead of strolling in from the hallway. Instead of asking friends to pay for me to get out like the previous time, I had demanded to be left in jail so that the court wouldn't get a false sense of my financial situation.

"Where's the money?" the judge demanded.

"I have no money," I replied.

She let me go immediately and I was summoned to appear again ten days later. At that point, she reversed her earlier opinion with a determination that I had experienced "a material change in circumstances." My child support payments were reduced to a shockingly low $50 a month.

If threatening me with jail—and then actually putting me there—was meant to instill fear through punishment, then what the court did to me had the opposite effect. I had always been motivated to provide for my family, just as I had provided for my mother all those years, even after my divorce from Monica. Like many men, I was frustrated that the law could be misused to, in effect, prevent me from being an involved parent. The court treated me as if I was merely a commodity.

In the midst of all this mayhem, there was at least one bright spot. Back when Karibu was approaching its zenith, I had been asked to serve on the board of trustees at the Mount. In spite of my recent misfortunes, I remained an active member. During one particular board event, I shared a personal story with a few other members and the Mount's president, Tom Powell, about my days hanging in the streets. Everyone enjoyed the story, and the president suggested I consider writing a book.

This time I couldn't tell myself I was too busy. I had more down time on my hands than I'd experienced since I was a young child, so I immediately cranked out a book proposal. After a few rejections, a small press in Chicago called Agate accepted it. I had a relationship with the owner, and we agreed on a contract with a small advance. The book's manuscript was due the following year.

Now I was left to confront myself, and this represented my greatest challenge. Over the years, writing had become increasingly difficult for me as my attachment to work grew stronger. On the rare occasions when I had down time, I filled it up with a range of tasks. I thrived on being active, and writing always led directly to procrastination. Even when I did put something down on paper, I rarely liked it.

If I was going to write something worthwhile, I had to get over my need to be in motion. My present circumstances made that easier in one way, but more difficult in another. I had the time to write, but that time was being imposed on me, in effect, under duress. The legal and financial turmoil I faced was like a thundercloud lingering over my head. It had always been my thought that after first getting well established, I would write from a place of comfort and tranquility, which some of the ancient philosophers suggested was necessary to produce the best work. Not being busy sucked my energy.

I was further demoralized by not being able to stay current

with the utility bills. It seemed like every other month I was making payment arrangements, some of which I wasn't able to keep. Every utility service we used was cut off at one time or another. I didn't want Trian getting involved with paying any household expenses on S Street, but she paid the utilities on a number of occasions when something got turned off unexpectedly. Those surprises usually resulted from my failure to call and discuss payment options with the utility companies. Sometimes I'd just shut down out of disgust with myself over not being able to pay the bills like I was accustomed to, and this only made things worse. On several occasions, Trian herself grew disgusted with my seeming inability to let her know what was going on.

Personally, my philosophy and viewpoint on life were undergoing an important change. Black Nationalism and Pan-Africanism were things I could now see only from my rearview mirror. Over the years, I'd developed an almost zealot-like commitment to ADO and Karibu. The nearly two decades spent working within the black consciousness movement had kept me preoccupied, but a deep and latent dissatisfaction had remained.

In particular, the more successful Karibu had become, the more pronounced my feeling of emptiness. During those times, it had never occurred to me that the political, economic, and cultural movements I embraced couldn't bring me inner fulfillment. In spite of my personal achievements, though, what Karibu achieved in terms of cultural significance and economic success failed to quench my insatiable thirst for something permanent and more edifying. I now knew, intimately, that no system of thought, including black radical thought, could give me any true fulfillment. The timeless moment I'd experienced had shown me that. I'd gained more understanding from that one brief uncovering than from all the knowledge I'd acquired during my life up to that moment. That understanding was only partial, however, and its occurrence ushered in a long period of suffering. Instinctively, I realized I was being drawn to seek a more comprehensive understanding through further inquiry.

All of this caused a significant shift in my reading habits in mid-2007. No more of the history books and biographies I'd favored for decades: now, nearly everything I wanted to read was of a philosophical or spiritual nature. I read the copy of Plato's *Republic* that had been sitting on my bookshelf for years. I checked out a few of the best-known "new age" spiritual books. Initially, they gave me an emotional boost, but some of their claims seemed, at best, negligent and irresponsible, and at worst, disingenuous and fraudulent. What I read from an Indian spiritualist named Ramana Maharshi, though, was of the utmost quality. The book I enjoyed most was *The Teachings of Sri Ramana Maharshi in His Own Words*. I found that what he had to say was sublimely profound, yet uniquely simple.

My studying became so intense that Trian insisted I consider going back to school. Though I'd always found reading immensely enjoyable and important to my personal development, I pointed out to her that true wisdom was obtained in life, not in a classroom. She countered that since I was doing all this reading anyway, I might as well get an advanced degree in philosophy or something. This became an ongoing debate between us for several years.

By the time it was 2011, I was writing only sporadically. Every time I got into a good writing groove, circumstances forced me to deal with some unpleasant, mundane aspect of my life. I just couldn't grasp what was happening. Losing what I had wasn't so bad; it was losing it and remaining in the same condition for such an extended period. I'd grown spiritually and gained true love, yet my life had become much more challenging, especially materially.

I was under a mountain of debt and, despite my loving relationship with Trian, there were times when our material circumstances created tensions in our otherwise happy marriage. At the onset of my travails in 2007, Brother Eric was the only friend who spoke to me about what I was about to go through. He'd just met Trian and was genuinely happy for me, but he pulled me aside to express a sentiment that many people around me were probably thinking: "Some dudes going through what you're going through would feel like they couldn't afford love."

I appreciated Brother Eric pulling my coat. But contrary to what some people may have felt about my relationship with Trian, I never saw her as being the *cause* of my financial hardship and suffering. To me, my relationship with Trian was my *reward* for facing my own ugliness. The foundation for my suffering had been set when I had first allowed myself, years before, to get trapped in the idea of who I had to become. Once I realized what I'd done to myself, I did what few people, unfortunately, seem willing to do: I worked to untangle myself from the mess I'd made, and paid the hefty cost for doing so. Though starting a new relationship before legally being out of the old one expedited my financial downfall, it was actually Trian's presence in my life that helped me achieve the miracle of getting out of a most difficult situation.

At times, however, I was angry from the pain I felt over my difficulties. I had lost a great deal. I was starting a new life without a blueprint to follow, and things didn't seem to be moving in a good direction for me. Yet I was still able to observe the foundation of a fulfilling life being set. I just needed a lesson in patience, and fortunately—despite the discomfort this lesson was forcing on me—I was getting one.

Gradually, years after Karibu's demise, some things began shifting in my favor. In 2010, that no-nonsense judge who had locked me up on my one-year wedding anniversary was still serving on the bench, and I filed for joint custody of my children. In early 2011, I was awarded joint legal custody, though I was still relegated to getting Zendaya and Talib only one day a week. Since I knew my time and attention were the most valuable things I could give them,

I began engaging in an uphill battle to get at least equal time with them. Eventually, I was able to secure one day a week and every other weekend during the school year, and three weeks over the summer.

My financial situation hadn't changed much. However, I began working as a substitute teacher in the DC public school system and managing a Liberty Tax office. My work was okay, but, besides the satisfaction of assisting people who were open to being helped, I didn't have any passion for what I was doing. I knew that to provide for my family well and pay off my debts, my energy would have to be spent on something that could be my fundamental passion.

For my whole adult life, I had thought black consciousness and Pan-Africanism were my passions. Those ideologies served as the foundation for everything I did. But an incident that happened less than a year before Karibu closed pointed toward another path, though I didn't really understand it at the time. I had a strange encounter with a man who I hadn't recalled ever seeing before, who approached me, pointed in the general direction of Karibu's office, and said, "Do you work over there?"

"Yeah."

"You're going to be travelling and speaking to young people," he said.

Then he walked up and shook my hand. I was polite but said nothing in response; I didn't know what *to* say.

As I looked at my life in the years after that encounter, though, in particular how I interacted with other people, I learned that what I most enjoyed was talking about self-inquiry and inner development. I kept envisioning myself speaking to groups of people about life itself, and telling them how what really mattered were those things that were permanent yet unseen.

Trian kept telling me that what I liked talking about was not common, and was in fact quite unsettling for some people. She continued urging me to find "my group," so I finally agreed to look into a few philosophy programs at area universities. I met with Dr.

William Griffith, a professor at George Washington University, and he saw that my interests spanned several disciplines—namely, philosophy, religion, and psychology. We discussed how I thought that too much of higher education was overly specialized, and he agreed, saying, "Philosophy departments no longer ask the big questions, because they can't be answered." I asked which school or program he thought might be a good fit for me, and he asked, "Have you heard of St. John's College in Annapolis?"

I was surprised and a little disappointed he hadn't mentioned one of the Ivy League schools. Later, I half-heartedly checked out St. John's website. The school was founded in 1696, and despite its name, it had no religious affiliation. St. John's offered undergraduate and graduate study on the Great Books of the Western tradition at its Annapolis campus, and the same for the Great Books of the Eastern tradition at a second campus in Santa Fe, New Mexico. Learning was based on reading, writing, and class discussions in small-group settings with one or two facilitators, known as tutors. The tutors didn't behave like authorities; instead they served to guide student discussions. Grades were deemphasized.

I was impressed by what St. John's had to offer, so I applied and was accepted. The school gave me some grant money for part of the tuition, and I discovered that federal loans for educational purposes were based on need, not credit rating. Well, I was definitely in need, so Sallie Mae gave me a loan to cover the rest. Just 45 minutes away in Annapolis, I found this little educational jewel that I had the good fortune to attend.

I started the graduate masters program in liberal arts in the summer of 2012 and finished at the end of the following summer. St. John's College was as quaint as it was unique: greenery all over, rabbits hopping nearby as you strolled from building to building, and a serenity that permeated every waking moment I spent on campus. During the summer semesters, I came home nearly every weekend to spend time with Trian and the kids. They also came to visit me several times. Trian especially loved it up there. David Alvaranga, who owned the Liberty Tax office I managed for a few years, gave me a car, so I was able to drive to classes during the fall and spring semesters.

Over four semesters, I studied philosophy, theology, literature, politics and society, and history. There were massive amounts of reading to complete, and almost as much writing. Among the writers who impressed me the most were Hume, Cervantes, Rousseau, and Nietzsche. Beyond a doubt, St. John's was my most rewarding formal educational experience.

St. John's was important to me in several respects. As with the Mount, the environment there offered me a peaceful respite. I made use of the old gymnasium's heavy and speed bags. I also befriended a fellow student, Rob Wells, who was a marathon runner. Over the years I'd run a few marathons myself, and we became running buddies. The breadth, intensity, and uniqueness of the graduate program put me in the proper mindset for writing. Going there was like being in training camp for finishing my book. After graduation, I began working on my book nearly every day.

I also kept trying to make sense of my life after coming to love. I realized that in truth, nothing could've prepared me for what I encountered after the loss of Karibu and my divorce. The fallout placed a heavy strain on my relationship with Trian. Several years into our marriage, we began getting into arguments over seemingly minor things, but my financial woes were at the root of the tension. We often dragged her mother into the mix to serve as an unofficial referee. As frustrating as things were at times, we always came back to a mutual understanding that our situation was only temporary, and there were no major problems in our marriage.

We were each adjusting to a role that neither of us was accustomed to. I'd been a provider even before I reached adulthood, and Trian had generally dated men who were very successful in their respective fields. My success, at least financially, was in remission, and trying to adjust to our circumstances was challenging for both of us. She was expecting me to take the lead, and I desperately wanted to as well, though I also didn't take issue with her being in that primary role.

In a very real sense, however, what was typically viewed as the "male" role of provider was of no use to me. I had to toss it in the trash bin. What carried more weight for me now was to face myself in the midst of dealing with the world. This was a costly endeavor, no doubt. I certainly had no qualms about earning money—one had to live—but my success, from now on, would be determined by how far I'd journeyed on the inside, rather than anything I'd be able to acquire on the outside.

My financial situation did begin to turn around. I finally filed for bankruptcy at the end of 2014 and started rebuilding my finances. I taught some writing courses at Montgomery College for three semesters. I took a full-time teaching position at Dunbar Senior High School in DC for a brief period before going into retail management.

The S Street house brought me nothing but good fortune. Trian helped me negotiate with the mortgage company to sell the house. In early 2015, she located a buyer. Not only was the mortgage paid off, but I was also able to repay a substantial amount of the money I owed to the friend who'd given me the loan for Karibu. Trian and I moved to Maryland.

Our children, as children always do, were growing up. After nearly following in his father's footsteps by becoming an NFL player, Jimmie moved in with us as he entered culinary school to pursue his passion for cooking. After graduating, he happened upon a really nice restaurant in Georgetown for his apprenticeship toward becoming a chef. Zendaya, who was now in high school, was smart, artistic, and quite athletically talented. Talib, a personable boy who seemed to never meet a stranger, was blessed with an inner maturity that seemed to resonate with everyone he encountered.

In my view, the best thing I could offer them was a sincere attempt to live what I was espousing. One weekday night in February of 2017, as I was putting Talib to bed, he dropped a heavy question on me that actually represented the completion of a circle in my life's journey. As he rested on the bottom bunk bed cuddled up in a blue-plaid blanket, I could hear in his voice the same concern and fear that had invaded my mind as a little boy when he asked, "What's going to happen when I die?"

By asking for my help in facing down a monumental human question, he was giving me an opportunity to offer him something that wasn't afforded to me at his age. I lay down beside him so we could feel each other's presence. In the clearest and plainest way possible, I explained that as humans we're attached to our bodies, and the thought of no longer being connected to what allows us to experience life in the physical world causes us to be fearful of dying. The human mind doesn't like to think about its own demise, so it seeks some guarantee of its continual existence. Since the mind can't reach beyond itself to acquire that assurance, it generally gives itself over to belief in life after death.

After encouraging Talib to seek out his own answers to life's big questions, I offered him my strongest evidence that our true being lives on beyond death. The fact that we exist in deep sleep, when the mind is not functioning and the body is motionless aside from its breath, demonstrates that our true being is constant, changeless, and not limited to the physical world. The daily life we cling to is merely an illusion our minds see as real. I encouraged Talib to consider that the purpose of living is to discover who we already are. Afterward, when he told me he felt better, I suspected it had more to with my presence than anything I'd said.

The struggles I've faced over the past decade have been difficult. But I've also derived great benefits from them. I've realized that everything I do in life has significance because there are consequences for my actions. In other words, there's a spiritual price connected to everything I do, or, as James Baldwin once wrote: "People pay for what they do, and still more for what they have allowed themselves to become. And they pay for it very simply: by the lives they lead."

I don't think suffering is always necessary, but it has been an important element in my own spiritual journey because it forced me to change my approach to life. For so much of my youth and most of my adult life, I accomplished nearly everything I put my mind to. My determined will had a knack for getting things done, and I thrived off of it as a result. But after experiencing that time-less moment, it's become, at times, painfully apparent that my life has changed.

From this, I've become intimately aware of an intelligence operating in my life that is greater than what exists in my mind. My former way of living left too much of what life has to offer on the table. I reasoned that if what created me is unlimited, and I'm merely a limited being, then it's best for me to forgo living life as I once did; I now understood that the unlimited source of life can lead me better than I could ever lead myself. Now, I look forward to the unknown opportunities life brings me, and this, I now know, is the truly appropriate way to live.

The very things I spent most of my life seeing as integral to my identity were blocking me from seeing what's truly real. My tun-nel-like focus, first on education and then on black consciousness, entrepreneurship, and sex, kept me busy for a time, but ultimately left me empty inside. Eventually, I came to embrace this unknown and unseen source that we're all connected to as the realest thing about me. Just as I told Talib, who we truly are is the nonphysical, eternal part of us—and this is the only thing, when it's all said and done, worth striving for. Our body and mind are important, though, in the effort to help us uncover who we truly are.

Uncovering this truth has become, in effect, my religion. Who or what God is had been an open question for me since I first pondered it as a little boy at St. Anthony's. After 30-plus years, my experiences helped me understand that whatever God may be is beyond our mental grasp. God can only be experienced—a truth that made itself known to me at a moment when my mind, without intention, was made still.

So whenever people ask me if I believe in God, I tell them that what we call God is too important for mere belief. Each and every one of us must look inside ourselves in the effort to uncover this greatest of mysteries. As I see it, at bottom, this is the preeminent purpose of life.

The example of Malcolm X was of enormous importance to my life. Malcolm was indispensible in my transition from the streets to college and beyond, because so many elements of his story spoke to my heart. I could relate to his growing up without a father, having a mentally-ill mother, and being fascinated with the streets—and despite those disadvantages, becoming educated and well spoken. Malcolm demonstrated that it was possible to be hip, intelligent, respectful, and committed to helping other people all at the same time. More than any other historical figure, he opened a doorway for me to step into the larger world.

As a young Malcolmite, I felt my grasp of his political and cultural ideology was pretty strong. I had read many books written by and about him and had sought out every available speech of his that had ever been recorded. I had even memorized several of these, such as "Message to the Grassroots." Malcolm's embrace of Islam aside, how he lived his life became the standard by which I judged my own life. As he was for so many of the more militant elements within the black community, Malcolm was my patron saint.

It wasn't until my fervent search for greater fulfillment began, more than 20 years after I was first introduced to Malcolm, that I looked at him anew. It was ironic that Trian, who knew very little about him, caused me to see beyond my hero's Black Nationalist and Pan-Africanist ideologies and learn more about his inner focus. I had been so caught up with Malcolm's revolutionary thought that I had never really considered his emotional and psychological development. When I showed Trian the 1972 Malcolm X documentary directed by Arnold Perl, she remarked on how miserable and ill-fated Malcolm appeared in the footage where he spoke about his feud with the Nation of Islam (NOI).

In his Pulitzer Prize-winning 2011 book *Malcolm X: A Life of Reinvention*, Manning Marable, more than any other biographer, details what he interpreted as the apparent dysfunction in Malcolm's marriage to Betty Shabazz. According to Marable, instead of being a place of refuge and rejuvenation, the marriage was a source of consternation and anxiety for Malcolm. Betty was no pushover, and there were occasions when Malcolm found it difficult to deal with her, so he practiced avoidance. There was infidelity on both sides, with Malcolm even expressing a desire to divorce Betty in order to marry a woman he dated before joining the NOI. Other Malcolm scholars have made similar disclosures about the marriage as well. These revelations indicate that Malcolm's busy schedule may, in part, have been inspired by a desire to mask his lack of personal fulfillment.

The primary culprit in Malcolm's tendency to neglect his family and his personal needs was his dedication to external movements. Nearly all his time and focus went into the NOI and the organizations he formed after his split with Elijah Muhammad: the Organization of Afro-American Unity (OAAU) and the Muslim Mosque Incorporated (MMI). James Baldwin summed up the spiritual quandary the NOI created for Malcolm and other adherents when he stated, "What Elijah Muhammad has done is very clever but also very sinister. It's easy to give people a false sense of superiority but it ultimately leads to moral bankruptcy."

If Malcolm had survived the turbulent 1960s, it would have been fascinating to see where his ongoing psychological and spiritual development would have taken him—and how the public and his admirers could have benefitted. His willingness to be open and honest about his missteps in life was an extremely rare trait for a religious or political figure.

Malcolm's famous statement, "The price of freedom is death," was meant to address the physical death people must be willing to risk in their effort to achieve physical, economic, political, and cultural freedom. However, there are also nonphysical analogues to death—and a more sublime freedom to be found in life—that Malcolm overlooked.

The degree to which Malcolm was willing to rid himself of any psychological handicap was the degree to which he opened the door to becoming free. His entire stint in the NOI was spent under psychological and spiritual confinement. In *To Kill a Black Man*, author Louis Lomax recounts an incident in which Malcolm admitted to a group of angry white Muslims, who had confronted him outside of a studio, that he knowingly preached the faulty belief that whites were devils because he felt that the NOI's separation movement offered the best opportunity for freedom for black people. He failed to appreciate that in a man's search for truth, to paraphrase Krishnamurti, he must *start* with truth. Physical, economic, and political freedom can make life more comfortable, but none of these brings fulfillment. Only truth can lead one to freedom and happiness.

Unfortunately, Malcolm's almost inhuman commitment to external movements was an impediment to the self-inquiry that was necessary for him to reach fulfillment. With someone like Malcolm, it was not an issue of commitment or intention, but of attention. He placed too much attention in the wrong area. The source of the problem he was facing was never external, yet he kept his primary focus there instead of continuing to deal with himself. The enormous personal strides Malcolm made in spite of the dysfunction he encountered during his youth, while in prison, and as a member of the NOI is an indication that he possessed the wherewithal to reach psychological freedom.

In a speech Baldwin delivered during the height of the civil rights struggle, he stated, "Black unity is a white invention." It took a while for me to unpack the meaning behind these words, but when I did, it forced me to revisit the black-consciousness ideology that had shaped my philosophy for so long.

Baldwin was attempting to point out the fallacy of using race as a basis for living. He explained that race was a product of European thought, created to address a pressing economic dilemma created by settling in the Americas. Those European pioneers were in desperate need of a cheap labor source to help them survive in the new world. Therefore, the term "black" was used to label, look down upon, and subjugate Africans into slavery, because most of the Europeans who came to America couldn't make it on their own back where they had come from. Since they viewed blacks as subhuman, "whites" could engage in slavery without believing they were committing a crime against humanity.

Understandably, Africans united based upon their common mistreatment due to their "blackness." Their respective native tongues were lost, forcing them to communicate among themselves and with whites in English. They also lost a lot of their cultures and customs.

Ever since the onset of white racist encounters with Africans and Africa, African people and their descendants have engaged in black struggle to fight against this oppression. After centuries of slavery, segregation, and other forms of racism, the angry memories from these experiences have become part of the collective consciousness of the descendants of African slaves.

Blackness and whiteness have an intricate and fundamental connection. Both are the creations of thought, the former being birthed from the latter. Neither contains any intrinsic value whatsoever, and they are only real in the extent to which they exist in our minds. Despite how noble black unity and struggle may appear, they are rooted in racism. Fundamentally, if whiteness is disorder, then blackness ultimately must be as well. At bottom, whiteness and blackness are opposite sides of the same coin of dysfunctional and narrow-minded thought.

In *The Price of the Ticket*, Baldwin eloquently warns us about the cost of race. Though racism is a problem Europeans created, blacks have become ever more preoccupied with it, to our own detriment. Our psychological pain from the past has caused seething bitterness among black people. Sadly, such prolonged anger and hatred foster self-destruction, which has had a pervasive impact on generations of African slaves and their descendants, and, I believe, has become one of the great impediments to more blacks becoming fully realized human beings.

Baldwin was correct when he stated, "There's only one race, and we're all a part of it." It is my hope that one day, sooner rather than later, black people will be able to live according to this precept. In my view, Baldwin's essays and speeches are proof that he was really a philosopher posing as a novelist and playwright. The depth of Baldwin's thought is as great as any philosopher produced by Europe, and may explain why he felt so compelled to criticize Plato's desire to exclude poets from the society he envisioned in *The Republic*.

To my mind, Baldwin's writings about race in the United States are the most insightful I have ever come across on the matter. When he warns blacks that we must face ourselves—especially since we've been demanding that whites face themselves—he is presenting us with a fundamental challenge as human beings. It was Malcolm who started me on my journey into black consciousness, but it was Baldwin who slipped me the key to move beyond it.

Contemplating the life and work of Malcolm X helped me understand the risks of trying to emulate someone else, no matter how great that person may be. If discovering who I am is the way to fulfillment, then by continuing to follow Malcolm, I ran the risk of making my hero's issues my own. I feel very fortunate that my overwhelming desire to know love forced me to prioritize my inner development. This undertaking led me to face my fears, my lingering pains, and my subconscious mind in my journey toward self-discovery. Ultimately, I learned that any true movement is an internal one.

Even though choosing *Simba Sana* emerged from my former association with black radical thought, I held onto the adopted name. First off, I liked the simplicity and rhythmic sound of it. Second, I discovered after getting married for a second time that my current and former names possessed essentially the same meaning. *Bernard* is a German word meaning "bear," a forest animal on equal footing with *Simba*, the lion of the jungle. The name *Sutton* has French origins, and travelled to England during the Norman Conquest of 1066. The Sutton family motto, *pour y parvenir*, means "to accomplish it." A continent away in Africa, *Sana*, meaning "to make or forge," carries the same message. For me, I guess running away from who I am isn't an option.

One thing became increasingly apparent in the years following 2007: the timeless moment I experienced set me on a journey, one that my unrelenting quest for love had set in motion years before. A nonstop journey toward fulfillment had commenced. A passage in the Gnostic Gospels speaks to the point. According to the Gospel of Thomas, Jesus once stated, "Let one who seeks not stop seeking until one finds. When one finds, one will be troubled. When one is troubled, one will marvel and will reign over all [i.e., will know God]."

Putting it another way, I had somehow accumulated karmic debt that could only be repaid with the destruction of my ego—a painful process, especially for someone whose ego had been boosted and pumped up through life experience. Just as I never stopped searching for love, I can never stop seeking happiness. I can never stop searching to find out who I am. I can never stop engaging in self-inquiry. The objective, the subjective, and the means of getting there are interconnected. They're really one and the same.

Today, I no longer follow any prescribed way of living. I have come to recognize that true wisdom is internally derived, infinitely more knowledgeable than the human mind, and rooted in a boundless truth—or simply, what is—that each one of us can arrive at and partake in.

True wisdom is universal. In other words, wisdom is what was true a thousand years ago, what is true today, and what is true everywhere. We tend to place too much importance on what exists in the physical world but is impermanent, while placing less importance on what's intangible yet permanent. The latter's immutability does not fade with the changing of circumstance or time. Wisdom is not beholden to time, space, or cause.

Some people feel it is unwise to divulge certain things about their life, because people tend to look at and treat you differently if the image they have of you is tarnished with disparaging or unflattering information. In my case, however, I could not share my story without, in effect, telling on myself. Besides, I have learned that what people think about me or how they treat me does not change who I am. Wisdom has enabled me to know that "I am that I am."

Showing vulnerability is strength, not weakness. It takes courage to be vulnerable and to speak truthfully, because to demonstrate such openness indicates that you're always willing to face yourself, regardless of the consequences. When it comes to dealing with something unpleasant, it's now my preference to be honest about it, even if I must suffer on the front end, rather than to be dishonest and pay for it on the back end. Such payments generally become costlier the longer you avoid dealing with them, and you have no idea how and when those payments are going to come due.

It wasn't until I was in my late 30s that I began to appreciate the importance of becoming a fully realized human being—a unique individual, imbued with an intimate understanding that you are part of a much larger whole. Putting it another way, I could see part of myself in everyone else.

At the onset of my journey to becoming fully realized, I began to move through life understanding that everything in the physical world was impermanent and devoid of any intrinsic value. Thus, there was no longer an incessant need to debate or argue about what was "right." There was an unwavering connection to the goodness that is Life itself, so much so that I could see that things, even awful and horrific things, somehow work themselves out for the best. My role as an individual was to give a premium effort and allow life to handle the rest. This type of understanding was beyond the intellectual or the conceptual, and therefore couldn't be explained. I had to experience it.

Once I seriously considered the task of becoming fully realized, then at least two other questions begged for my attention. First, how could I fulfill my life's purpose, and second, what difficulty, if any, was involved in such an endeavor? For many years, I was largely unaware of the former question. But I was always pervaded by the feeling that the way to create a better life lay beyond mere theory or simply following a particular dogma.

On June 26, 2000, I read an article in the *Washington Post* by Libby Copeland entitled, "Our Lady of Perpetual Help: In the Church of Feel-Good Pop Psychology, Spiritual Rebirth Means Starting at O," which discussed how *The Oprah Winfrey Show* served as the launching pad for a number of self-help authors and their books. What caught my attention were some quotes from Dr. Vicki Abt, a professor at Pennsylvania State University, who stated:

We don't reach self-actualization, most of us . . .
America and Oprah Winfrey are popularizing this
ridiculous, naive optimism that life isn't tough or

> that life can get better . . . The fact is, we don't know
> how to fix the human dilemma. And the notion
> that there's an easy fix, or a fix at all, doesn't help
> Americans . . . Most of us are mediocre at best,
> average by definition, and being exposed to this
> nonsense makes us more mediocre.

I was skeptical of self-help books in general, and Dr. Abt's words touched a fiber in me, so I called her office. She was very gracious, and when I asked her to provide me with some deeper insight into what she meant, she stated simply, "It's very difficult to change your life." Elaborating further, she explained that there were others books, such as Tocqueville's *Democracy in America* and Proust's monumental, multi-volume novel *Remembrance of Things Past*, that could offer people a better appreciation of just how difficult changing one's life can be. She felt that many of our modern-day self-help books give people the false impression that the task is easier than it truly is.

Some years after our conversation, I watched two renowned spiritualists on Oprah's show, on different occasions, speaking about reaching a higher state of consciousness. In each episode, Oprah expressed a concern over how difficult it was for a person to follow their advice with success, but both of them failed to acknowledge her comment. I found their nonresponse to be quite concerning. It was as if taking a moment to offer viewers some practical guidance would somehow tarnish the pretty picture they were using her show to craft. Or perhaps they ignored her comment because they really couldn't offer any direction on how to carry out their recommendations.

From my own experience, and the stories of others I've either read or somehow come to know, I fully embraced Dr. Abt's point of view. When I ran into Christopher "Chrissy" Turner, one of the former leaders of the 8th & H Street Crew, on a spring afternoon in 2016, I gained an even better appreciation for how difficult the journey can be. Coming out of the North Capitol Street post office, I recognized Chrissy as he was entering. Fit, tan-complexioned, and about 5'7" or a little more, he looked very much the same as when we were teenagers, except for his clean-shaven head.

I called him several months later. He'd been working steadily since coming home in 2011 after serving 26 years for Catherine Fuller's murder, a crime I still believed he and the other guys, all of whom were still incarcerated, didn't commit. In fact, the prosecution's witnesses had recanted their testimony years afterward and efforts were being made by concerned groups to get the convictions overturned. In March of 2017, the Supreme Court, in an unusual move, decided to hear the case despite its only going through two lower courts instead of the typical eight or nine. For Chrissy, being in prison all those years was especially difficult, because people thought that since he had a good work history and was the only one of the bunch with a high-school diploma, he'd ultimately be found innocent. "The marshals had my release paperwork ready; that's how certain they were that I was going home," he told me. He went on to tell me that upon entering prison, the prison guards became the focal point of his rage over being held unjustly; he had a kill-or-be-killed mentality.

Over time, his mentality about the whole thing changed. He let go of the anger and began helping other inmates. Some needed guidance using the law library to work on their individual cases. Others just needed help dealing with day-to-day prison life. In all the prisons he stayed in, and there were more than a few, Chrissy used his natural leadership abilities to bring inmates together.

"How do you look at the time you served now?" I asked.

"Joe, it saved my life. When I think about some of the good dudes I was close to who lost their lives? Knowing me, if I was out there I wouldn't have let those things ride."

The tone of his voice was filled with conviction as he spoke; his determination seeped through the phone. He'd crossed my mind a number of times over the years, and I'd wondered how he'd fared; after we hung up, I didn't have to wonder any more. As ugly as it was, Chrissy's time in prison had elevated his consciousness. He'd been painfully blessed with an intimate understanding to which most people only render lip service. Back in high school, when Underdue and I visited him at the DC jail before his conviction, he came across as a dude with a strong character, so I wasn't surprised that he'd found his way forward in life, prison notwithstanding.

Invariably, I think, the journey to wholeness requires a certain degree of suffering. Whenever suffering is unavoidable, its purpose is to bring those of us experiencing it closer to our true being. It is a painful blessing that most of us seek to avoid. Though Chrissy's situation was an extreme case, it seems that every life encounters *some* level of suffering.

If we're going to change our world, we must be willing to make new discoveries about ourselves, and not just the external world. The problems in our world are here because we created them. Our insatiable desire to be pleasured, coupled with the inner fears we all harbor, have led us to create corrupt societies. The ongoing existence of the world's problems stems from our unwillingness to face ourselves. This crucial step must occur on an individual level. More of us must serve as examples by how we live, not merely by what we say. The journey to wholeness is a difficult one, and it will only get easier if more people embark upon it.

The Dalai Lama is someone I really respect in this regard. He's open, humble, and doesn't present himself as a person who is unaffected by what's happening in his life and the world at large. In *My Spiritual Journey*, his personal story of spiritual growth, he admits to not being as confident when speaking about Buddhism in a place where people from a different religion are in the majority.

And in *Beyond Religion*, he states, "Even I find myself complaining from time to time!"

The Dalai Lama's writings feature spiritual constancy that doesn't waver with the changing of time and circumstance. He doesn't propagate the unrealistic notion that he is always bubbling over with happiness. He acknowledges that life is not always happy, even for those who may be fully realized, but he also asserts that all of us possess the innate ability to go through life with a relative sense of calm. His personal story of displacement from his homeland of Tibet exemplifies how to work toward one's purpose, in spite of or maybe even because of experiencing misfortune.

Life stories such as the Dalai Lama's are great for reaching our heart, the place where our true self resides, because they offer readers the chance to share in a meaningful experience. Stories are less about prescription and more about openness, vulnerability, and sharing. A great tale can be life changing for the reader. Plato's numerous stories about Socrates are a case in point. Those anecdotes are imbued with so much wisdom that they have encouraged discussion and sharing among people for thousands of years.

The Autobiography of Malcolm X is still so pertinent, in part, because it's so wide-ranging. He details his personal struggles with an exciting flair, bringing his readers through his various transformations, from dysfunctional child, to street hustler, to prison inmate, to grassroots organizer and Muslim minister, to international humanist. Through it all, Malcolm's story makes him accessible.

Fictional accounts have their place as well. I think the *The Lord of the Rings* is a great example of a story replete with spiritual potency. Frodo Baggins and his fellowship's yearlong battle against the seemingly insurmountable forces of darkness demonstrate how difficult the struggle toward goodness and fulfilling one's purpose can be. Frodo had to confront his darkest demons to carry out his commitment to destroy the One Ring, while Aragorn had to overcome his fears in order for mankind to play its instrumental role in saving Middle-earth. Even Gandalf, the wise old wizard, had to put aside his reluctance to battle the demonic Balrog by venturing into the Mines of Moria, travelling through darkness to light, and claiming his rightful place in his Order. The battle to defeat darkness carried each of them to the brink of destruction.

In my own life, the level of pain I experienced because of my efforts toward self-discovery was intense and long-standing. At times I almost regretted embarking on the journey. All of the things I'd spent years working to acquire had been taken from me. My circumstances were so financially and emotionally dire that, despite having found a loving relationship, there were times when I felt abandoned. One feeling I had to confront over and over was that I'd done something to improve my life and was suffering as a result of it. I'd never before suffered for such an extensive period of time for doing what I felt was right. There were certainly times when I encountered difficult situations, but those problems had been rectified relatively quickly. In this case, however, following my heart had placed me in a painful and seemingly intractable situation. Once I made the move toward self-discovery, there was no turning back. My love for myself, my wife, and our children helped to sustain me during those times.

After the pain and astonishment over my predicament started to subside, a purpose behind all of the difficulty emerged. I realized that most of my adult life had been spent not following my passion—because I didn't know what that passion was.

When I was building Karibu, my will and ambition drove me to get things done, and I was very much disciplined in living this way. My life was filled with work, but everything was like a blur. As soon as I achieved a goal, the sense of satisfaction I felt from the accomplishment was short-lived; it seemed as if I was only as good as what I was going after. At bottom, I felt empty. In truth, I was attempting to run from myself by chasing a myth of who I had to become, instead of discovering who I already was.

My journey toward self-discovery led me to uncover my passion, the thing I did when all the inessential things were no longer grappling for my attention. Being forced to spend a significant amount of time in solitude, I started paying more attention to myself. It became apparent that most of the time, I was either engaged in conversation or was reading to prepare myself for conversation. Though I didn't know how to get out of my quagmire, I believed my passion, my outer purpose, would serve as my guide, so I was forced to trust it. There was no other option.

My passion for making inner discoveries and sharing them with others would help to deliver me out of the quagmire in which I felt trapped. Exactly how to do this, though, was beyond me at the moment. For the first time in my life, there wasn't a ready-made idea that I could work on to get me through a difficult situation. Patience, diligence, and a willingness to confront my fears would serve as my companions. I was forced to live in the moment, and the only thing thought could tell me about anything beyond the present is that there was still some space between the cup and the lip.

If my experience taught me anything about living, it's that my inner purpose must be aligned with my outer purpose. How I live my daily life dictates whether I'm in conflict or in harmony with my inner self. Doing what I'm passionate about helps me maintain a harmonious way of living. Even at my lowest point, I spent time engaging in my passion, the thing I enjoy doing for itself. Thus, it represents the key to connecting my inner and outer existence.

I can't fulfill my purpose, and thereby reach true happiness, without being fully realized, and the key to being happy is not to pursue happiness but to eliminate the impediments that stand in the way of it. The ways I thought before, my views on certain things, and some of my long-held positions all served as obstacles that I had to dispense with in order to experience something infinitely better. To knowingly or unknowingly live in discomfort, misery, and unhappiness goes against the purpose of life.

Doing what I love, not being in conflict with myself, having a loving family, and being intimately connected to God are what I'm seeking. At the end of it all, the only thing worth having is that which is permanent; everything else is secondary.

Acknowledgments

FIRST OFF, I WANT TO THANK DOUG SEIBOLD FOR HAV-
ing confidence in this book. The personal time he committed to
this project and the support he has given me during the years I've
taken to write it have been reassuring.

Though I could not have visualized it at the time, a book given
to me by a man named Emmanuel Williams shifted my reading toward matters of an inner nature and became the true starting point
for my memoir. I began writing my own book in earnest after a
suggestion from Tom Powell, who at the time was the president of
Mount St. Mary's University in Emmitsburg, Maryland, my alma
mater. This wasn't the first time someone suggested that I pen my
story, but my business had recently closed, so I was stripped of my
long-standing excuse for not pursuing the effort. During the writing stage, Mark Boss, a friend of more than 25 years, expressed the
importance of vulnerability if I truly wanted to share my story. The
conventional wisdom is that people, men especially, would be wise
to hide their faults and problems, even from those close to them.
Mark, on the other hand, advocated a different viewpoint, and I'm
forever grateful for his insight.

Throughout the entire process of creating this book, my wife has given me unwavering support, in spite of, at times, challenging circumstances. I must also acknowledge the support of Charlotte Reid, one of the best people I've ever come to know. Her experience and foresight have had an indelible impact on this book. She also introduced me to stylist Michele Lopez and photographer Robert Shanklin, and I'm very appreciative of their expertise.

There are a number of people I must acknowledge who have helped me to this point in my life: the Artis family, Greg and Beverly Mosso, Don Brooks, Benjamin "Bummy" Morrow, Looby "Butch" Chance, Willie Houser, Brenda McCutcheon, Anthony "Tonyson" Carter, Raymond Underdue, Raymond Singleton, Keith "Kubweza" Johnson, Kwabena Lumumba (Brother Eric), Gilbert Davidson, Joel Dias Porter, aka DJ Renegade, Brian Gilmore, Patrick Carter, and Mary Cox.

Finally, I want to note all of the children who have come into my life, including Jimmie Johnson III, Jasmin Hicks, Ashley Morrow, and Amika Underdue.